The Aam Aadmi Party

The Aam Aadmi Party

The Untold Story of a Political Uprising and Its Undoing

Sayantan Ghosh

juggernaut

JUGGERNAUT BOOKS
C-I-128, First Floor, Sangam Vihar, Near Holi Chowk,
New Delhi 110080, India

First published by Juggernaut Books 2025

10 9 8 7 6 5 4 3 2 1

P-ISBN: 978-93-5345-876-8
E-ISBN: 978-93-5345-399-2

Typeset in Adobe Caslon Pro by Mukul Chand

Printed at Thomson Press India Ltd

For Ma, Baba, Aishiki and Anindita

Contents

PART 4
ONE-MAN SHOW

PART 5
THE AAP UNDER FIRE

PART 6
EXPANSION AND PROSPECTS

Introduction

It was the winter of 2016, a season when Delhi's chill seeps into your bones and the city wears a shroud of mist. As an intern with the *Times of India*, I found myself shadowing a seasoned reporter to a crime scene in the Seemapuri slum of East Delhi. A murder had allegedly occurred there, from a dispute over ration supplies, casting a pall of fear and sorrow over the neighbourhood.

Amidst the sombre atmosphere, I encountered Geeta Jatav, a 73-year-old woman sitting outside her humble abode, wrapped in a faded off-white saree that seemed to mirror the foggy sky. She was a neighbour to the house where the tragedy had unfolded. My senior, sensing the gravity of the scene, advised me to avoid the crime site itself, suggesting instead that I speak with the neighbours to gather their stories.

Geeta's eyes, though weary, held a spark of resilience as she began to speak, '*Khun se mujhe darr nahi lagta, bahut murder dekhi hay maine. Mere bete ko satra admi milke pita tha, pata hay kyun? Woh ration mafia ka virodh kia tha* (I am not scared of murders as I have seen many. Seventeen people once beat up my son, do you know why? Because he protested against the ration mafia),' she recounted, her voice steady and unwavering.

She paused, her gaze drifting to some distant memory, then continued, '*Nahi dari thi, pata hay kyun? Arvind Kejriwal the hamare sath is ladai mei. Tab woh koi CM ya leader nahi the, lekin ration mafia ke khilaf ladh rahe the. Har hafte aate the, mere bete ka bhi wo log ilaj karwaya. Aaj kal nahi ata hay kyun ki woh toh mukhyamantri ban gaya hay. Lekin humlog abhi bhi uske saath hay, ehsan chukani hay* (Do you know why I was not scared that day? Because Arvind Kejriwal was with us. He was not a CM [chief minister] or a big leader at that time, but he used to fight against the ration mafia. They used to come every week, they even did my son's treatment. But he no longer comes here now, as he has become the CM. But we still support him, as there are several favours to return.)'

She confided in me that day, revealing the harsh reality of Seemapuri – where murder is a grimly familiar occurrence among the impoverished Dalit and Muslim families. The area is a stronghold for mafias, yet the battle against these criminal forces began with Arvind Kejriwal's intervention. Back when he was spearheading the NGO Swaraj, Kejriwal took a stand against the ration mafia and championed the Right to Information (RTI) Act. It struck me profoundly how individuals like Geeta share a deeply personal connection with the now former CM of Delhi – a bond forged in the crucible of their shared struggles and aspirations.

Geeta's words wove a tapestry of courage and gratitude, revealing the depth of her community's bond with Kejriwal. Despite their daily struggles, the people of Seemapuri felt a profound sense of indebtedness to him. It was in that moment, amidst the echoes of her story, that I understood the true essence of their connection to the Aam Aadmi Party (AAP) and Kejriwal. The trust and loyalty Kejriwal had cultivated were not just political capital but a testament to his enduring impact on their lives – a beacon of hope in their relentless fight for justice and dignity.

Reflecting on that pivotal conversation, I realize now that it marked the inception of my journey into the intricate world of the AAP. This dialogue continues to resonate with me, serving as the catalyst for my deep dive into the party's ethos and dynamics.

The lack of material on the AAP's history and evolution was a challenge, but it was also an opportunity. My coverage of the party over the years had granted me an insider's view, and it was during this time that a seasoned member of the party suggested I meet Raghu (name changed for confidentiality). Once an integral part of the AAP's leadership, from the time before the party was formed, Raghu has since distanced himself from it as well as from the AAP's national convenor, Kejriwal.

Raghu was not alone in his estrangement. Several early supporters and comrades of Kejriwal have parted ways with him, both before and after the AAP's inception. While some voiced their discontent publicly, others, like Raghu, chose silence. Their stories were whispers in the political corridors, waiting to be heard.

Raghu and I decided to meet at a coffee shop and wine bar named Perch in Khan Market, Lutyens' Delhi – an area synonymous with the power and prestige of the capital. Raghu arrived, a man whose distinctive features could tell a thousand tales, yet he preferred anonymity. Our conversation unfolded over cups of coffee, revealing the layers of the AAP's journey of transformation from a social movement to a political force. His insights were invaluable, and shed light on the internal dynamics and shifts within the party. My conversations with Raghu (over a period of time) are the source of many incidents mentioned in this book.

I began covering the AAP as a rookie journalist from 2017 at the *Millennium Post* newspaper. The AAP, although not as structurally complex as national political entities like the Bharatiya Janata Party (BJP) or the Indian National Congress (INC), presented unique hurdles, particularly during the 2019 Lok Sabha elections. Despite its grassroots origins and relatively straightforward organizational framework, the AAP's media interactions were notably restricted, posing significant challenges for journalists like me.

The AAP's approach to the media was a study in contrasts. On the one hand, a faction within the party believed that their status as Delhi's ruling party guaranteed perpetual media attention. This confidence was rooted in their significant presence in the capital, which houses major national media outlets. On the other hand, another faction argued that the party's historical association with media professionals and intellectuals inherently equipped them with the wisdom needed to manage media relations effectively.

At the Delhi Secretariat and within the party's inner circles, interactions with journalists were often superficial. While we were offered tea, coffee and engaging conversations peppered with gossip and sarcasm, substantial news was rarely shared. The real stories were reserved for elite media houses, notably the *Times of India* and *Hindustan Times*, whose extensive readership perhaps justified the preferential treatment they got.

However, these observations did not deter me from pursuing stories that mattered. Covering the AAP in Delhi provided an opportunity to explore the city's streets, lanes and neighbourhoods, bringing to light the perspectives of ordinary citizens and their interactions with the ruling party.

The 2019 general election campaign was a significant event, particularly in East Delhi, where the contest garnered considerable attention. The BJP fielded the famous cricketer Gautam Gambhir, while the AAP's candidate was Atishi Marlena (a close associate of Kejriwal). Atishi's decision to drop her surname 'Marlena' and adopt 'Singh' during the 2019 campaign was a strategic move to counter the BJP's attacks on her. She quietly shed the moniker 'Marlena' from her digital footprint and public persona as well. This strategic decision distanced her from her middle name's overt nod to communist luminaries Karl Marx and Vladimir Lenin, and also potentially quelled rumours that she was a Christian. Born into a Punjabi Rajput family, Atishi's cultural heritage stood distinct from the implications of her former middle name. This calculated rebranding underscores the complexities of identity politics and the scrutiny that public figures face. Atishi's choice reflects the delicate balance between personal heritage and perceived affiliations, highlighting the tension between authenticity and strategic self-presentation in the public eye.

One memorable assignment for me was covering an AAP rally for Atishi in Kondli (a Dalit slum in East Delhi). Here, I met Sukhdev, a 58-year-old manual scavenger, who expressed his support for the AAP, stating, '*AAP party ke log zyada imandar hote hain* (AAP members are more honest).' This sentiment was echoed by many others who believed in the AAP's integrity and clear intent, despite the party's poor performance in both the 2019 and 2024 Lok Sabha elections, where they failed to secure a single seat in Delhi.

The AAP's appeal lay in its grassroots origins and its image as a party of the people. Founded in 2012 out of the India Against Corruption (IAC) movement, the AAP positioned itself as a party dedicated to anti-corruption and good governance. This resonated with many Delhi residents, particularly those from lower socio-economic backgrounds who felt neglected by traditional political parties.

Throughout my coverage, it became clear that the AAP's strength was its ability to connect with the common man. Whether through public rallies, *mohalla sabha*s (community meetings) or their flagship policies like free water and subsidized electricity, the AAP maintained a strong rapport with the electorate. This grassroots engagement was a key factor in their continued relevance in Delhi politics, despite setbacks at the national level.

Through interactions with the AAP leaders and supporters, I gained a deeper understanding of the party's philosophy and its approach to governance. This firsthand experience of witnessing the AAP's growth and the dynamics within the party enriched my journalistic journey.

From Journalism to Political Insights Commentary

My initial encounters with the AAP were strictly as a journalist. However, I was presented with an unexpected opportunity to cross over to the other side, so to speak. The former speaker of the Delhi Legislative Assembly, Ram Niwas Goel, established the Delhi Assembly Research Centre (DARC), and I was fortunate enough to be awarded a fellowship there in 2019. This role elevated me to the position of associate fellow at DARC, where, due to my prior experience, I was stationed at the office of the then deputy CM, Manish Sisodia.

My responsibilities primarily involved media coordination. I facilitated interactions between the media and key leaders, assisted ministers with their media engagements and crafted press statements and releases for the CM, the Deputy CM and the party. This role granted me access to the party's inner workings, allowing me to observe it from an insider's perspective. However, despite this access, I remained an outsider in many ways, as the AAP's ideology was rapidly evolving during that period. I never formally joined the party but worked closely with its leaders, including top figures like former CM Kejriwal, former Deputy CM Sisodia and other prominent AAP members.

In the 2020 Delhi Assembly elections, I worked tirelessly behind the scenes for the party. The experiences I had, the stories I heard and the people I met provided me with a fresh perspective on the party, which is captured in this book.

After completing two years of my fellowship, I chose not to extend my tenure. By then, I felt a strong pull to return to my family in Kolkata. However, before I could do so, another opportunity took me to Jaipur, where I embarked on a completely different professional journey. Deliberately, I distanced myself from the AAP leadership, adhering to my belief that once you leave a space, especially a workplace, it is best not to remain entangled in its affairs. Nonetheless, my interest in the AAP persisted from afar, as I continued to study and write about their politics, offering my insights as a columnist and political commentator.

My journey from journalist to researcher has been instrumental in shaping my understanding of the AAP, and I am grateful for the opportunity to share my insights with readers.

Party with a Difference?

The rise and struggles of the AAP present a fascinating case study. Founded on the principles of anti-corruption and transparency, the party's predicament in 2024 seems paradoxical, with its senior leadership embroiled in the Delhi liquor policy case. The AAP's journey from its inception to its current state is a testament to the volatile nature of Indian politics. The party emerged from the IAC movement led by Anna Hazare in 2011, with Kejriwal and his colleagues promising a new kind of politics – clean, transparent and accountable. This promise resonated with a significant section of the populace, leading to the AAP's remarkable electoral success in Delhi. Their victory in the 2015 Delhi Assembly elections was unprecedented, with the party winning 67 out of 70 seats. This mandate was seen as a rejection of traditional politics and an endorsement of the AAP's vision.

However, the subsequent years have been challenging for the AAP. The party's governance model – which emphasized healthcare, education and public utilities – won accolades but also attracted scrutiny. The very ideals that brought the AAP to power became points of contention. Accusations of corruption and administrative overreach began to surface, tarnishing the party's image. The liquor policy case became a significant blow, leading to the arrest of key leaders and raising questions about the party's commitment to its founding principles of clean governance.

The AAP's strength has always been its grassroots appeal. Its policies on free water, subsidized electricity and improved public education and healthcare have had a tangible impact on the lives of Delhi's residents. Critics argue that the AAP's populist measures strain the state's finances and are unsustainable in the long run. Proponents, however, view these policies as necessary interventions to uplift marginalized communities and provide basic amenities to all citizens.

In the broader context of Indian politics, the AAP's journey underscores the complexities of sustaining a political movement rooted in idealism. Its challenges highlight the difficulties of maintaining transparency and accountability, while navigating the murky waters of political power. The allegations of corruption and the subsequent arrests of its leaders have cast a shadow over the AAP's claims of being a clean and ethical alternative to traditional political parties. During an interview for this book, former AAP member and journalist Ashutosh reflected poignantly, 'AAP was born out of a desire to make a difference, to be a beacon of change. Yet, today, it stands indistinguishable from any other political party in India.'

There is an undeniable aura surrounding Kejriwal within the AAP, a magnetic presence that has grown to define the party itself. As I pen these words, Kejriwal has stepped down as Delhi's CM, following an interim bail granted by the Supreme Court. True to his vow, he seeks a moral *agni pariksha* – a trial by fire – choosing only to reclaim his post if the people of Delhi re-elect him in the 2025 Assembly polls. In his stead, Atishi has assumed the CM's office, yet the shadow of Kejriwal looms large. So profound is this symbolic power that she governs with an empty chair beside her, dedicated to Kejriwal – a gesture that speaks volumes about his omnipresence.

Aurangzeb Naqshbandi, a seasoned journalist who has chronicled the AAP's journey since its inception, once remarked to me, 'You might call Atishi's act optics, but in reality, it reflects something far deeper. Today, Kejriwal's persona has eclipsed the party itself. His cult within the AAP is as powerful as Prime Minister Modi's within the BJP. The AAP is no longer just a party – it is Kejriwal-centric politics, with everything revolving around him, and nothing existing beyond.'

This statement captures the essence of a leadership so compelling that even in physical absence, Kejriwal remains the gravitational centre, a political figure whose cult has become synonymous with the AAP's very identity. The AAP's fall from grace is a cautionary tale of the dangers of unchecked ambition and the importance of adhering to one's core values. The party's journey serves as a reminder that the pursuit of power can often lead to compromise and corruption. As the AAP navigates this treacherous political landscape, it must confront its own demons and rediscover its lost ideals. Only then can it hope to reclaim its position as a champion of anti-corruption and a beacon of hope for the common man.

About this Book

This book embarks on a captivating journey to unravel the transformation of the AAP, chronicling a less-documented chapter of contemporary political history. It refrains from passing judgement on whether the AAP is right or wrong, good or bad, instead presenting facts to the readers. The narrative is divided into six distinct sections, each meticulously exploring different facets of the AAP's evolution.

The initial chapters delve into the inception of the AAP, tracing its roots back to Anna Hazare's IAC movement. This section captures the fervour and momentum that propelled the AAP into Delhi's political arena, highlighting its early achievements and setbacks. The third chapter offers a thorough evaluation of the AAP's tenure in Delhi, followed by profiles of key individuals whose contributions are integral to the party's history. Here I took the opportunity to tell the story of how the Rashtriya Swayamsevak Sangh (RSS), the ideological parent of the BJP and its affiliated organizations like the Vivekananda International Foundation (VIF) played a crucial role behind the IAC movement.

A significant portion of the book is dedicated to the 'Delhi Model of Governance', dissecting its various aspects. The narrative intertwines the persona and popularity of Kejriwal with a governance model characterized by schemes the party touts as welfare initiatives, while critics label them as populist measures. The book also delves into the contentious liquor policy issue, which led to the arrest of the AAP's top brass, including Kejriwal, presenting the facts without passing judgement.

I have also focused on the AAP's political strategy and leadership beyond Delhi, particularly its rise in Punjab, where it secured its first state election victory outside the capital. This part also addresses the controversies surrounding the party, providing a balanced view of the issues and facts. The narrative pays homage to the thousands of grassroots cadres whose stories are woven into the fabric of the AAP's journey. Additionally, it explores the party's innovative use of media, drawing from my personal experiences with the AAP.

The book concludes with an analysis of the party's prospects, and delves into the 2025 Assembly elections, which Kejriwal has termed his *agni pariksha*. This final reflection encapsulates the blend of idealism and pragmatism that defines the AAP's journey, acknowledging both its significant strides and the complexities of governance it faces. Through this comprehensive exploration, the book aims to provide readers with a nuanced understanding of the AAP's impact on Indian politics.

Today, as the AAP stands tall as a national political force within just a decade, governing two states and establishing a presence in four crucial others, there is an undeniable curiosity about its remarkable journey. While there are no comprehensive books documenting this odyssey from its inception, a few pivotal works have chronicled the AAP's meteoric rise in the political arena. In India, there exists a notable void in literature on contemporary political history, and the AAP is an integral part of this narrative. This book aims to fill that gap, offering a nuanced perspective on the party's evolution.

It is essential to acknowledge that although this book focuses on the AAP and its journey, it inevitably delves into significant political stories from various states and other political parties, all through the lens of the AAP's trajectory. By doing so, it not only charts the course of the AAP but also provides a broader understanding of the political landscape in which it operates.

I would like to add that as an associate fellow, I was appointed by the Delhi Legislative Assembly and not by any political party. I state unequivocally that this book does not disclose or refer to any official documents, reports, or outcomes of work prepared for the Legislative Assembly or the Government of Delhi.

Any references to my experience with the Aam Aadmi Party (AAP) are based solely on interactions and observations related to the party in its political capacity, and not in connection with any official or governmental function. Conversations or anecdotes involving AAP office bearers mentioned herein pertain exclusively to their role within the party and not as public representatives or government officials.

In my official capacity, I was accountable only to the Delhi Legislative Assembly and the office of the MLA or Minister to whom I was assigned. At no point did party functionaries who were not elected public representatives fall under my reporting hierarchy or official responsibilities.

It is important to clarify that any overlap between the government and the party referred to in this book is purely incidental and reflects the complex political realities of the time. None of the content herein draws upon or reveals confidential, classified, or internal work of the Delhi Government or Legislative Assembly.

Part 1

Origin Story

1

Anna vs Arvind

On 18 November 2024, my phone buzzed with a news notification informing me that the Delhi Transport and Environment Minister and senior AAP leader, Kailash Gahlot, had resigned from the party.[1] It was a news that felt like a jolt that reverberated through my thoughts. I had known Kailash Gahlot since 2015, the year he actively entered politics after contesting and winning from Najafgarh. A soft-spoken, dedicated individual, Gahlot had never veered from the directives of the AAP's high command. His work, particularly in revitalizing Delhi's transport infrastructure, had earned him widespread respect as a policymaker who prioritized action over rhetoric.

Eager to uncover more, I turned to X (formerly Twitter), where Gahlot's resignation letter had already ignited conversations. In the letter, he voiced his discontent, lamenting the erosion of the AAP's foundational values. Within a day of his resignation, Gahlot joined the BJP, sparking a storm of political speculation. Yet, for me, one line from his letter lingered: 'Challenges from within, to the very values that brought us together to AAP.'[2] He suggested that the AAP had lost the moral compass it once prided itself on.

This sentiment of shifting values is not new. Over a decade ago, Anna Hazare, the face of the IAC movement, had publicly declared his disillusionment with Kejriwal. Hazare accused him of abandoning the original ideals of transparency and anti-corruption that had fuelled their movement. The movement that once stood as a symbol of ethical reform in politics seemed mired in ideological compromises and internal discord. Hazare said, 'It is obvious. Despite the rift, we have one single aim. This (rift) is not like (what happens with) political parties. He (Kejriwal) will go his way and I will go mine. I have always stated that I don't want to form a political party and contest elections. My path is different. I had made it clear at Jantar Mantar.'[3]

In Gahlot's resignation letter, another poignant detail stands out – the mention of 'personal ambition' within the AAP. This phrase resonates deeply, as it reflects a broader and more intricate narrative within the party's history. The friction caused by individual aspirations has not only shaped Gahlot's departure but also mirrors the ideological rift that once defined the relationship between Kejriwal and his mentor, Hazare.

There has been extensive writing on the IAC movement, detailing the roles of Hazare and Kejriwal and the formation of the AAP. However, what has always fascinated me is the relationship between Hazare and Kejriwal. The dynamic between the two is a subtle yet layered story of transformation. They were once a celebrated duo – *guru* and *shishya* – united in their crusade against corruption during the IAC movement. However, this camaraderie gradually eroded, giving way to a contentious relationship marked by disillusionment and discord. Hazare later became one of Kejriwal's most vocal critics, accusing him of abandoning the movement's ethos in favour of personal and political gain.

As I reflect on this complex history, the image of Hazare's pointed critiques lingers. His disappointment with Kejriwal's governance style is not just about policy differences but about a perceived betrayal of the moral foundation upon which their movement was built. To delve deeper into this evolving relationship, I turn to my notes from an enlightening conversation with Dhruv (name changed), who had witnessed these dynamics unfold firsthand. I had the chance to meet Dhruv during the 2019 Lok Sabha election campaign. Through his insights, the tangled threads of ambition, ideology and betrayal begin to transform into a story of a partnership that once inspired millions but now stands as a cautionary tale of fractured ideals.

Dhruv, who resides in Canada, had come to Delhi for a family function and decided to attend some AAP rallies due to his old association with Hazare's movement.

Over a cup of tea at the Cha Bar in Connaught Place, Dhruv shared his insights with me. 'Arvind met Anna during the early 2000s, when the Right to Information protest was gaining momentum. At that time, several organizations across India were working on eradicating corruption and making the government accountable,' he recounted.

Dhruv explained that, during this period, Kejriwal was an Indian Revenue Service (IRS) officer running an NGO named Parivartan. His efforts to expose corrupt IRS officers and his relentless work for the betterment of the slum dwellers in Sundar Nagri were well-known among activists. 'When Anna and Arvind met, they not only collaborated on RTI but also worked closely on drafting the Jan Lokpal Bill in later years. Anna had an aura but also an ego, and it was clear to us that Arvind was never very fond of Anna,' Dhruv said.

Dhruv mentioned that during the late 2000s, RTI activism peaked, and news of the murders of RTI activists and whistleblowers was rampant. Arvind Kejriwal, lawyer Prashant Bhushan, Supreme Court judge Santosh Hegde and former Law Minister Shanti Bhushan came together to draft a bill to protect whistleblowers and fight corruption. Shanti Bhushan had first proposed the draft Lokpal Bill in 1968, but it was not fully passed.

From late 2010 to early 2011, Kejriwal and others travelled state by state, discussing their plan to launch a mass movement against corruption and to pressurize the government to pass the Jan Lokpal Bill. Activists from Maharashtra suggested that Hazare could become the face of the movement, as he was already an anti-corruption crusader and a popular name in Maharashtra.

According to activists close to Kejriwal, he was initially hesitant to involve Hazare due to the latter's ego and straightforwardness. Kejriwal reached out to figures like Baba Ramdev, Sri Sri Ravi Shankar and others to involve them in the anti-corruption movement because they had a huge following. But he was sure that they could not be the face of the IAC movement.[4]

It's essential to recognize that the IAC movement, which electrified the nation, was not originally conceived by Hazare but was largely the vision of Kejriwal. Before Kejriwal and his team approached Anna, there was no blueprint for such a large-scale anti-corruption campaign under Hazare's name. Kejriwal, with his organizational acumen and clarity of purpose, imagined a movement that could channel public frustration against systemic corruption into a force of change.

Kejriwal's ambitions were boundless, and he saw the IAC movement as the beginning of something transformative. In contrast, Hazare, rooted in Gandhian principles, approached the movement with a different mindset. For him, protests, fasting and grassroots agitation were the ultimate tools of moral persuasion – the measured and patient pathways to reform. This divergence in temperament and vision became evident as the movement progressed.

In order to grasp the breakdown between Hazare and Kejriwal, it's vital to revisit the chain of events that unravelled their once-solid camaraderie. Hazare's hunger strikes under the IAC banner comprised three notable fasts in 2011 (discussed in detail in the next chapter). The inaugural fast occurred in April, followed by another in July and culminated in a less successful one in December. The unyielding support and enthusiasm around the first two Delhi fasts gradually waned by the time they reached Mumbai (previously Bombay).

By early 2012, the discord within the IAC movement was publicly evident. Hazare, abandoning the IAC banner, embarked on a state-wide tour in Maharashtra.[5] Despite the apparent discord, neither Hazare nor Kejriwal openly opposed one another, maintaining a veneer of unity. However, the cracks became glaringly visible during a critical internal meeting of the IAC's core committee in Delhi.

During this period, predating the official announcement, whispers about Pranab Mukherjee being a potential presidential candidate under the United Progressive Alliance (UPA) were rampant. In a bold move, Kejriwal – supported by his close-knit team including Manish Sisodia, Gopal Rai and Sanjay Singh – in an internal meeting of the core committee proposed that the IAC should stand against Mukherjee's candidacy, citing corruption allegations.[6] Hazare, however, was blindsided by this proposal, which wasn't on the agenda and felt like an abrupt hijacking of the meeting's purpose. Reliable sources recount Hazare's public chastisement of Kejriwal, declaring that if the IAC took a stance against Mukherjee, he would dissociate from the movement. The meeting concluded in disarray.

Come April 2012, post this heated confrontation, Kejriwal, alongside Sanjay Singh, made an unanticipated sojourn to Himachal Pradesh, where the state was gearing up for its Assembly elections. 'We were startled when we heard about their presence in Himachal. Only a select few of Arvind's team were in the loop, leaving the core committee in the dark. When confronted, Arvind claimed Anna sent him to explore potential candidate support,' an insider remarked. However, according to the sources, when questioned, Hazare denied issuing any such instructions.

Upon their return, Kejriwal and his loyal associates – Prithvi Reddy, Mayank Gandhi, Manish Sisodia, Gopal Rai and Sanjay Singh, among others – clandestinely broached the idea of forming a political party. Kejriwal was acutely aware that Hazare would never endorse such a move, but he was resolute in his conviction that the time was ripe to venture into politics.

An insider revealed, 'Arvind indicated it was time to engage disenchanted IAC supporters and rally them. Surprisingly, his team also suggested refocusing leadership on Arvind and centralizing efforts on Delhi, as the Mumbai fasts and protests fizzled out.'

By mid-2012, it was clear that Kejriwal had outgrown his pretence of deference to Hazare. With grand designs in mind, those close to the movement sensed that a significant shift was imminent. In a dramatic turn, Kejriwal announced that he would be on an indefinite hunger strike from the end of July 2012.[7] During the preparations, it became evident that Hazare had not been kept in the loop. Nevertheless, Kejriwal's team extended an olive branch, seeking Hazare's support. With little choice, Hazare accepted, aware that outright refusal could mean ceding leadership of the IAC movement to Kejriwal.

An incident during this period offers insight into the brewing betrayal felt by Hazare. He agreed to support the strike on the condition that placards denouncing Pranab Mukherjee be removed. He added that he would join the fast later to allow the government time to act on their demands, which included probes against then Prime Minister (PM) Manmohan Singh and other cabinet ministers. Hazare joined the fast on the fourth day, but insiders noted Kejriwal's irritation. In the protest rally, the placards and banners against Mukherjee were removed by team Kejriwal. But suddenly, in a fiery speech upon Hazare's arrival, Kejriwal condemned Mukherjee, further deepening the rift.[8]

Kejriwal then distributed copies of his book, *Swaraj*, calling for a total revolution – a thinly veiled reference to forming a political party. The message was unmistakable: Kejriwal was now steering the IAC and Hazare's influence was waning. Many viewed this move as typical of Kejriwal: use someone until they were no longer needed.

This fast seemed orchestrated to pit Kejriwal directly against the government. Insiders believed the script was predetermined. When Kejriwal's health began to fail, he remained obstinate about ending the fast. It was then that his confidant, Yogendra Yadav, reached out to civil society figures, drafting a letter urging Kejriwal to consider forming a political alternative rather than succumbing to hunger. The seeds of a political party were sown on 3 August 2012. While Hazare opposed the idea, he begrudgingly supported the notion of a political alternative.

An insider commented, 'Arvind was poised to launch a political party, but Anna ji was attempting to manipulate the situation. Arvind conducted an opinion poll following Anna ji's directives, which showed public support for a new party. Anna ji rejected the poll and suggested forming a panel of prominent civil society figures for their opinion. Again, the majority endorsed Arvind.'

According to the insiders, the decisive fracture came when Kejriwal convened a panel of 42 prominent figures – including Kiran Bedi, Santosh Hegde, Yogendra Yadav and V.K. Singh. On 19 September, only six (this includes Bedi, Singh and Hegde, among others) of the 42 members opposed the formation of a party. Hazare stormed out, declaring he would disassociate from the movement if a political party was formed, and insisting that his name and image not be used. The schism between Kejriwal and Hazare became public and has persisted ever since.[9]

A key question about the genesis of the AAP is: Why did Anna Hazare refuse to support Arvind Kejriwal's idea of turning the movement into a political force? Was it ego that divided them, or were they simply disillusioned in different ways, driven by their own restless ambitions?

The IAC movement had shaken the Congress-led government to its core, forcing it to engage in discussions with the movement's leaders. Hazare seemed to believe that the movement's impact would fade into irrelevance if they abandoned their non-political stance, while Kejriwal, ever the pragmatist, recognized that real change would require political power – power that could only be wielded from within the system.

A senior member of the AAP, who spoke to me on condition of anonymity, offered a candid reflection on those turbulent times:

> It's been a decade since we first met Anna Hazare. When we were forming AAP and Anna refused to support us, we thought he was being stubborn, impractical. But now, standing where we are today, I see the difference between Arvind and Anna was flexibility. Anna was a man of

unyielding ideals, unwilling to compromise even an inch. But look at him now – he's being used by political leaders in Maharashtra for their own ends.

He paused thoughtfully before continuing, his voice steady yet reflective.

Arvind was relentless, but not for the sake of accolades or authority. His drive wasn't about earning a title or sitting in a plush office. It was something deeper – a burning hunger to transform the ideals of the IAC movement into tangible change. He saw what others didn't: that without a political framework, the movement's fire would burn out. The energy, the passion, the unity of people from all walks of life – brought together by the hope of a corruption-free India – would dissipate. They'd return to their routines, their struggles, their personal ambitions. And all that would remain of the IAC would be the memory of an extraordinary uprising, a 'what-if' etched in history.

He paused again, as if measuring the weight of his words, and then continued: 'Arvind understood the cost of inaction. He realized that movements, no matter how powerful, are fleeting without an anchor in governance. His leap into politics wasn't a betrayal of the movement – it was, in his eyes, its natural evolution. Without it, the ideals of the IAC would be nothing more than whispers lost to time.'

He said that the people who were part of the movement understood Hazare's ideology and respected it, but also knew that if they didn't act, the opportunity would be lost forever. He said:

Kejriwal wasn't willing to lose that momentum. That's why AAP was born. Today, when Anna criticizes Arvind and the party, it hurts each one of us who were part of the IAC. But we also understand, we never held it against him. He chose his path, and we chose ours. In the end, it wasn't about ego or disillusionment; it was about the choices we made in the face of an uncertain future.

For Kejriwal, the birth of the AAP was not just a choice but a necessity – a calculated move to translate the fervour of the IAC movement into real political change. To him, a political platform was the logical next step, a way to institutionalize the fight against corruption and bring about tangible governance reforms. However, for Hazare, this transition symbolized a departure from the purity of the movement's ideals. He saw the shift as a betrayal of the principles of apolitical activism that the movement was founded upon, a deviation from its essence.

One of the early participants in the IAC movement shared a memory with me that underscored this growing rift. 'There was a meeting,' he recalled, 'where Anna's team and Arvind sat down to discuss the way forward. Within 10 minutes, Arvind abruptly walked out. He didn't say much, but it was clear to all of us that he was deeply upset. The reason? Anna had expressed that venturing into politics was a selfish move, a path that would compromise the integrity of the movement.'

Hazare's opposition to the formation of the AAP stemmed from several key concerns. Primarily, he feared that politicizing the anti-corruption agenda would undermine its effectiveness. The IAC movement's strength had been its ability to rise above the political fray, uniting people under a common cause without the taint of party politics. Hazare worried that by entering the political arena, the movement would lose this universal appeal and become just another political party – vulnerable to the same compromises and corruptions it had originally sought to challenge.

Moreover, Hazare was deeply concerned about the practical realities of forming a political party. He understood the necessity of compromise in politics, the pressures of electoral success and the inherent risks of candidates succumbing to the very corruption they were supposed to fight. His scepticism was, perhaps, based on a profound understanding of these challenges, and he feared that the purity of the IAC movement's intent would be eroded by the harsh realities of political life.

Kejriwal's trajectory within the IAC movement was marked both by his ambitious vision and an unyielding desire to lead from the front. Known among his circle for his persuasive charm, Kejriwal had an exceptional ability to bring people to his point of view. A section of IAC's early members believed that Kejriwal was confident he could similarly influence Hazare, the movement's moral compass. However, Kejriwal underestimated Hazare's steadfast commitment to his principles and was ultimately unable to sway him.

In the initial months after the AAP was formed, Hazare cautiously lent his external support. But as the party's actions unfolded, his disillusionment grew. The party's ticket distribution process, which included candidates with questionable backgrounds, starkly contradicted the ideals of integrity and transparency championed by the IAC movement. Despite Kejriwal's public rhetoric about decentralization, the party and decision-making increasingly revolved around him. This divergence from IAC's foundational principles made it impossible for Hazare to continue his tacit support.

The bond between Hazare and Kejriwal, once rooted in mutual respect and shared ambition, unravelled as their paths diverged. Anna, deeply committed to Gandhian principles and social welfare, could not reconcile with Kejriwal's pragmatic (some might say opportunistic) political strategies. While Kejriwal's vision and decisiveness had been instrumental in building the IAC movement's momentum, his shifting values and centralized leadership style created an enduring tension. This tension, born of differing worldviews, became the defining element of their complicated relationship.

2

RSS Support

In March 2011, Hazare was preparing to launch his first major *dharna* and fast as part of the IAC movement. This was set to begin in the first week of April at Jantar Mantar, Delhi. However, Kejriwal was anxious about the level of public participation. Team Kejriwal reached out to various individuals, including celebrities, to join the agitation. Many agreed, as the issue of fighting against the corruption of the Congress government resonated widely. But the question remained: what about grassroots support?

A senior journalist, privy to these developments, explained things under the condition of anonymity, saying, 'Kejriwal had several concerns. Firstly, Hazare was adamant about an indefinite hunger strike and was unwilling to settle for just a dharna. Kejriwal and his team realized that to sustain such an indefinite hunger strike, they would need substantial logistical support, funds and a consistent presence of people.' The journalist added that while many well-wishers and even NRIs were enthusiastic about the agitation and provided funds to the IAC, Kejriwal was seeking more grassroots support. He knew that at the time most of the agitators were from the middle and upper-middle classes, whose commitment for an indefinite period was uncertain.

In mid-March, Kejriwal met with a group of anti-corruption volunteers who had been involved in other agitations led by figures close to the RSS, such as Baba Ramdev and Sri Sri

Ravi Shankar. They suggested that Kejriwal contact Ajit Doval, who was then the founding director of the RSS-linked think tank VIF, established in 2009. The foundation was actively fighting against corruption, particularly black money. Doval was a well-known figure among anti-corruption activists, and sources familiar with the developments indicated that Kejriwal sought support from Doval and his team.

The RSS operates several frontal organizations under its patronage. In 1970, noted RSS *Pracharak* Eknath Ramakrishna Ranade – a disciple of RSS founder K.B. Hedgewar and a close confidant of the second *Sarsanghchalak* (RSS chief) M.S. Golwalkar – founded Vivekananda Kendra. In 2009, Vivekananda Kendra launched its think tank, VIF, with Doval as the founding director. Later, his son Shaurya became the director of the foundation. Many RSS-linked ideologues, including S. Gurumurthy, co-convenor of Swadeshi Jagaran Manch, were associated with the VIF.[1]

Kejriwal was well aware of the history of the VIF and its links with the RSS and the BJP. Following initial conversations between Kejriwal and some members of the VIF, Kejriwal, Hazare and Kiran Bedi (who was also part of the IAC movement) were invited by Doval to attend a two-day seminar organized by the VIF in early April 2011. During this seminar, Kejriwal also met Baba Ramdev and several top RSS functionaries, including RSS ideologue K.N. Govindacharya. Within a week of this seminar Hazare started his fast at Jantar Mantar.[2]

A source close to the RSS revealed, 'After that meeting, Kejriwal met Govind ji [Govindacharya] and sought his support for the IAC movement.' In that brief encounter, it became evident that the RSS would provide ground support in terms of crowd mobilization. Sources confirmed that as the IAC movement gained momentum, many patrons close to the RSS, VIF and another RSS-linked organization, India Foundation, extended their support in various ways, such as by organizing *langars*, managing footfall and more.

It is crucial to acknowledge that the RSS's support was not solely for social causes but also for political reasons. At that time, the BJP was cornering the UPA government led by Congress under then PM Manmohan Singh. The RSS was working on the ground to create a larger narrative. In an interview, senior journalist and political editor of *The Hindu*, Nistula Hebbar, noted, 'The RSS always takes a long view of any sociopolitical development. They realized that providing grassroots support to IAC would be beneficial in many ways. The BJP had been raising the issue of corruption politically but was not gaining traction on the ground, which the IAC did. Therefore, the Sangh decided to support it from the background.' She also acknowledged that Kejriwal had a good relationship with many RSS ideologues, including Govindacharya.

Hazare ended his fast on 9 April 2011, as the government agreed to form a joint committee to draft the Jan Lokpal Bill.[3] Several meetings of the joint committee took place until mid-June 2011. On 7 June, Hazare boycotted the joint committee meeting over several disagreements. It was then that Kejriwal realized that more protests would be needed on a much larger scale. This time, with a bigger venue and much more support, Hazare started his second fast at Ramlila Maidan on 19 August.[4] But before this mega event, Kejriwal and representatives of the RSS had several meetings to strengthen the protest.

According to a source close to these developments:

> There was discontent within the RSS, as some leaders like Prashant Bhushan, Yogendra Yadav and Medha Patkar openly expressed their displeasure with the presence of RSS volunteers. But Kejriwal tried to pacify the situation. In an effort to do so, he took the lead in organizing a day-long joint fast of Baba Ramdev and Anna Hazare against black money and corruption.

For the very first time, Baba Ramdev and Hazare shared the protest stage together on 3 June 2011.[5] The talks between the RSS and Kejriwal resumed after a brief stalemate. When Kejriwal started planning the bigger phase of the protest at Ramlila Maidan, he met Govindacharya in July 2011.[6] It was the first formal meeting between a top RSS ideologue and Kejriwal.

Govindacharya was not only close to the RSS but also to the BJP, having served as a general secretary of the party. During their interaction, Kejriwal informed Govindacharya that there was a sentiment within a section of the IAC that the direct presence of RSS ideologues and BJP leaders should be avoided. Govindacharya understood the sentiment and ensured that the RSS would continue to support the movement from the background. According to people close to these developments and media reports, Govindacharya stated that while there were several different groups organizing protests on the same issue – such as Baba Ramdev, Sri Sri Ravi Shankar, Hazare and others – each protest had its own priorities. However, he added that they should work in tandem with each other and not stand against each other.

In an interview to the *Economic Times*, Govindacharya mentioned about this interaction with Kejriwal. He said:

> I remember very distinctly, July 6, 2011, at a meeting held at the office of the NGO run by Kejriwal, it was decided that *mudde samaan, manch alag* (same issues, different platforms). It was agreed that whether it is Ramdev, Anna Hazare, Kejriwal, Jayprakash Narayan's Loksatta or R.K. Mishra's Navbharat Party, we would not engage in competitive politics with each other.[7]

In the following month, Kejriwal also met with RSS ideologue and one of the key patrons of the VIF, S. Gurumurthy. In an article, Gurumurthy vividly recounted his conversation with Kejriwal. He wrote, 'A common friend, Darshak Hathi, had accompanied Kejriwal. Darshak was part of the India Against Corruption (IAC) team in its critical work of drafting the Lokpal Bill, meeting the Prime Minister and other ministers. He was also instrumental in mobilizing the Art of Living volunteers who were initially IAC's backbone.'[8]

The article made it clear that not only were RSS pracharaks directly involved in the IAC movement, but that they were also part of crucial decision-making processes. During that meeting, Kejriwal accepted that RSS ideologues and BJP leaders could attend the IAC rally, but that they would have to be there as part of the audience.[9]

After the second hunger strike led by Hazare, Kejriwal believed the groundwork for a large-scale protest had been laid. The massive turnout and public support had pressured the government to discuss the Jan Lokpal Bill in Parliament. However, Kejriwal continued to face dissent within the IAC for involving the RSS in the movement. In response, he began distancing himself from the RSS. In a surprising move, pictures and names of Baba Ramdev and Sri Sri Ravi Shankar were removed from the IAC website.[10] Despite attempts by the RSS, through various NGOs and ideologues, to resolve the situation, Kejriwal remained adamant. The top leaders of the RSS were irked by the IAC's distancing and denial of their role. A year later, RSS Chief Mohan Bhagwat openly criticized Hazare, stating, 'It is a fact that the Sangh workers in individual capacity did play an active role in the anti-corruption crusade by the civil society headed by Hazare … It baffles me as to why the former did not acknowledge the fact.'[11]

In December, Hazare announced a three-day fast in Mumbai.[12] Maharashtra, with the RSS headquarters in Nagpur, has always been a stronghold for the organization. The RSS, wanting to retaliate against Kejriwal, completely stayed away from the fast. Internally, some members from the IAC movement sought support from Sri Sri Ravi Shankar and Baba Ramdev, but even they denied their support. The withdrawal of RSS support hit the IAC movement hard, and the Mumbai protest did not see the expected turnout. Within 48 hours, Hazare withdrew the fast due to the lack of support.

From these incidents and interactions, it becomes clear that the RSS was actively involved in the IAC movement, and that it was Kejriwal who maintained the bond with the RSS. Many early members of the IAC movement, like Prashant Bhushan, often expressed that they and many others were not informed about the active participation of the RSS.[13] The fact is that Kejriwal knew that members like Bhushan would never accept the active participation of the RSS, and therefore, they were not informed about many of these interactions.

In an interview with *India Today*'s Rajdeep Sardesai, Bhushan said:

> In hindsight, there are two things that I do regret. One is not seeing that the movement was to a large extent supported and propped up by the BJP–RSS for their own political purposes to bring down the Congress government and get themselves in power. I have no doubt about it [RSS–BJP role] today. He [Anna Hazare] was also probably not aware of it, Arvind was aware of it, I have very little doubt of that.[14]

An IAC member, former AAP member and journalist, Ashutosh, admitted that the active participation of the RSS and its volunteers was indeed a crucial factor within the IAC, but he defended that RSS members were never a part of the key decision-making process. He said, 'It is an open secret today that RSS members and volunteers joined the IAC movement. But we always limited their presence to the audience. They were never part of the core committee which used to take all the decisions.'

Meanwhile, the AAP members, despite knowing the reality, have always been tight-lipped about the involvement of the RSS in the IAC movement and, more importantly, the closeness of Kejriwal and the Sangh. The pertinent question is: when the RSS and its ideologues gave unconditional support to a movement like the IAC, how could it be possible that they were not part of any decision-making process?

3

IAC to AAP

In the opening chapter of this book, I detail how the seeds for a political party were sown during Kejriwal's hunger strike in July 2012, leaving Hazare perplexed. As Hazare distanced himself from the notion of forming a political organization, the path was cleared for Kejriwal and his supporters to move forward with launching their own political entity. This marked a turning point, signalling the transition from a grassroots movement to a structured political venture led by Kejriwal.

The formation of the AAP from the IAC movement is a narrative that embodies the transformation of grassroots activism into a formal political entity. This evolution was both inevitable and challenging. To fully appreciate this metamorphosis, it is essential to delve into the motivations that drove the movement, the ideological commitments of its leaders and the key events that catalysed the formation of the AAP.

As I began to trace the early days of the AAP, I encountered significant challenges. Everyone seemed to have a different version of events. Current AAP members predominantly focused on Kejriwal, casting him as the central figure and hero of the entire movement. However, those who were involved in the IAC movement but later distanced themselves from the AAP (or never joined it) offered a contrasting narrative. They believed that the movement was a culmination of the people's growing frustration with the corrupt Congress government and other politicians, which eventually led to the creation of the AAP as a political vehicle for these grievances.

To better understand the AAP's early days, I met Ashutosh at his Noida residence. 'Corruption was rampant at that time, and there was widespread public anger,' Ashutosh explained. 'The idea behind AAP was to show the people of India that politics could be different – that a political party could stand against dynastic politics and be free of corruption. We genuinely believed that a cleaner, more accountable political system was possible. Although things have changed within the party over time, our original motivation and goals were sincere.'

Before the launch of the AAP, its founders adopted a series of resolutions that would define the party's identity and principles. They resolved to focus on five foundational ideals: participation, accountability, transparency, decentralization and integrity – echoing the ethos of the IAC movement.

To maintain these principles, they established four key commitments: the party would contest elections without resorting to corruption, steadfastly reject communalism, avoid caste-based politics and would refuse alliances with other political entities, either for power or other purposes. These resolutions underscored the party's commitment to clean governance and moral clarity.[1]

The group also agreed on the establishment of an internal *lokpal* – a watchdog headed by a retired judge – to address complaints against party leaders or elected representatives. This was seen as a way to uphold the integrity of the party. Additionally, they pledged that the party would remain grounded, standing by the people in all circumstances.

These foundational principles set the tone for the AAP's early days, marking it as a party dedicated to challenging the entrenched political system and empowering ordinary citizens. With these resolutions, the party laid the groundwork for its vision of clean, transparent and accountable governance.[2]

The AAP was officially launched on 26 November 2012.[3]

The early days of the AAP were marked by a sense of urgency and idealism. The party quickly began to organize itself, building a network of volunteers and supporters across the country. Its message of clean governance and citizen empowerment resonated with many – particularly with the urban middle class, who had grown disillusioned with the existing political options. The AAP's emphasis on transparency, its rejection of traditional political hierarchies and its commitment to grassroots activism set it apart from other political parties. This was a party that promised to break the stranglehold of the old political elites and give voice to the common man.

One of the key figures in the AAP's success has been **Manish Sisodia**, a former journalist and social activist who emerged as one of the most prominent faces of the party, particularly in the realm of education. As deputy CM of Delhi, Sisodia has been instrumental in revolutionizing the state's education system. His background in journalism gave him a nuanced understanding of public issues, which he channelled into creating policies that emphasized quality education for all.

Another key figure in the party's early days was **Prashant Bhushan**. Bhushan's reputation for legal activism, particularly in holding the powerful accountable through the judiciary, lent credibility to the AAP's anti-corruption stance. As a member of the party's political affairs committee, Bhushan played a crucial role in shaping the AAP's policies and strategies, ensuring that the party remained true to its founding principles of transparency and accountability. His involvement highlighted the importance of legal expertise in navigating the complex political landscape of India.

Kumar Vishwas, a poet and professor, brought a unique cultural and academic perspective to the AAP. Vishwas's background in literature and his oratory skills made him a charismatic figure within the party, helping connect the AAP's message with a broader audience. His ability to engage with people through poetry and speeches added a distinct flavour to the party's campaign, making politics accessible and relatable to the common man. Vishwas's contributions demonstrated how cultural and academic insights could be harnessed to inspire and mobilize support for political change.

Pankaj Gupta, an IT professional turned political strategist, was instrumental in building the AAP's organizational structure and election strategies. With his background in information technology, Gupta brought a modern, data-driven approach to the party's operations, helping to streamline processes and improve efficiency. His strategic thinking was key to the AAP's success in the highly competitive electoral landscape, ensuring that the party was not only ideologically sound but also logistically prepared for the challenges of modern politics.

Gopal Rai, a social activist with a deep connection to grassroots movements, focused his efforts on labour issues and the empowerment of marginalized communities. Rai's work within the party emphasized the importance of inclusivity and social justice, ensuring that the AAP's policies addressed the needs of the most vulnerable sections of society. His commitment to these causes reinforced the AAP's image as a party of the people – dedicated to uplifting those who had long been ignored by the political establishment.

Sanjay Singh, a seasoned politician and social worker, played a pivotal role in expanding the AAP's reach beyond Delhi. His experience in grassroots politics and his ability to connect with diverse communities helped the AAP establish a presence in other states, broadening the party's appeal and influence. Singh's efforts were crucial in transforming the AAP from a regional movement into a national political force.

Shanti Bhushan, a respected senior advocate and former union law minister, brought a wealth of legal and political experience to the AAP. As one of the party's founding members, Shanti Bhushan's involvement provided a strong moral and legal foundation for the party's anti-corruption stance. His long-standing commitment to judicial activism and his role in drafting the Jan Lokpal Bill made him a vital figure in the party's early formation. Shanti Bhushan's presence in the AAP not only lent it credibility but also highlighted the party's commitment to upholding the rule of law and ensuring justice for all.

Yogendra Yadav, a renowned psephologist and academic, provided the party with critical insights into electoral politics and policymaking. Yadav's expertise in analysing voter behaviour and his deep understanding of political theory helped the AAP craft policies that were not only popular but also pragmatic. His contributions were essential in guiding the party through the complexities of electoral strategy and governance, ensuring that the AAP's ideals were translated into effective political action.

Together, these individuals formed the backbone of the AAP, each contributing their unique talents and perspectives to create a party that sought to redefine Indian politics. Their collective efforts helped shape the AAP into a political force that continues to challenge the status quo and advocate for a more just and equitable society. The formation of the AAP from the IAC movement is not just a chapter in a book, it is a chapter in the ongoing saga of India's quest for a more equitable and just society.

Senior journalist and former AAP member Ashutosh told me during an interview:

> None of us entered politics because we craved power. Just look at people like Yogendra Yadav, Prashant Bhushan, Ashish Khetan and so many others. They were already well-established in their respective fields. There was no allure of power for them. We didn't romanticize the idea of holding office. What drove us was the desire to take the ideals of the India Against Corruption movement and translate them into political reality. That's why we decided to form the party – not for power, but for a purpose, to change the system from within.

His words captured the ethos of the AAP's early days – idealism over ambition, purpose over power.

4

Uncertain Beginnings

After the formation of the AAP, one of the immediate challenges was accommodating members of the IAC movement who opted to join the party. The IAC had branches across the country, and many activists from various states expressed interest in becoming part of this new political venture. Although Kejriwal was clear in his strategy to initially focus the party's activities in Delhi, it was essential to include members from other states to uphold the inclusivity and spirit of the movement.

In mid-November 2012, Kejriwal convened a meeting with his close confidants in Delhi to discuss the party's organizational structure. It was proposed that the AAP would have three primary components:

1. the National Council, comprising representatives from all states;
2. the National Executive, limited to 30 members and responsible for discussions and decision-making;
3. the Political Action Committee (PAC), the apex body tasked with political strategy and decisions.

The first National Council meeting, attended by over 300 members, was held in Delhi on 24 November 2012. This meeting marked a significant milestone, as the National Executive was entrusted with drafting the party's constitution. Kejriwal was elected as the national convenor, and the party finalized its symbol – the *jhadu* (broom), symbolizing a commitment to clean governance. Thus, the AAP's journey began.

A former AAP member speaking anonymously told me during 2017 when I started to trace the roots of the party, 'The structure was designed so that ultimate authority rested with the PAC and the national convenor. Over time, it became evident that other bodies had minimal influence. Initially, the party also introduced an internal Lokpal, but this position was effectively sidelined and eventually rendered obsolete. Today, the role no longer exists.'

After establishing its organizational structure, the AAP faced its first major challenge – the 2013 Delhi Assembly elections. While the party enjoyed momentum from its roots in the IAC movement, Kejriwal and his team were uncertain whether this support would translate into votes.

Kejriwal and Sisodia, experienced in grassroots activism, identified issues that had long plagued Delhi residents – electricity and water bills. Internal discussions led to a bold promise: slashing electricity and water bills by 50 per cent. While some leaders initially doubted the feasibility, a committee was formed to study the proposal. The findings revealed that Delhi's surplus budget, maintained under Sheila Dikshit's government, could support such a policy. This encouraged the party, but Kejriwal pushed for a more pointed political narrative.[1]

According to a party insider privy to these discussions, Kejriwal linked high utility bills to alleged cronyism between Dikshit's government and electricity companies, creating a compelling campaign narrative. 'She's catering to crony capitalists,' he argued, galvanizing public anger. This strategy laid the foundation for the AAP's direct outreach to voters through grassroots mobilization.

Kejriwal's leadership style also became evident during this period. As mentioned previously, decisions increasingly revolved around him and a close circle of confidants, leaving others in the organization sidelined. For instance, his proposal to launch a hunger strike – aimed at drawing attention to the utility bill issue – sparked internal debate. Many felt it could overshadow essential organizational tasks like building grassroots networks and selecting candidates.

Despite reservations, Kejriwal's determination to lead from the front defined the AAP's campaign. His rhetoric, paired with actionable promises, resonated deeply with Delhi voters, setting the stage for the AAP's rise as a political force. However, his approach also hinted at emerging tensions within the party's ranks, foreshadowing the challenges the AAP would face in balancing idealism with pragmatism.

The AAP's preparations for Kejriwal's indefinite hunger strike in March 2013 were met with mixed responses. Volunteers, initially focused on the Delhi Assembly election preparations, were redirected to mobilize support for the fast. Kejriwal chose Sundar Nagri, a slum where he had previously worked as an NGO activist, as the protest venue – a symbolic gesture to demonstrate his connection to grassroots issues.

The hunger strike began with moderate success. The initial days saw a good turnout, but the crowd began to dwindle, leaving primarily the AAP volunteers in attendance. Unlike Hazare, Kejriwal lacked the charismatic pull of a mass mobilizer, as his reputation had been built in the background. However, the AAP leaders recognized that only Kejriwal could galvanize the party's grassroots traction. Frustrated by the low footfall, Kejriwal escalated his campaign, calling for a *satyagraha* against Dikshit's government and urging Delhi residents to stop paying electricity bills. This bold move rekindled public interest, but the government remained unresponsive, and Kejriwal's health began to deteriorate.[2]

Behind the scenes, party leaders convened to address the situation. An insider recalled, 'We urged Arvind to end the fast, as many signatures had already been collected in support of slashing utility bills. But Arvind was adamant – he wanted over a million signatures before considering withdrawal.' With limited reach, achieving this goal seemed daunting.

The AAP volunteers were tasked with door-to-door campaigns to engage diverse demographics, from the economically disadvantaged to residents of middle-class housing societies and RWAs (residents welfare associations). This outreach not only bolstered support for the hunger strike but also established goodwill with key voter bases, laying a foundation for future governance.

As signatures surpassed the one million mark, Kejriwal ended his fast, signalling a symbolic victory.[3] With the hunger strike behind them, the AAP resumed its preparations for the electoral battle ahead, fortified by the momentum of their grassroots efforts.

This time, the AAP faced the monumental task of deciding how to field candidates for Delhi's 70 constituencies. Unlike traditional political parties, which often select candidates based on financial prowess and winnability, the AAP aimed to revolutionize the process with a transparent policy. Crafted by minds like Atishi Marlena Singh and Yogendra Yadav, this complex policy was designed to ensure fairness and integrity. Interestingly, within a year, the party would abandon this policy, reverting to conventional methods of candidate selection.

What I gathered from the founding members of the party is that the AAP's innovative approach allowed any individual from a constituency to become a candidate by gathering signatures from at least a 100 supporters. Candidates then had to complete a detailed form disclosing any criminal or political history. An internal committee meticulously reviewed these reports, narrowing down the candidates to five per constituency. These names and their forms were published on the AAP website, inviting public feedback. Citizens could submit evidence of corruption or wrongdoing, which the party would consider before finalizing the candidate.

Despite the complexity, the AAP adhered to this process for its first election, upholding the IAC's demand for transparency.

The party also committed to publishing detailed donation records on their website during the 2013 Delhi election campaign.

However, reality soon set in. Several AAP candidates had assets exceeding ₹1 crore. The *Indian Express* reported that nine candidates had declared assets over ₹1 crore, with Shazia Ilmi leading with over ₹30 crore. This wealth highlighted the socio-economic diversity within the party, despite its anti-corruption stance.[4]

A senior journalist covering the AAP's early days noted that the media repeatedly questioned Kejriwal about selecting wealthy candidates over those from lower economic strata. Kejriwal often evaded these critical questions.

The AAP's supporters, mostly enthusiastic and principled individuals from the IAC movement, appreciated the party's initial decisions on candidate selection and donation transparency. There was a palpable excitement among Delhi's people, AAP supporters and volunteers from various states eager to support the party in its first election. Kejriwal and his team, with the help of well-wishers, arranged food and accommodation for the volunteers.

Buoyed by this enthusiasm, Kejriwal announced his candidacy against Delhi's sitting CM, Sheila Dikshit. Arvind's core objective was clear: he aimed to position himself as the direct challenger to Sheila Dikshit. His entire political narrative in Delhi was built around opposing the then chief minister, and he believed that if he didn't confront her head-on in the electoral battle, the central message of his party would be undermined. This bold move surprised everyone, as top leaders typically contest from safe constituencies. Neither the Congress party nor Dikshit fully grasped the AAP's rising influence and public resonance. Dikshit dismissed the AAP as a non-entity in several interviews, attempting to discredit Kejriwal. She once remarked:

> When AAP was created, they touched the emotions and feelings of people, and their talk was something reflective of what people were feeling. But, as it appears now, that was really a self certification. And today their face has

> totally changed They influenced people in such a way that people started believing that they will really change ways, thoughts and means of the system, but they are exposed now. So now time will see what happens next.[5]

Kejriwal's identity politics became prominent in this election, framing it as a battle between him and Dikshit. Posters across Delhi claimed, 'If you vote for corrupt, women will continue to get raped.' Both the Congress and the BJP criticized this campaign, but Kejriwal remained steadfast, doing what he believed was best.[6]

Finally, the high-decibel election took place, forever altering the political landscape of Delhi. The BJP emerged as the largest political party, securing 32 seats, followed closely by the AAP with 28 seats, Congress with 8 and others with 2. While no party had the numbers to form a government outright, the verdict was clear: Delhi had rejected the Congress government and Sheila Dikshit's leadership. The people of Delhi were clamouring for change, and they saw the AAP as the vehicle to deliver on their promises.

Senior journalist Aurangzeb Naqshbandi aptly described the election as a watershed moment in Indian politics. He said, 'A political party that rose from a social movement jolted the Congress in Delhi. AAP's rise happened because it siphoned off Congress voters. Arvind Kejriwal's ascent was historic; he wasn't a seasoned politician but an activist who successfully led his party to victory. This triumph established him as the undisputed leader of AAP.'

The pressing question for the AAP was whether to form the government. Both the BJP and the Congress had their strategies to expose the AAP. The BJP took a principled stand, declaring they would not form the government, leaving the onus on the AAP.

Kejriwal initially believed the party should accept Congress's support to form the government. However, principles within the party were still alive, and leaders like Yogendra Yadav, Prashant Bhushan and Kumar Vishwas opposed seeking Congress's support. They argued that the AAP should either remain in opposition or call for fresh elections. Kejriwal feared that not staking a claim would cause the party to lose momentum.[7]

In this dilemma, the Congress announced its willingness to provide outside support to the AAP. This move solved the problem, as it was Congress offering support rather than the AAP seeking it. Despite internal opposition, Kejriwal, in his characteristic style, decided to proceed. However, the party soon realized that a section of the AAP was resentful. From the inception of the IAC movement they had fought against Congress and its corruption, including against several Congress leaders who had become MLAs (member of Legislative Assembly) in this election.

An insider revealed:

> Several senior leaders proposed that we seek suggestions and opinions from the people. Following this, Kejriwal and senior leaders crafted a question and reached out to the public for their input. The question was: should AAP form the government? We held several *mohalla sabha*s and shared the question through emails, messages and other platforms to gather responses. As expected, the majority supported AAP forming the government with outside support from Congress.

On 28 December 2013, a massive crowd gathered at Ramlila Maidan in Delhi, the same venue where Hazare had led the IAC movement's second hunger strike in 2011.[8] This time, the enthusiasm was even higher as Kejriwal took the oath as Delhi's CM. The election had not only changed the political dynamics of Delhi but also marked the rise of a new political force. Kejriwal's bold decision to contest against Sheila Dikshit had paid off. His victory was seen as a testament to his courage and determination to take on established political figures.

The first test for the AAP was complete, but the real challenge lay ahead: governing Delhi.

5

Calculated Exit

After Kejriwal ascended to the role of CM for the first time, he faced a myriad of challenges. Having toppled the formidable Sheila Dikshit, he was now seen as a giant killer, and the pressure to prove himself as a superior administrator was on. The AAP leaders were acutely aware that their government, propped up by the Congress's outside support, was on shaky ground. The Congress, not a natural ally, had backed the AAP to expose its inability to fulfil promises. Kejriwal had limited time and a plethora of promises to deliver. Additionally, the 2014 Lok Sabha elections loomed large, necessitating crucial decisions.

One of Kejriwal's landmark moves was the reduction of electricity tariffs, offering a 50 per cent subsidy for households consuming up to 400 units per month.[1] This decision directly benefited thousands of Delhi residents, showcasing his commitment to alleviating the financial burden on citizens. Alongside this, he launched a policy to provide 20,000 litres of free water per month per household – addressing basic needs and generating goodwill among the electorate.[2]

To tackle corruption, Kejriwal introduced an anti-corruption helpline, empowering citizens to report instances of bribery in government offices.[3] This initiative reflected his roots in the IAC movement and also his resolve to instil accountability within the bureaucracy.

However, Kejriwal's tendency to make unilateral decisions within the government and the party began to surface. According to AAP insiders, senior leaders observed this tendency but tolerated it, believing that the urgency of the situation justified his actions as long as he delivered on the manifesto. This dynamic shifted dramatically when Kejriwal decided, unilaterally, that the party should stage a dharna demanding control over the Delhi Police.

In the early weeks of Kejriwal's tenure, then Cabinet Minister Somnath Bharti conducted a controversial raid in his constituency, alleging that foreigners were running a drug and sex racket under the police's nose. Bharti's aggressive behaviour and use of slurs against the foreigners went unchecked by Kejriwal, despite internal disapproval. Another incident involved then Cabinet Minister Rakhi Birla, who demanded the arrest of a woman's in-laws for allegedly burning her. When the police did not act, Kejriwal demanded the suspension of the officers and control over the Delhi Police, leading to a dharna at the end of January 2014, just 20 days into his tenure.[4]

A former AAP member remarked:

> Many top leaders felt Kejriwal's decision was wrong. It was time to build the government, not protest. We had protested enough. It was unnatural for a CM to sit in dharna. It sent the wrong message to the people, and it was clear that, being the national capital, the police would never come under the Delhi government. His image was under question, and the opposition began labelling AAP as an anarchist party.

Kejriwal's early tenure was marked by bold decisions and significant achievements, but also by internal strife and controversial actions that tested the party's unity and public perception. The balance between governance and activism proved to be a delicate one, shaping the trajectory of both Kejriwal and the AAP in the years to come.

The 2014 Lok Sabha elections marked a turning point for the AAP, catapulting it from a Delhi-centric movement to a national political contender. Buoyed by its success in the 2013 Delhi Assembly elections, the AAP leadership faced a critical decision – should they contest the Lok Sabha elections on a broad national scale or restrict their efforts to key urban constituencies? The resolution of this debate would shape the party's strategy and influence its future trajectory.

Kejriwal was determined to seize the momentum. For him, this was not merely an election but an opportunity to amplify the party's anti-corruption agenda on a national platform. He believed the AAP should field candidates in as many constituencies as possible. A few AAP insiders told me that this vision clashed with the perspectives of other senior leaders, including Yogendra Yadav, who argued for a more focused approach. Yadav suggested targeting urban seats, where the party's support base was stronger, ensuring a more strategic allocation of resources.

An internal meeting called by Kejriwal in early January 2014 highlighted these tensions within the party. While Kejriwal expressed his view in favour of widespread participation, he sought inputs from party leaders and grassroots volunteers. A National Executive meeting was convened on 4 January 2014 to finalize the party's strategy.[5] However, AAP insiders recalled that the meeting took an unexpected turn when Kejriwal unilaterally announced his preference for contesting over 400 seats nationwide, citing Shanti Bhushan's endorsement of this approach. The abruptness of this decision bypassed standard procedural norms, leaving several leaders disgruntled but unable to openly challenge the momentum building around Kejriwal's vision.

A former AAP member, who did not wish to be named, told me, 'This episode marked a significant moment in the party's evolution. Kejriwal's approach raised concerns among many of the senior leaders about the erosion of internal democracy within the AAP. The unilateral nature of the decision underscored Kejriwal's growing centralization of power, setting the stage for future conflicts within the party.'

As preparations for the 2014 elections began, the party faced a daunting reality: it lacked the organizational structure, funding and leadership capacity to contest on such a grand scale. The AAP volunteers and state units scrambled to build networks, mobilize resources and connect with voters across the country. While enthusiasm ran high, logistical challenges mounted, stretching the party's limited resources thin.

A key turning point in the AAP's strategy was Kejriwal's resignation as CM of Delhi after 49 days in office. Officially, Kejriwal cited the failure to pass the Jan Lokpal Bill as the primary reason for stepping down. The Congress and the BJP had opposed the bill, preventing its passage in the Delhi Assembly. However, insiders suggest that the decision was also influenced by the looming Lok Sabha elections. Running a government while leading a nationwide campaign was deemed impractical.

According to an AAP insider, 'Kejriwal was clear that the government would struggle due to lack of support from the Congress. He believed that resigning on the Lokpal issue would send a stronger message to the electorate than staying in power without achieving this key goal.' Kejriwal's resignation, framed as a moral stand against systemic corruption, was designed to reinforce the AAP's commitment to its founding principles.

This decision, however, was not without controversy. During my conversations with AAP leaders, I found out that some senior leaders (Yogendra Yadav, Prashant Bhushan and others) within the party opposed the resignation, arguing that it could be perceived as an abandonment of governance responsibilities. They recommended discussing the matter within the National Council and Executive before proceeding. However, Kejriwal was resolute, viewing the resignation as a strategic move to galvanize support for the Lok Sabha campaign.

The resignation was executed amidst high drama in the Delhi Assembly. When the Jan Lokpal Bill was tabled, opposition parties vehemently opposed it, creating a deadlock.[6] This set the stage for Kejriwal's exit, which he used to highlight the challenges of battling entrenched political corruption.

Following his resignation, the AAP fully shifted its focus to the Lok Sabha elections. Campaigning began in earnest, with Kejriwal and other leaders travelling across the country to connect with voters. Despite their best efforts, the party's foray into national politics exposed its vulnerabilities. The lack of a cohesive strategy, coupled with insufficient groundwork in many constituencies, hindered its ability to resonate with voters outside its core urban support base.

The AAP faced internal and external challenges. Its cadre and supporters were demoralized after contesting over 400 seats nationwide with limited resources. The party's anti-Congress narrative, a cornerstone of its identity, was insufficient against the BJP's dominance. Most AAP candidates across the country lost their deposits, with the party failing to secure a single seat in most places. Despite a high-octane campaign in Maharashtra, the results there were dismal. Punjab emerged as the sole exception, where the AAP won four seats, offering a glimmer of hope in an otherwise crushing defeat. The results emphasized the limitations of its rapid expansion and the need for a more measured approach in future elections. The campaign's outcomes also deepened internal rifts, with some leaders questioning the wisdom of contesting on such a grand scale without adequate preparation.

One of the boldest but most controversial moves was Kejriwal's decision to contest against BJP's prime ministerial candidate, Narendra Modi, in Varanasi. While the campaign attracted immense media attention, it was clear from the start that victory was unattainable. The failure in the 2014 elections came at a time of tectonic political shifts. The BJP, under Narendra Modi, achieved a sweeping victory, while the Congress was reduced to a shadow of its former self. These national dynamics reshaped Delhi's political landscape as well. The BJP emerged as the AAP's primary challenger, creating a new battleground.

The 2014 Lok Sabha elections was a defining moment for the AAP. While the results were disappointing, the experience offered valuable lessons. It underscored the importance of strategic planning, organizational capacity and internal cohesion. For

Kejriwal, the election reinforced the need for a more structured approach to decision-making and party governance.

This chapter in the AAP's journey reflects the challenges of transitioning from a regional movement to a national political force. It highlights the tensions between ambition and pragmatism, and the growing pains of a party striving to redefine Indian politics. While the 2014 elections were a setback, they also laid the groundwork for the AAP's eventual successes, shaping its evolution as a party rooted in the ideals of transparency, accountability and citizen-centric governance.

6

'Get Rid of Gaddars'

As discussed previously, the 2014 Lok Sabha election marked a significant setback in the AAP's early years. Furthermore, the BJP and the Congress painted the AAP as anarchist, emphasizing Kejriwal's abrupt resignation after 49 days in power. Many voters viewed this resignation as a betrayal, leading to widespread scepticism about the AAP's governance capabilities.

Realizing this, Kejriwal adopted a direct, people-centric approach, acknowledging his mistake and apologizing for resigning prematurely. He assured voters that if given another chance, he would complete his term. This strategy of humility and accountability resonated with Delhiites, paving the way for the AAP's historic victory in the 2015 Assembly elections, where it secured 67 of 70 seats.

Rather than revisiting the well-documented details of the AAP's 2015 campaign strategy, it is essential to focus on the organizational and ideological shifts during this period. These changes laid the foundation for the AAP's evolution, influencing its approach to governance and expansion in subsequent years. The 2014 loss was not just a moment of reckoning but a catalyst for transformation, demonstrating how setbacks can lead to a reinvention that reshapes a party's future.

By 2015, two significant developments had taken place within the AAP. First, Arvind Kejriwal's impatience with internal dissent had reached a boiling point. Prominent figures like Prashant Bhushan, Shanti Bhushan, Yogendra Yadav, Prof. Anand Kumar and Ajit Jha – all well-established professionals – were increasingly at odds with Kejriwal's unilateral decisions. These individuals, who had initially worked under Kejriwal's leadership, found themselves marginalized as Kejriwal began to break the fundamental principles of the AAP.

Simultaneously, Kejriwal had cultivated a close-knit group of loyalists who formed his inner circle. This coterie included his personal secretary Bibhav Kumar, Aswathi Muralidharan and Ashish Talwar, among others. Kejriwal's reliance on this group grew, and he began to trust their advice implicitly, often to the exclusion of other voices within the party.

A former AAP member remarked, 'We were shocked and surprised that Kejriwal was taking strong exceptions to whatever Prashant ji or Yogendra bhai were saying. He was very vocal against these people in front of many leaders. At the same time, those closer to him were circulating news alleging that Prashant ji and Yogendra bhai were harming the party.'

As the 2015 Delhi Assembly election approached, Kejriwal knew that the AAP could not afford to alienate key figures like Bhushan and Yadav. However, it became evident within party circles that he might take a strong stand against these individuals after the election.

The infighting between these two camps became more pronounced over the issue of candidate selection for the 2015 elections. In earlier chapters, I have discussed how the AAP had developed a strategy for selecting candidates for the 2013 elections, based on key principles of transparency and integrity. By 2015, as mentioned earlier, these ideals had eroded. Kejriwal appointed his confidant Ashish Talwar to head the candidate selection process, effectively sidelining other voices within the party.

A former AAP leader noted in an interview:

> Arvind broke every protocol of the party. He did not listen to the PAC or any others in the party, nor did he consult his views in the national executive. As the national convenor, he unilaterally handled candidate selection. We were shocked to see that many candidates were selected based on their popularity and financial resources. There were also several candidates from other parties like Congress or BSP [Bahujan Samaj Party], and candidates with corrupt pasts.

Prashant Bhushan and Yadav protested against Kejriwal's unilateral decisions and questioned why individuals with dubious records were given tickets for the 2015 election. Kejriwal remained evasive, downplaying these issues. For the sake of the upcoming election, the two stayed silent, but former Cabinet Minister Shanti Bhushan was not willing to accept these actions. He went to the media and openly criticized Kejriwal for abandoning the AAP's principles.

Shanti Bhushan stated, 'He gave a large number of tickets to people who had amassed a lot of wealth by questionable means and were prepared to buy votes by distributing money and liquor. He (Kejriwal) also accepted tainted money and abandoned all principles of inner party democracy.'[1]

Meanwhile, Prashant Bhushan submitted a list of around 12 AAP candidates to the party's internal Lokpal, demanding their removal. He said, 'There were a lot of complaints about the kind of candidates selected, especially those who had been para-dropped into the party recently. Some of them were referred to the party Lokpal, who recommended the removal of two candidates.'[2]

Despite the growing infighting, the campaign for the 2015 Delhi Assembly election continued. The Congress had lost its support base and was not very visible on the streets of Delhi. The BJP made a strategic error by parachuting former IAC member and ex-IPS officer Kiran Bedi into Delhi, making her the face of their campaign. Bedi lacked grassroots connections with the people of Delhi, and in this context, the AAP won a resounding mandate.

Kejriwal became the CM for the second time, now wielding absolute power in governance, as the BJP secured only three seats and the Congress none. This was also the time when Kejriwal sought absolute control within the AAP. A plan was devised to oust Prashant Bhushan, Yogendra Yadav, Shanti Bhushan, Ajit Jha and Anand Kumar. Kejriwal and his team executed this plan step by step.

Insiders revealed that Kejriwal was determined not to tolerate any opposition within the party. To build this sentiment, a National Executive meeting was called on 26 February 2015.[3] It was initially decided that this meeting would discuss crucial issues like candidate selection, where there were clear indications of corruption. However, individuals like Kumar Vishwas did not allow Yadav or Prashant Bhushan to speak, effectively hijacking the meeting. Mayank Gandhi, a PAC member present at the meeting, wrote, 'Pankaj Gupta read out a note by an absent Arvind. In this note, Arvind accused Prashant and Yogendra of anti-party activities and offered to resign as AAP's convenor.'[4]

This note from Kejriwal completely changed the mood of the National Executive meeting. A clear sentiment against Yadav, Bhushan and others was built. Within weeks, on 4 March, another National Executive meeting was convened by Kejriwal. Insiders reported that Kejriwal was not present at this meeting either. The clear intention of the meeting was to remove Yadav and Bhushan from the PAC. As the meeting began, people again started speaking against the two. Many insiders noted that the AAP social media team worked relentlessly to discredit these individuals. The mood was already set, and when the voting took place on the agenda of removing Yadav and Bhushan from the PAC, 11 members approved, 8 voted against and some abstained.[5]

This marked a significant turning point in the AAP's internal dynamics, as Kejriwal consolidated his power and sidelined dissenting voices within the party. The events of 2015 highlighted the challenges of maintaining ideological purity and internal democracy within a rapidly growing political movement.

The first stage of ousting the dissenting leaders from the PAC was executed with precision. Many within the AAP believed that this would be the end of the internal strife, and that Kejriwal would not pursue the matter further. However, they were gravely mistaken. Kejriwal's ultimate goal was to *completely* expel the dissenters from the party, ensuring that no one would dare to challenge his authority in the future.

On 28 March, Kejriwal convened a meeting of the AAP's National Council. As the agenda became clear – that Kejriwal intended to remove Yadav and Bhushan from the party – the two proposed their resignation, contingent upon the party making certain corrections and passing a resolution to that effect. Kejriwal, however, was adamantly opposed to this idea. He tasked leaders like Gopal Rai and Sanjay Singh with rallying National Council members to support his proposal to expel the dissenters.

Insiders recall that the meeting took place at a resort on the outskirts of Delhi. All MLAs were instructed to bring their supporters to voice their dissent against the targeted leaders. A former AAP leader present at the meeting recounted:

> We knew the meeting would be heated, but we didn't anticipate the extent. When Kejriwal decided to bar the party's internal Lokpal, former Admiral L. Ramdas, from attending, it became clear that this meeting would break every protocol and ideal of the party. Many of us personally requested Kejriwal not to take any drastic actions that would set a bad precedent for a party built on principles of integrity and fairness.

The meeting was marked by several dramatic events, both inside and outside the venue. Leaders were prohibited from carrying pens, phones or other items. Mayank Gandhi, who was present, wrote in his book, 'Arvind thundered, "I have given my sweat and blood to this party and will not allow it to break up. Either get rid of Yogendra and Prashant or release me from all responsibilities and positions within the party."'[6]

After this impassioned speech, Kejriwal walked out of the meeting. Immediately afterward, a resolution was read, calling for the expulsion of Prashant Bhushan, Yogendra Yadav, Prof. Anand Kumar and Ajit Jha from the party. To the surprise of many insiders, the resolution had already been signed and approved by the National Convenor. It was evident that the entire process was a farce.

In the days following the meeting, the atmosphere within the AAP was tense. Supporters of Bhushan and Yadav were disillusioned, while Kejriwal's loyalists celebrated their leader's decisive action. The media coverage of the event was intense, with many questioning the future of a party that had promised to be different from the rest.

This marks the end of the first part of this book, which has examined the party from its inception to this stage. A party founded on the ideals of honesty, integrity and transparency had, in less than two years, transformed into a political entity like any other. The incidents described above leave no doubt that the AAP had become a party where only one person mattered: Arvind Kejriwal. The metamorphosis of the party, however, had just begun. In the subsequent chapters and sections of this book, I will trace how this transformation deepened over time.

The 2015 Delhi Assembly election campaign and its aftermath made it clear that the founding principles of the AAP, borrowed from the IAC movement, no longer held any significance. Kejriwal systematically dismantled any opposition within the party. After this incident, no one dared to question Kejriwal in the same manner again. It was clear that those who did so would be removed and humiliated.

While the rise of the AAP is a significant chapter in India's political history, the fall of the party from its founding principles is equally crucial. It serves as a stark reminder of why honesty, fairness and transparency struggle to survive in Indian politics. The story of the AAP's transformation – from a movement of idealists to a party driven by the ambitions of a single leader – is a cautionary tale for all who seek to bring about political change.

Part 2

Policy, Politics and Populism

7

Delhi Model of Governance

As discussed in Chapter 6, in the early months of 2015, Indian politics witnessed a seismic shift when the AAP swept the Delhi Assembly elections, winning 67 of 70 seats. This overwhelming mandate was not just a victory, it was a tidal wave that altered the course of governance and politics in the capital and beyond. The insider perspective reveals that while the AAP was confident of a win, the sheer magnitude of the victory was beyond their wildest expectations. This landslide, however, also came with its own set of challenges and realizations, prompting the party to recalibrate its approach to governance and political strategy.

Kejriwal strode into the Delhi Secretariat in 2015, buoyed by a sweeping electoral mandate and flanked by six of his most trusted allies – Manish Sisodia, Gopal Rai, Satyendar Jain, Jitender Singh Tomar, Sandeep Kumar and Asim Ahmed Khan.[1] Armed with an overwhelming majority, the AAP appeared poised to deliver on its promises, with Kejriwal eager to transform Delhi's governance model. However, what Kejriwal did not foresee was the labyrinth of governance challenges that lay ahead.

The days following the election win were a whirlwind of excitement, strategy sessions and a palpable sense of mission. However, the euphoria soon gave way to the harsh realities of governance. The new government quickly found itself in the crosshairs of the central government. The first significant confrontation occurred with a Central Bureau of Investigation (CBI) raid at the Delhi Secretariat, targeting the office of the CM himself.[2] This move was perceived by Kejriwal as a politically motivated attack, and he did not shy away from expressing his outrage, accusing PM Narendra Modi of orchestrating a vendetta. The raid was more than just a personal affront – it was a stark reminder of the limitations of power in a federal structure where Delhi, had its hands tied in many areas of governance.

The initial months of 2015 were a period of intense introspection for the AAP. Kejriwal, known for his combative approach, began to recalibrate his political stance. The party started identifying key areas in Delhi where they could make a tangible difference, irrespective of the limitations imposed by the central government. Education and healthcare emerged as two sectors where the AAP could exercise substantial control and deliver on its promises to the people of Delhi.

In its manifesto for the 2015 Delhi elections, the AAP had pledged a transformative overhaul of the education and healthcare systems. The party vowed to construct 500 new schools, with a particular emphasis on secondary and senior secondary education. Additionally, the AAP committed to reshaping the existing educational framework to cultivate job providers rather than job seekers. In the realm of healthcare, the party had promised the creation of 900 new primary health centres (PHCs) and the addition of 30,000 more beds in Delhi hospitals. With these ambitious goals, the AAP aimed to address the pressing needs of the city's residents.[3]

Having already prioritized the reduction of power and water bills during its initial 49-day tenure, this strategic pivot to education and healthcare underscored the party's commitment to improving the quality of life for Delhi's citizens through comprehensive reforms in these critical sectors. The AAP termed this as the 'Delhi Model of Governance'.

At the time, there were few governance models for Kejriwal to emulate. While Narendra Modi's 'Gujarat Model' emphasized industrial development, Delhi's lack of a robust industrial base necessitated a different approach. Thus, Kejriwal's administration leaned heavily on welfare-oriented governance, now commonly referred to as the 'Delhi Model'.

Two major sociopolitical dimensions underpin the Delhi Model of Governance: tactical governance and cosmopolitan sub-nationalism.

Tactical Governance

Before going into the policy discussion, it is important to look at why the AAP thought about this model.

As we know by now, by 2015 the AAP had firmly established itself as a formidable force in Delhi's political landscape, winning two Delhi Assembly elections while losing the 2014 Lok Sabha polls in the city. Over time, this electoral pattern became predictable (until 2025) – the AAP dominates the Assembly elections, but the BJP prevails in the parliamentary polls.

Examining the elections from 2013 to 2024 revealed consistent trends. The BJP maintained a core vote bank of approximately 32 per cent in Delhi, while the AAP's core voter base stood at about 18 per cent. What bridged the gap during Assembly elections was a significant section of floating voters (around 15 per cent on average), who shifted allegiance from the BJP in parliamentary contests to the AAP in state elections. These voters were often swayed by the AAP's localized governance and welfare promises.

By 2015, Kejriwal and the AAP leadership recognized that their rising popularity stemmed from demographics that had traditionally supported the Congress, such as Muslims (13 per cent of Delhi's population) and Dalits (16 per cent). Studies, like those conducted by Lokniti-CSDS (Centre for the Study of Developing Societies), revealed that unauthorized colonies, slums and lower-caste communities were critical to this shift. These groups were drawn to the AAP's pro-people initiatives (such as slashed electricity and water bills), which directly impacted their daily lives.[4]

The AAP realized that unlike many Indian states where regional identity politics has played a decisive role, Delhi required a nuanced approach. When Mamata Banerjee came to power in

West Bengal in 2011, after toppling the 35-year reign of the Left front, she leaned heavily on Bengali nationalism and identity politics. She portrayed herself as the saviour of Bengali culture and heritage, a narrative that people of the state responded to.

Identity politics have never worked in Delhi. The city is a mosaic of diverse cultures, with its residents hailing from various parts of India. Delhi is a vibrant cosmopolitan city, home to a rich tapestry of ethnic and cultural communities. Among its key demographic groups, *Purvanchali*s – migrants from eastern Uttar Pradesh, Bihar and Jharkhand – constitute approximately 35–40 percent of the population, making them one of the largest segments. Close behind are the Punjabis, including both Hindus and Sikhs, who account for about 30 per cent of the city's population. The Haryanvi community, representing Delhi's native and surrounding rural population, makes up around 10 per cent of residents. Other prominent groups include Bengalis, (comprising 2 per cent) of the population and South Indians (who form approximately 5 per cent). The Northeast community also adds to Delhi's diversity, contributing around 2 per cent to the population.[5]

Beyond these major ethnic groups, Delhi is also home to several other migrant communities and religious segments, each adding its unique cultural flavour. Together, these communities make Delhi a true melting pot, reflecting the essence of India's diversity in a single city.

A senior AAP leader explained to me the party's strategic shift after their landslide victory in the 2015 elections, 'We realized that to win the hearts of the people, we needed to focus on issues that touched them every day – education and healthcare. These are universal concerns that everyone, regardless of class or background, cares about deeply. That was where we started.'

The AAP's realization was both simple and profound: people respond to tangible changes in their immediate environment, and few things are as central to daily life as the schools and hospitals. In 2015, the party inherited a system that, by their account, had been neglected by previous governments, particularly the Congress, which had ruled the city for years. The state of education and healthcare infrastructure was, in their view, deplorable.

'The Congress government had ruined the educational infrastructure, or rather, they had done little to develop it,' the senior leader said. This perception became the foundation for the AAP's governance model – a model that focused on delivering visible improvements in sectors that affected the maximum number of people.

'Upon assuming power,' said Aurangzeb Naqshbandi, 'the AAP recognized that the Congress government under Chief Minister Sheila Dikshit had made significant strides in infrastructure development such as roads and flyovers. However, the Congress had neglected crucial sectors like healthcare and education. This gap is precisely why the AAP chose to focus on these areas.'

In addition to that, as Ambar Kumar Ghosh (a fellow at the Young Researchers' Network at the European Democracy Hub in Brussels) observed, PM Narendra Modi's presence in Delhi was nothing short of ubiquitous. Unlike states like Tamil Nadu or West Bengal, where cultural and linguistic differences diluted Modi's influence, Delhi was a different story altogether. Here, Modi's convoy was a familiar sight on city streets, his speeches at the Red Fort an annual occurrence and his presence at national events impossible to miss. This omnipresence cemented Modi's status as a beloved figure in Delhi, making any direct confrontation with him a potentially costly move for politicians, as it risked alienating voters who held Modi in high esteem.

This apprehension led Kejriwal and the AAP to rethink their political strategy. They understood that a head-on clash with Modi would not work in Delhi, and instead they pivoted towards 'tactical governance'. Kejriwal knew that to penetrate a diverse Delhi, the party needed to focus on governance that delivered tangible results to people. The AAP shifted its focus from confrontation to delivery, crafting policies that addressed the immediate needs of Delhi's residents.

From auto drivers and daily-wage labourers to small business owners, Kejriwal managed to connect with a wide swathe of the population by focusing on everyday issues. One of the key aspects was breaking down economic barriers through policies that resonated with both the poor and the middle class. In the months leading to the 2020 election, free electricity up to 200 units and free water became the cornerstone of the AAP's governance, allowing the party to gain favour across economic classes. Later, initiatives like the transformation of government schools and mohalla clinics providing free healthcare became hallmarks of the AAP's governance. These measures were not merely policy interventions but symbols of the government's commitment to the welfare of the people, particularly the most vulnerable ones.

These 'freebies', as some critics called them, were instrumental in building the AAP's strong base of support.

As senior journalist Aurangzeb Naqshbandi told me:

> The AAP's core support comes from the lower economic strata, lower middle class and middle class segments. These groups are directly benefiting from the government's schemes, and this has solidified their loyalty. The improvements in healthcare and education infrastructure have also played a crucial role in supporting these communities. For instance, a woman who works in my home purchased an air conditioner, confident that the electricity subsidy would make it affordable. This is an example of how these policies lead to real empowerment.

Kejriwal's vision for Delhi was one of inclusion, addressing the needs of the many over the few. By focusing on governance rather than identity, the AAP managed to carve a unique space for itself in Delhi, making Kejriwal not just a politician, but a leader who was seen as being close to the people and their everyday struggles.

Ambar Kumar Ghosh explained to me during an interview that the AAP's tactical governance strategy focuses on core issues – education, healthcare, electricity and water – that resonate deeply with people from all walks of life. Ghosh notes that the AAP's focus on these core issues has contributed significantly to its popularity, which was reflected in the outcomes of Delhi's

Legislative Assembly elections in 2015 and 2020. By successfully addressing these fundamental needs, the AAP has improved the lives of many.

However, the Delhi Model has not been without criticism. Detractors label it overly populist, arguing that while these initiatives provide immediate benefits, they fail to tackle deeper systemic issues. For example, while government schools in Delhi have shown remarkable improvement, broader challenges like inequity in access to quality education remain unaddressed. Similarly, while mohalla clinics have enhanced healthcare access, they do not resolve deeper issues such as the shortage of doctors and inadequacies in public hospital infrastructure.

The emphasis on direct benefits has led some to question whether the model prioritizes short-term gains over long-term solutions. Yet, for the AAP, this approach succeeded in consolidating support among target demographics and establishing a unique governance identity.

One aspect deliberately excluded from this chapter is the controversial subject of freebies or *revdi*. Although such populist measures became a significant part of Kejriwal's second-term governance strategy, they were not a core feature of the Delhi Model in its initial formulation. The focus here is on the foundational policies and their sociopolitical implications, leaving the discussion around populism to a subsequent chapter.

Cosmopolitan Sub-nationalism

Unlike traditional forms of sub-nationalism – which focus on a singular ethnic, linguistic or regional identity – cosmopolitan sub-nationalism aims to create a collective identity that includes *all* of the region's diverse communities.

For the AAP, this concept has been central to their political strategy in Delhi, a city that is both the capital of India and a melting pot of cultures, languages and communities from across the country (as mentioned earlier). Delhi is home to Punjabis, Bengalis, Tamils, Muslims and numerous other groups, each with their own unique cultural identities. The AAP's challenge

– and opportunity – has been to craft a sense of belonging and pride that transcended these individual identities and fostered a unifying vision for Delhi.

The AAP's version of cosmopolitan sub-nationalism focuses on creating a civic pride in being a 'Delhiite' by emphasizing governance and local development. It is an inclusive model, where the focus is on what binds the citizens of Delhi together – the city itself and their shared aspirations for better public services and quality of life.

In this framework, cosmopolitan sub-nationalism allows the AAP to cater to a wide demographic without alienating any particular group. In a way, the AAP's cosmopolitan sub-nationalism is a reflection of Delhi itself – diverse, dynamic and deeply interconnected with the rest of India. It focuses on inclusivity, using governance and civic responsibility as the main unifying elements rather than relying on traditional markers of sub-national identity. This strategy helped the party maintain its relevance and appeal in a city where traditional identity politics could easily alienate large sections of the population.

'By framing AAP as synonymous with the people of Delhi,' says Ambar Kumar Ghosh, 'Kejriwal has successfully tapped into the city's diverse population, establishing the party as an indispensable part of Delhi's civic identity, one that is inclusive and positive in its vision for the city.'

Core Policies under the Delhi Model

Education as the Cornerstone

The decision to prioritize education was not just a policy choice – it was a statement of intent. The AAP's approach to education reform was both innovative and bold. Under the leadership of Sisodia, and with the intellectual support of advisors like Atishi, the party launched a series of initiatives aimed at revamping the infrastructure, curriculum and overall environment of government schools in Delhi.

One of the first and most critical steps taken by the AAP government was to address the crumbling infrastructure of Delhi's government schools. The state of these schools was dismal, with overcrowded classrooms, dilapidated buildings and poor sanitation facilities being the norm. In response, the AAP government allocated an unprecedented 22.8 per cent of its budget to education – the highest percentage for any Indian state.[6] This bold financial commitment laid the foundation for sweeping infrastructural improvements that would significantly enhance the learning environment for students across Delhi.

Shailendra Sharma, former principal advisor to the director of education of the Delhi government, explained that the government's efforts led to the construction of over 20,000 new classrooms, equipped with modern amenities like smart boards, projectors and ergonomic benches. He said:

> These smart classrooms have revolutionized the way students engage with their lessons, making education more interactive and enjoyable. But the improvements didn't stop at classrooms; the government also ensured that every school had access to clean drinking water, well-maintained toilets and playgrounds, fostering an environment conducive to both learning and physical well-being. The addition of facilities such as swimming pools, gyms and libraries in several schools underscores the government's commitment to providing a holistic education, nurturing well-rounded individuals who excel in both academic and extracurricular pursuits.

Beyond infrastructure, the AAP government launched the Chunauti initiative in 2016 to address the pressing issues of low learning levels and high dropout rates.[7] Recognizing that a one-size-fits-all approach was inadequate, Chunauti introduced a system that grouped students according to their learning levels, enabling personalized educational support. This tailored approach allowed teachers to focus on bringing weaker students up to grade level through targeted interventions. Regular assessments and strong community involvement were key components of this initiative, ensuring that students received the necessary support both at school and at home. The results were significant – improvements in reading abilities among students and a reduction in dropout rates – and highlighted the success of this targeted approach.

Sharma explained that in 2018 the AAP government introduced another pioneering reform: the Happiness Curriculum. In a world where academic pressure often eclipses other aspects of a child's development, this initiative was a bold move towards creating a more balanced education system. Aimed at students from nursery to eighth grade, the Happiness Curriculum focused on emotional and mental well-being, teaching mindfulness, social–emotional learning, critical thinking and relationship-building. Daily sessions included activities such as meditation and storytelling, designed to help students reflect on their thoughts and emotions. The impact of this was profound, with students reporting improved mental well-being, better relationships with peers and teachers, and a greater sense of inner peace. The curriculum has even garnered international acclaim, with institutions like Harvard University recognizing its innovative approach.

Continuing its streak of groundbreaking reforms, the AAP government introduced the Entrepreneurship Mindset Curriculum (EMC) in 2019.[8] Designed for students from ninth to twelfth grades, this curriculum aimed to instil an entrepreneurial spirit, encouraging students to become job creators rather than job seekers. The EMC included practical elements such as the 'Business Blasters' programme, where students were given seed money to develop and implement their business ideas. This hands-on experience fosters creativity, innovation and problem-solving skills, allowing students to experiment with real-world business concepts. The success of the EMC has been notable, with many students launching startups in diverse fields supported by incubation centres and mentorship programmes. This initiative not only equipped students with practical skills but also contributed to the broader economy by nurturing a new generation of entrepreneurs.

Recognizing that the success of educational reforms hinges on the quality of teaching, the AAP government also invested heavily in teacher training programmes. The AAP's education department collaborated with organizations like the British Council and Tata Trusts to provide training and academic support to teachers. This included workshops, mentoring and coaching to enhance pedagogical skills. Another game-changing initiative by the AAP government was the introduction of regular parent–teacher meetings (PTMs) across government and MCD (Municipal Corporation of Delhi) schools.

Sharma said:

> Before this intervention, communication between teachers and parents in government schools was often lacking, leaving many parents unaware of their children's academic progress and challenges. The AAP government recognized the importance of parental involvement and made PTMs a cornerstone of its educational reforms. These meetings have become a vital platform for open dialogue, allowing parents and teachers to collaboratively address academic and personal issues facing students.

The impact of these PTMs was transformative. Teachers were better equipped to adopt personalized approaches for each student, while parents felt more connected and involved in their children's education. This increased parental involvement had a positive influence on students' academic outcomes and overall well-being. Moreover, PTMs were instrumental in identifying and addressing issues such as absenteeism and behavioural problems early on. The AAP government further expanded this initiative with Mega PTMs 2017 onwards, which saw overwhelming participation and reinforced the shared responsibility of parents and schools in a child's educational journey.[9]

Sharma explained that there were three key aspects to the AAP government's work in education: infrastructural development, training of teachers and principals from leading institutions (like IIM, Harvard Institute and so on) and curriculum development.

Through these various initiatives, the AAP government not only transformed the physical infrastructure of Delhi's schools but has also redefined the educational experience for students. By prioritizing emotional well-being, entrepreneurial thinking and active parental involvement, alongside infrastructural improvements, the AAP set a new benchmark for public education in India. The reforms not only improved academic outcomes but also created a more inclusive and supportive educational environment, ensuring that students in Delhi are better prepared for the challenges of the future. This holistic approach to education reform made Delhi's public schools a model for others to emulate, showcasing the transformative power of visionary governance in the realm of education.

However, the AAP government's education model was also the subject of significant scrutiny due to various allegations and challenges. While the government highlighted improved infrastructure and impressive results, a closer examination revealed issues requiring attention.

In November 2022, the Delhi vigilance department submitted a report to the Chief Secretary alleging serious irregularities in the construction of 2,405 classrooms across 193 government schools. A similar report was earlier submitted by the Central Vigilance Commission in February 2020, highlighting potential discrepancies. Although the AAP government dismissed these allegations as baseless, no formal probe has been concluded, leaving doubts unresolved.[10]

Moreover, academic performance data challenges the narrative of consistent success in Delhi's schools. In the 2023–24 academic year, over 100,000 ninth-grade students failed their annual exams in government schools. These ninth-grade failures rose from 88,409 in 2022–23 to 101,331 in 2023–24. Similar trends were observed in eighth and eleventh grades, with over 46,000 and 50,000 students failing, respectively.[11] This sharp increase points to systemic issues affecting student learning outcomes despite infrastructure improvements.[12]

The dropout rate in Delhi government schools further complicates the picture. A report by the Praja Foundation highlighted concerning trends between 2013 and 2017. Of 2,19,377 students enrolled in ninth grade in 2013–14, 44 per cent did not reach twelfth grade by 2016–17.[13] The transition rate from ninth to tenth grade stood at just 56.95 per cent, contrasting sharply with the 98.55 per cent transition rate from seventh to eighth grade. [14] This disparity underscores the impact of the no-detention policy, which promoted students up to ninth grade regardless of learning outcomes. Consequently, many students failed to clear crucial secondary-level examinations.

Transforming Healthcare in Delhi

After coming to power in 2015, the AAP government set in motion a wave of transformative reforms in the healthcare sector. These reforms not only enhanced the accessibility and quality of healthcare services in the capital but also established a new benchmark for public health initiatives in India. Delhi's former health minister, Satyendar Jain, took up these initiatives. By focusing on inclusivity, accessibility and innovation, the AAP government redefined healthcare delivery, making it more equitable and effective. Here, we delve into three major healthcare reforms introduced by the AAP government: the establishment of mohalla clinics, the expansion of hospital infrastructure, and the provision of free essential medicines and diagnostics.

One of the most revolutionary health reforms introduced by the AAP was the creation of mohalla clinics – neighbourhood clinics that redefined primary healthcare by making it accessible, affordable and efficient. Launched in 2015, these clinics were envisioned as the first line of defence against health issues for the urban poor and marginalized communities, offering them quality healthcare within their localities.[15]

Each mohalla clinic was staffed with a doctor, a pharmacist and a clinic assistant, and provided a range of services, including consultations, basic treatment and essential medicines – all free of charge. In addition, these clinics offered over 200 types of diagnostic tests, ensuring that patients received comprehensive care without the burden of high medical expenses. By 2022, more than 553 Mohalla Clinics had been established, with many functioning out of rented spaces.[16]

The impact of mohalla clinics has been profound. These clinics significantly reduced the patient load on tertiary hospitals by addressing common ailments at the primary level. This decentralization of healthcare not only improved patient outcomes but also made healthcare more accessible to those living in densely populated and under-served areas. The success of mohalla clinics garnered international attention, with several countries expressing interest in replicating this innovative model of primary healthcare.[17]

The concept behind the clinics is as simple as it is powerful – bringing healthcare to the doorstep of the community. In many cases, these clinics were located within walking distance of the residents they serve, eliminating the need for long and costly journeys to distant hospitals. This proximity was especially beneficial for the elderly, children and those with chronic illnesses, who require regular medical attention. Furthermore, by providing free diagnostic services, the clinics made early detection and timely treatment of diseases more accessible, thereby preventing complications and reducing the overall burden on the healthcare system.

However, while the AAP government frequently highlighted the success of its flagship mohalla clinics initiative, allegations of malpractice and irregularities raised serious concerns about its implementation. During my visit to Delhi during 2024, I observed that several mohalla clinics were closed, casting doubts on the accessibility and functionality of these healthcare centres.

One of the most significant allegations was the large-scale fraud involving pathology and radiology tests. Reports suggested that several clinics conducted and recorded fake diagnostic tests for non-existent patients.[18] This alleged malpractice was facilitated by the use of fabricated or non-existent mobile numbers to register patients, with some numbers repeated multiple times or left blank. An inquiry by the vigilance department revealed that thousands of diagnostic tests were recommended through questionable means, leading to unwarranted payments to private diagnostic firms for tests that were never conducted.[19]

Further, there are claims of unethical practices within the clinics. Some doctors and staff were accused of marking attendance through pre-recorded videos, rather than physically attending to patients.[20] In certain instances, unauthorized personnel were reportedly found dispensing medicines and offering medical consultations in the absence of qualified doctors.[21] These practices raised legitimate questions about the quality and integrity of services provided under the mohalla clinics programme. These allegations highlight the need for stronger oversight and accountability to ensure that welfare schemes like the mohalla clinics achieve their intended objectives without compromising on quality or integrity.

In response to these allegations, Delhi's lieutenant governor (LG), V.K. Saxena, recommended a CBI probe into the matter. Meanwhile, the AAP government has defended the initiative, emphasizing its benefits and the millions of patients who have benefited from the scheme. Simultaneously, the government took action against several doctors and staff members implicated in these irregularities, signalling a willingness to address the concerns.[22]

It is also pertinent to remember that the COVID-19 pandemic exposed significant gaps in Delhi's healthcare infrastructure, debunking the myth of its robustness. Despite initial confidence in the system, the crisis revealed critical shortages in ICU beds, trained medical staff and essential equipment in public hospitals.[23]

A report by the Brookings Institution highlighted that while private healthcare was expensive and inaccessible for many, public facilities were overwhelmed. The lack of preparedness was evident, as more than 50 per cent of the COVID-19 beds in government hospitals remained vacant during the peak, while people struggled to find beds in private hospitals.[24]

The situation was so dire that even government ministers sought treatment in private hospitals. The Delhi High Court criticized the deplorable conditions in the government-run hospitals, noting the presence of dead bodies in wards where patients were being treated.[25]

Despite these challenges, Delhi did implement some effective measures, such as establishing a plasma bank and combining hotel and hospital facilities for COVID-19 patients. However, the overall experience underscored the need for substantial improvements in the city's healthcare infrastructure.

Revolutionizing Delhi's Power Sector

Since its inception, the AAP government made significant strides in transforming Delhi's power sector. Their focus on providing affordable and uninterrupted electricity set new benchmarks in public service, making Delhi a model state in power distribution and infrastructure.

One of the most notable reforms has been the introduction of free electricity for consumption up to 200 units since 2019,[26] a pioneering move that benefited millions of Delhi residents. This initiative, combined with a 50 per cent subsidy for those consuming between 201 and 400 units, made Delhi the only state in India where such a progressive tariff structure was in place. Remarkably, despite the financial challenges brought by the COVID-19 pandemic, the Kejriwal government continued to offer these subsidies, significantly easing the burden on households during a time of crisis.

A senior AAP functionary told me during a conversation in 2022:

> The AAP government has also prioritized enhancing Delhi's power infrastructure, resulting in a drastic reduction in power cuts across the city. Their efforts have ensured 24x7 electricity supply, a feat achieved through extensive upgrades to the power grid and distribution networks. This commitment to improving infrastructure has positioned Delhi as the only state with no electricity tariff hikes over the past six years.

According to the AAP government, it embraced sustainable energy solutions by developing solar power infrastructure. Over the past year between 2020 and 2021 more than 21 megawatts (MW) of solar rooftop plants were installed across 150 Delhi government schools.[27] These installations not only generate significant electricity savings – amounting to approximately ₹8.8 crore annually – but also contributed to environmental sustainability by reducing reliance on non-renewable energy sources.

While the AAP government boasted about its work in the power sectors, Delhi's power distribution companies (DISCOMs) grappled with severe financial stress, largely due to the persistently low power tariff rates.[28]

The Delhi Electricity Regulatory Commission (DERC) maintained the same tariff rates for the past six years, from 2016 to 2021, creating a significant revenue shortfall for the DISCOMs. The tariffs did not align with the rising costs of power procurement, leading to an increasing gap between the average cost of supply and the average revenue realization.[29]

The reliance on costly imported coal and high short-term tariffs further exacerbated this issue. Despite efforts to curb aggregate technical and commercial losses, these measures were not sufficient to bridge the financial gap.

Moreover, the practice of posting regulatory assets, essentially deferred costs to be recovered in the future, added to the financial burden. The slow recovery of these assets strained DISCOMs finances. Additionally, delays in payments from state government departments and other consumers led to substantial debt accumulation. Operational inefficiencies and allegations of financial mismanagement within the DISCOMs also contributed to their precarious financial state.[30]

Revitalizing Delhi's Water Sector

The AAP government embarked on a transformative mission to overhaul Delhi's water sector, addressing long-standing challenges with innovative and inclusive solutions. Recognizing water as a fundamental right, the AAP government implemented a series of ambitious reforms to ensure equitable distribution and sustainable management of this critical resource.

According to an AAP functionary closely associated with water reforms, 'The AAP government has provided piped water connections to over 934,000 homes, many of which had never before experienced reliable access to clean water. This expansion has brought much-needed relief to millions of residents, particularly in underserved and marginalized communities, showcasing the government's commitment to inclusivity and equity.'

In addition to expanding access, the AAP government placed a strong emphasis on improving the quality and reliability of the water supply. Under the guidance of the Delhi Jal Board (DJB), the government implemented advanced water treatment technologies and carried out extensive infrastructure upgrades to reduce leakages and wastage. These efforts ensured that more residents received a consistent supply of clean, safe water.

The AAP functionary also said:

> The government has also prioritized the rejuvenation of water bodies and the augmentation of groundwater resources, recognizing the critical need for sustainable water management. The AAP government has backed its commitment with substantial financial investments, allocating ₹7,195 crore to the Delhi Jal Board. This funding has facilitated the construction of new water treatment plants, the expansion of existing facilities, and the development of an extensive pipeline network to secure Delhi's water future.

Despite facing challenges such as inter-state water disputes, the AAP government remained steadfast in its efforts. Through legal interventions and public awareness campaigns, the administration actively worked to secure Delhi's rightful share of water, setting a precedent for other regions to follow. This resolute approach underscored the government's dedication to ensuring a sustainable and equitable water supply for all of Delhi's residents.

It is equally important to recognize that multiple allegations were made against the DJB regarding recruitment practices and various other issues. In 2022 the LG of Delhi has called for a CBI investigation into these matters.[31] The investigation that followed implicated senior AAP officials, indicating a potential major scandal and related complications for the party.

A close examination of the AAP government's policies in Delhi reveals a fundamental truth: the intent behind many of its initiatives was sincere and, in several cases, transformative. The AAP government brought long-overdue attention to critical sectors like education and healthcare – areas that had languished under previous administrations. Government schools were upgraded, mohalla clinics introduced and affordability became a policy priority.

However, this narrative of reform was accompanied by a parallel story of controversy. Several of these schemes, despite their promise, were clouded by allegations of irregularities and corruption. The gap between intent and execution became glaring. While the vision was ambitious, the implementation was often marred by operational shortcomings, raising questions about governance and accountability. In the end, it was not the policies themselves but the failure to deliver them transparently and effectively that dented the AAP's credibility.

8

Experiments: Attack or Defend?

The years 2015–19 marked a period of intense experimentation and turbulence for the AAP and Kejriwal. Politically, the party oscillated between aggressive attacks on the BJP – particularly PM Narendra Modi and then BJP President Amit Shah – and periods of relative silence, focusing instead on defending its governance record.

As discussed previously, after assuming office for his second term as Delhi's CM in 2015, Kejriwal faced a significant internal crisis. Key leaders Yogendra Yadav and Prashant Bhushan were expelled from the party following disagreements. Despite these internal rifts, the AAP gradually initiated its governance agenda. However, by late 2015, the party faced its first major external challenge when the CBI filed a case against Rajendra Kumar, Kejriwal's secretary.

The CBI accused Kumar of using his official position to favour a private firm in securing government tenders. The raids extended to the Delhi Secretariat, including the CM's office, sparking a massive political showdown. A CBI spokesperson stated, 'The CBI has registered a case against Rajender Kumar[sic]. […] After taking warrants, searches are being conducted in the office and residence of Rajender Kumar [sic].'[1] The incident incensed Kejriwal, who lashed out at the PM, calling him a coward and a psychopath in a fiery tweet.[2] This marked the beginning of a phase where Kejriwal launched relentless verbal attacks on Modi and the central government, escalating the confrontation between the AAP and the BJP.

During this period, Kejriwal was reportedly determined to leverage the Delhi government's Anti-Corruption Branch (ACB) to take on the central government. A senior AAP leader, speaking anonymously, reflected on the challenges: 'It was a tough time for AAP. The central government, through the Lieutenant Governor, frequently obstructed Delhi's governance. Meanwhile, Arvind insisted on filing cases against sitting Union ministers and Delhi officials through the ACB. Anyone perceived to have links with the LG or the centre became a target of investigations.'

This confrontational strategy backfired in some ways, particularly within the bureaucratic machinery. According to the same source, Kejriwal's approach created unease among Delhi's administrative officials. 'If there were even rumours that an official had visited the LG's office, Arvind would order an ACB probe. We began losing the confidence of officials, which made governance more difficult,' the leader added.

The early months of 2016 marked a significant turning point in the growing tensions between then Delhi CM Arvind Kejriwal and the BJP-led central government. Speculations about Kejriwal planning to file a case through the ACB against a sitting Union cabinet minister were rife, though the Delhi CM denied such claims.[3] However, the situation escalated when then LG Najeeb Jung removed S.S. Yadav, an officer seen as an ally of Kejriwal, and replaced him with M.K. Meena as the ACB chief.[4] Shortly after, the central government issued a notification barring the ACB from investigating central government officials, including IAS (Indian Administrative Service) officers posted in Delhi. This marked the beginning of a series of flashpoints between Kejriwal's government and the BJP.

The following year, 2017, proved to be a critical one for the AAP as they faced electoral challenges in Punjab, Goa and MCD elections. Despite high-profile campaigns, the AAP suffered significant setbacks in all three. The Punjab Assembly election, a key focus for the AAP, ended in disappointment as the party failed to secure a majority. In the Delhi MCD elections, the AAP's vote share plummeted dramatically from 54 per cent in the 2015 Assembly polls to just 26 per cent.

This sharp decline caught the party off guard. In contrast, the BJP, which had secured 32 per cent of the vote in 2015 Delhi, slightly increased its vote share to 36 per cent, enabling it to sweep all three MCD zones. Notably, the Congress party made a remarkable recovery, increasing its vote share from 9 per cent in 2015 to 21 per cent in the MCD elections. This shift highlighted that the AAP's loss of 28 per cent vote share had partly benefited Congress, which was resurging in the capital's political landscape.

A senior AAP leader admitted, 'The Punjab results were disappointing, but the MCD outcome was shocking. We expected to maintain the momentum of our 2015 victory, but we lost miserably. It was clear that the party needed a shift in its political strategy.'

Following the MCD elections, Kejriwal called an informal meeting with his close confidants at his residence. According to one attendee, Kejriwal was visibly upset by the results and refrained from visiting the Delhi Secretariat for several days. The leader recalled, 'His close aides advised us to accelerate all pending government work. They also instructed us not to directly attack the Prime Minister or Amit Shah without Kejriwal's explicit permission. Arvind ji remained silent throughout the meeting.'

This marked a dramatic shift in the AAP's political approach. Kejriwal believed that his aggressive rhetoric against the PM had alienated a significant section of voters, many of whom shifted allegiance to the Congress. The party then adopted a more subdued stance, with Kejriwal toning down his attacks on the BJP and focusing on governance. This recalibration was aimed at regaining lost ground and rebuilding the AAP's political momentum in the capital.

Less than a month after the elections, senior AAP leader and Delhi Water Resources Minister Kapil Mishra was suspended from the party over allegations of corruption. Mishra retaliated by accusing CM Kejriwal of accepting bribes – the first such direct charge against Kejriwal from within his party.[5]

Despite the gravity of the allegations, Kejriwal's response was strikingly subdued. He issued a brief statement: 'Truth will prevail.'[6] There was no fiery rebuttal, no press conference and notably, no accusations directed at the BJP, which many expected given the AAP's previous combative style. This silence marked the beginning of a calculated transformation in Kejriwal's political approach.

A journalist who has covered the AAP since its inception told me, 'It was a pivotal moment. Kejriwal became reclusive and distanced himself from the press. The daily press conferences he once led were reduced to governance-related updates handled by Deputy Chief Minister Manish Sisodia. Political statements were left to party spokespersons.'

According to senior AAP leaders, this shift was part of a larger strategy as Kejriwal set his sights on the 2019 Lok Sabha elections. By 2017, PM Narendra Modi had established himself as a formidable and popular political figure. Kejriwal believed that persistent attacks on Modi could alienate voters further, jeopardizing the AAP's chances in the general elections.

In early 2018, Kejriwal took this recalibration a step further, transitioning from an aggressive politician to a more subdued '*aam aadmi* (common man)' persona. He began issuing public apologies to prominent leaders he had previously targeted. The first apology was to Shiromani Akali Dal leader Bikram Singh Majithia[7], whom Kejriwal had accused of drug-related corruption during the Punjab campaign. Similar apologies were made to BJP leaders Nitin Gadkari and Arun Jaitley, among others.

Kejriwal wrote to Jaitley[8]:

Dear Shri Arun Jaitley Ji,

I had made certain statements about you and your family in December 2015 and thereafter in connection with your tenure as the president of the Delhi and District Cricket

Association. These allegations also form part of the subject matter of proceedings currently pending adjudication before the Hon'ble Delhi High Court an Ld. CMM, Patiala House Court, New Delhi.

These allegations made by me were based on information and papers furnished to me by certain individuals who represented to have first-hand insight into the affairs of DDCA. However, I have recently discovered that the information and the imputations contained therein are unfounded and unwarranted and I was clearly misinformed into making these allegations.

Therefore, I unequivocally withdraw all the allegations made by me in question whether made in print, electronic or social media against you. I offer my sincere apology to you and your family members for any harm caused to your reputation as a consequence of my allegations.

Though we belong to two different political parties, I believe that we should end the unsavoury litigations between us and serve the people of our country to the best of your ability.

With warm regards
Arvind Kejriwal
Sh. Arun Jaitley
2, Krishna Menon Marg,
New Delhi-110011

This was a different Kejriwal than what many of the AAP leaders knew. This series of apologies created unease within the party. Many senior AAP leaders began questioning Kejriwal's leadership style and its impact on the party's morale. A former AAP leader recounted, 'Four senior leaders who had been with Kejriwal since the India Against Corruption movement met him to express concerns. We told him that the apologies and his silence were demoralizing party members. He didn't respond, and nothing changed.'

In addition to that, by August 2018, key figures in the AAP began distancing themselves from Kejriwal and the party. Ashish

Khetan, a close confidant of Kejriwal and head of the Delhi Dialogue Commission, resigned citing personal reasons.[9] Around the same time, senior leader and former journalist Ashutosh also stepped down, tweeting, 'Every journey has an end. My association with AAP, which was beautiful/revolutionary, has also ended. I have resigned from the PARTY/requested PAC to accept the same. It is purely from very personal reasons. Thanks to the party/all who supported me throughout.'[10]

While the resignations appeared personal, a senior journalist argued that they were also linked to dissatisfaction over the AAP's decision-making, particularly regarding Rajya Sabha nominations. The journalist said, 'From the 2015 Assembly elections, ticket distribution showed AAP wasn't prioritizing candidates' backgrounds. Many hoped Kejriwal would course-correct with Rajya Sabha nominations, but he didn't. Instead of experienced insiders like Ashutosh and Khetan, Kejriwal chose senior leader Sanjay Singh and two outsiders: N.D. Gupta, a chartered accountant, and Sushil Kumar Gupta, a Haryana-based businessman with no prior connection to AAP.'

This decision fuelled speculation about Kejriwal's evolving leadership style, highlighting a perceived disconnect between him and the party's founding principles. The period marked a turning point for the AAP, as internal dissent grew and questions about its future trajectory became more pronounced. Party insiders revealed that leaders from various assembly constituencies reported growing complaints from grassroots workers, particularly at the booth level, who felt ignored and disillusioned. The prevailing sentiment was that the party had lost its momentum.

This dissatisfaction coincided with a challenging political landscape for the AAP. The 2019 Lok Sabha elections loomed large, and there were serious concerns about the party's ability to contest effectively in Delhi, let alone in other states. In Punjab, another key base for the AAP, internal strife was rampant. Senior party leaders were leaving, and Kejriwal's controversial apology to Bikram Singh Majithia had further alienated party members and supporters in the state.

A senior AAP member recounted a pivotal meeting of the PAC at Kejriwal's residence. In the meeting, leaders acknowledged the urgency of the situation. Deputy CM Manish Sisodia was tasked with working alongside senior leaders to identify an issue that could reignite enthusiasm among the party's base. It was also decided that they would conduct surveys to gauge public sentiment ahead of the Lok Sabha elections.

'We lacked strong political issues to energize supporters,' the senior leader said. 'Manish ji suggested that the best strategy would be to leverage our ongoing tensions with the Lieutenant Governor of Delhi, as it was a familiar and effective narrative for mobilizing the public.'

In June 2018, Kejriwal and his cabinet – including Sisodia, Gopal Rai and Satyendar Jain – launched a direct protest by staging a sit-in at the LG's residence.[11] The move was strategically designed to revive the party's fighting spirit and to galvanize supporters in preparation for the elections.

Simultaneously, Kejriwal sought to strengthen the AAP's position on the national stage by reaching out to opposition leaders, excluding the Congress party. It marked a rare moment of outreach for Kejriwal, who had previously maintained a more insular approach. Leaders like West Bengal CM Mamata Banerjee, Kerala CM Pinarayi Vijayan, Andhra Pradesh CM N. Chandrababu Naidu and then Karnataka CM H.D. Kumaraswamy voiced their support. Banerjee and other opposition leaders even visited Kejriwal's residence to meet his family, signalling solidarity with his cause.[12]

The protests against the LG provided the AAP with a much-needed rallying point. Supporters gathered in large numbers outside the LG's residence, turning the sit-in into a high-energy political spectacle. A senior leader reflected, 'The protests recharged our supporters. We hit the streets with full force and held a massive dharna. It felt like a comeback moment for the party.'

For journalists covering the Delhi government, the June 2018 sit-in was a significant moment, marking the AAP's re-emergence into the spotlight after a prolonged period of silence. I distinctly recall receiving an unexpected call from an advisor in the CM's Office (CMO) just days before the dharna. The advisor informed me of a 'breaking story': a special session of the Delhi Legislative Assembly had been convened.

Though the news of the Assembly session was already circulating among journalists, it became apparent that the AAP was gearing up for something substantial. When the session began, Deputy CM Sisodia led the proceedings with an impassioned speech, revisiting key legislative bottlenecks that had plagued the Delhi government. Bills such as the Jan Lokpal Bill and policies for regularizing unauthorized colonies were highlighted – these were measures that were passed by the Delhi Assembly but stalled by the LG or the central government.

Sisodia's remarks encapsulated the frustration of the AAP leadership. 'Jan Lokpal Bill could not be passed as Delhi is not a full state. Had Delhi been a state, the Lokpal Bill would have been created within six months of us coming to power[.] All corrupt officers would have been jailed,' he declared.[13] The narrative was clear: the lack of full statehood was not just an administrative hurdle but a deliberate tool of obstruction by the central government.

For seasoned observers, this marked a pivotal shift in the AAP's political strategy. The issue of statehood was elevated from an administrative grievance to the party's central electoral plank for the upcoming 2019 Lok Sabha elections. It was a calculated move to rally public support and redefine the party's narrative. A senior AAP leader later confided, 'The 2019 Lok Sabha election was around the corner, and we needed a national issue tied to our core struggle – the tussle with the centre. Statehood became that issue.'

The demand for full statehood was not new. It had been a recurring theme in Delhi's political discourse, championed by various parties over the years, including the Congress under Sheila Dikshit and by the BJP itself. However, it had always been an uphill battle. The practical challenges of granting statehood to Delhi are immense. As the seat of India's central government, Delhi houses top bureaucrats, ministers, diplomats and Supreme Court judges. Altering its governance structure will have wide-ranging implications for national administration and security.

A veteran journalist then told me, 'Kejriwal knows full statehood is an old, unresolved issue with little realistic scope. It's a narrative, not a solution.' Yet, Kejriwal remained undeterred. While some within the AAP expressed reservations about the effectiveness of the statehood narrative, he was convinced it would resonate with voters. The party framed the issue as a matter of local empowerment, positioning it against the BJP's alleged high-handedness in undermining the Delhi government's autonomy.

However, questions loomed. How would Kejriwal, who had been noticeably restrained for over a year, mount an effective campaign against a dominant BJP? His silence over the past several months had already raised eyebrows among party insiders and observers alike.

The answer came shortly after the Assembly session. In a rare press conference at his residence, Kejriwal broke his silence. Addressing the media, he said:

> People keep saying Kejriwal has not said anything in the past year. An undue advantage of the silence was being taken. The attacks on us have intensified over the last three months. The BJP is rattled by our good work, mainly because they are being questioned by the people as to why their governments are not delivering in areas like education and healthcare as ours has in just three years.[14]

This was classic Kejriwal – mixing defiance with a subtle pivot in tone. While he criticized the BJP, his focus remained on showcasing his government's achievements, particularly in education and healthcare. It was a stark departure from his earlier combative rhetoric, which had often targeted PM Narendra Modi directly.

9

An Alliance That Never Was and the 2019 Jolt

As discussed, by mid-2018, the AAP had unveiled its strategy for the 2019 Lok Sabha elections: a campaign centred on the demand for full statehood for Delhi. Additionally, it became clear that Kejriwal was preparing for a more aggressive political comeback.

This strategy had emerged following internal surveys that revealed mixed sentiments among the AAP's supporters. According to the AAP sources, one part of the survey indicated that Kejriwal's toned-down approach was not resonating with the public, many of whom still associated him with his fiery and combative style. 'People wanted the old Kejriwal back,' an AAP leader confided.

In addition to that, the same survey revealed that the party's chances of success in the Lok Sabha elections were slim – only about 30 per cent if they contested alone. If the AAP joined forces with the Congress, however, the odds reportedly improved to a more favourable 50–50 chance. This presented a conundrum for the AAP, a party born out of opposition to the Congress, with Kejriwal himself having accused its top leaders, including former PM Manmohan Singh, of corruption.

A source in the AAP recalled that, despite internal resistance, Kejriwal convened a meeting at his residence in August 2018 to deliberate on an alliance with the Congress. Many senior leaders expressed concerns, particularly about the impact on the AAP's grassroots workers, who had already grown disenchanted due to the party's evolving political strategy. Sources told me that one leader remarked in that meeting, 'If we join hands with the Congress, our workers, who are already unhappy, will lose faith in us entirely.'

Nevertheless, Kejriwal's stance prevailed, as it often did within the party. He decided to pursue an alliance, not just in Delhi but also in Punjab, Goa and Haryana. Rajya Sabha MP Sanjay Singh was tasked with leading the discussions with the Congress, while Kejriwal would reach out to opposition leaders such as Mamata Banerjee and Pinarayi Vijayan to explore the possibility of a broader anti-BJP alliance.

The Congress also signalled interest and appointed P.C. Chacko, then in charge of the Delhi Congress unit, to spearhead talks.[1] However, the Delhi Congress was staunchly opposed to an alliance. Many leaders, including Sheila Dikshit, lobbied against it, even reaching out to Sonia Gandhi to voice their objections. The situation became more complicated when Dikshit was appointed president of the Delhi Congress in January 2019. Known for her strong political stature, Dikshit was unequivocally against any tie-up with the AAP. A senior AAP leader recalled, 'When Sheila ji returned as Delhi Congress president, we knew the alliance was as good as dead.'

For over three months, discussions between the two parties dragged on without resolution. Dikshit publicly declared her opposition, stating in an interview, 'There was never any tie-up plan with AAP. We were never interested in any alliance with them. They are a party which is itself very arrogant.'[2] This statement marked the beginning of a public breakdown in talks, with both sides trading accusations.

Kejriwal claimed that the Congress had agreed to an alliance but later reneged on its commitments. 'Everything was decided and fixed. [...] But from the next day Congress leaders stopped answering our calls,' he alleged.[3] Rahul Gandhi, on the other hand, accused Kejriwal of being inconsistent, tweeting, 'An alliance between Congress and AAP in Delhi would mean the rout of the BJP. [...] But Mr. Kejriwal has done yet another U-turn!'[4]

The stalemate was also influenced by the Congress's reluctance to include the AAP in any alliance beyond Delhi. Meanwhile, the AAP insisted on a broader arrangement that covered states like Punjab and Goa, where the two parties were in direct competition.

While the Congress talks faltered, Kejriwal found support among other opposition leaders. In February 2019, the AAP hosted a rally in Delhi attended by Mamata Banerjee and other prominent figures. Even the Congress sent Anand Sharma as its representative, despite the ongoing tensions. Nationalist Congress Party Chief Sharad Pawar[5] also attempted to mediate, hosting a dinner where he encouraged Kejriwal and Rahul Gandhi to find common ground. However, these efforts proved futile.

Kejriwal also made appearances at major opposition events, including Banerjee's rally in Kolkata.[6] Despite the lack of a formal alliance, he positioned himself as part of the larger anti-BJP front, even as his relations with the Congress remained strained.

In Delhi, the AAP fielded candidates across all seven parliamentary constituencies: Pankaj Gupta (Chandni Chowk), Dilip Pandey (North East Delhi), Atishi (East Delhi), Brijesh Goyal (New Delhi), Guggan Singh (North West Delhi), Balbir Singh Jakhar (West Delhi) and Raghav Chadha (South Delhi). The candidates were selected for their clean image and alignment with the AAP's focus on governance, education and healthcare.

Kejriwal's campaign was centred on two key narratives: the demand for full statehood and warnings against the BJP's alleged authoritarian agenda. He claimed that if the BJP returned to power, it would undermine the Constitution and eliminate elections altogether.

However, the national mood following the Pulwama attack and India's retaliatory strikes in Balakot overshadowed the AAP's campaign. The BJP capitalized on a surge in nationalism, with PM Narendra Modi and then-BJP president Amit Shah emphasizing themes of security and patriotism. Modi's rallying cry of '*ghar mein ghuskar marenge*' (We will enter your home and kill you) struck a chord with voters, leaving little room for statehood to gain traction.

The AAP's campaign faced internal hurdles as well. Many party workers were disillusioned with the candidate selection process, arguing that none of the nominees had significant grassroots connections. 'If sitting MLAs had been fielded, the outcome might have been different,' an insider remarked.

Meanwhile, the Congress fielded a strong lineup of candidates, including Sheila Dikshit (North East Delhi), Ajay Maken (New Delhi) and Vijender Singh (South Delhi). This further split the anti-BJP vote, significantly weakening the AAP's prospects.

The election results were devastating for the AAP. The BJP swept all seven Delhi seats, securing 56.86 per cent of the vote share. The Congress garnered 22.51 per cent, while the AAP's share plummeted to a mere 18 per cent – its lowest ever in Delhi.

A senior AAP leader reflected, 'The results showed that voters who opposed BJP preferred Congress over us. Our alliance talks with Congress created confusion among our supporters, and we failed to convey why statehood mattered.'

The 2019 Lok Sabha elections were a wake-up call for the AAP. The results underscored the need for a strategic reset, both in terms of policy and politics. The party recognized that it had to reconnect with its grassroots base and present a more cohesive narrative. Kejriwal, too, understood the importance of re-engaging with day-to-day politics and reclaiming his role as an aggressive, hands-on leader.

With the 2020 Delhi Assembly elections looming, the AAP undertook a significant course correction, focusing on local governance issues like education, healthcare and infrastructure – areas where it had a proven track record. This recalibration proved critical, setting the stage for the party's eventual resurgence at the state level. The lessons of 2019 were clear: alliances are tricky, narratives must resonate and leadership must be both strategic and adaptive. For the AAP, the Lok Sabha elections may have been a setback, but they were also a crucial learning experience that shaped the party's future trajectory.

10

Populism and Prashant Kishor

The 2019 Lok Sabha elections were a moment of reckoning for the AAP. The outcome was not just a defeat – it was a wake-up call that forced the party to confront some hard truths about its strategy, voter base and political alliances. While the AAP appeared to learn little from its misstep of pursuing an alliance with the Congress in 2019 – a mistake it repeated with similar outcomes in 2024 – it took a critical lesson from the voter demographics that abandoned it. The party realized that its reliance solely on its governance record in education and healthcare was not enough. It needed a stable, targeted voter base, directly benefiting from its schemes, to ensure political longevity.

Kejriwal looked towards governance models like that of Mamata Banerjee in West Bengal for inspiration. Banerjee's initiatives such as Kanyashree and Sabooj Sathi had solidified the Trinamool Congress's (TMC) support among women voters. Despite the TMC's poor performance in the 2019 Lok Sabha elections – securing only 22 of 42 seats – its female voter base remained intact. Kejriwal recognized that building such a loyal constituency was vital for the AAP's future.

After the 2019 debacle, the AAP's internal analysis highlighted two significant voter groups that had drifted away: Dalits and women.

Delhi's Dalit community, constituting 17 per cent of its population, had historically supported the Congress and the BSP. However, the AAP's rise in 2013 disrupted these traditional allegiances. In its debut Delhi Assembly elections, the AAP had secured 36 per cent of Dalit votes, emerging as the community's new preference. The BJP and the Congress had trailed with 29 per cent and 23 per cent, respectively.[1]

The 2015 Delhi Assembly elections cemented this support. The AAP won an overwhelming 58 per cent of Dalit votes, sweeping all 12 reserved constituencies in Delhi. The BJP's share dropped to 27 per cent, while the Congress further dwindled to 9 per cent.[2] The AAP's promises of affordable education, healthcare and utilities resonated deeply with Dalit voters, contributing significantly to its landslide victory.

However, by 2019, this equation had shifted dramatically. In the Lok Sabha elections, the AAP's Dalit vote share plummeted to 22 per cent, while the BJP captured 44 per cent and the Congress regained some ground with 20 per cent.[3] The reasons for this shift were multifaceted. The BJP's strong emphasis on nationalism and welfare schemes appealed to Dalits, while the AAP's declining grassroots connect and failure to sustain its momentum alienated this key demographic.

Women voters presented another challenge for the AAP. The 2015 Delhi Assembly elections had already highlighted a gender gap in the AAP's appeal. According to a CSDS-Lokniti post-poll survey, while the AAP had a significant lead over the BJP among male voters, its lead among women was just 19 percentage points. Women were more inclined towards the BJP, which outperformed the AAP among this demographic compared to male voters.[4]

Although precise data on women's voting behaviour in the 2019 Lok Sabha elections in Delhi is unavailable, internal AAP surveys indicated that women voters did not rally behind the party in large numbers. A senior AAP leader admitted, 'Women did not vote for us in large numbers even in 2015. Our vote share decreased across all demographics in 2019, and women were no exception.'

After the lessons of 2019, the AAP had a new strategy for the two groups. For Dalits, this meant renewed outreach and a focus on issues that mattered to them – jobs, social justice and affordable living. For women, it required a deeper understanding of their needs and a commitment to policies that improved their daily lives, such as safety, education for their children and access to healthcare.

The AAP's post-election introspection also revealed another alarming trend: a disconnect between its MLAs and the party's Lok Sabha candidates. In constituencies like Chandni Chowk, New Delhi and North East Delhi, the AAP's candidates lost their deposits despite the party having sitting MLAs in all assembly segments within these constituencies.

This underperformance pointed to a lack of grassroots engagement and accountability among some MLAs. Kejriwal took note. In an internal meeting, he reportedly stressed the importance of thorough grassroots surveys to assess MLA performance. 'If any MLA is not performing, they will not get a ticket in the 2020 Delhi elections,' he declared. This was a clear message: complacency would not be tolerated, and the AAP's success depended on rebuilding its connection with voters at the ground level.

While the party grappled with the fallout of its disappointing 2019 Lok Sabha election performance, it also faced critical challenges. Key questions loomed over its strategy: How should internal surveys be conducted to determine which MLAs deserved tickets? What policy changes could appeal not only to women and Dalits but also to a broader cross-section of voters? Most crucially, what fresh political strategy could reignite the party's prospects?

Before the 2019 Lok Sabha elections and the 2017 Punjab Assembly elections, the AAP had conducted internal surveys, but their credibility was often questioned. In Punjab, several sitting MLAs were denied tickets based on survey findings, only for the party to later discover that some of those leaders enjoyed significant grassroots support. These decisions, influenced by internal sabotage, highlighted the pitfalls of unreliable data and poor strategy.

In Delhi, the stakes were even higher. With the 2020 Delhi Assembly elections shaping up as a do-or-die battle, the AAP needed to make bold decisions to regain its footing. The party was in no position to risk ticket distribution or rely on questionable survey methods.

One pivotal decision in this aspect was Kejriwal's move to engage Prashant Kishor and his Indian PAC (I-PAC). Kishor's reputation as a master strategist was well established by then. His work in the 2017 Punjab Assembly elections had played a key role in the Congress's victory under Captain Amarinder Singh. The AAP leaders believed Kishor's strategy was a major factor in their own defeat in Punjab, despite having had a strong grassroots presence.

By 2019, Kishor had also led successful campaigns for Jagan Mohan Reddy's Yuvajana Sramika Rythu Congress Party in Andhra Pradesh. Kejriwal was impressed with Kishor's ability to craft professional, data-driven strategies, and saw him as the right choice to guide the AAP in the high-stakes 2020 Delhi elections.

A senior AAP leader explained, 'Kejriwal told us the 2020 election was crucial for the party's survival. He believed that professional support from someone like Prashant Kishor could ensure not just reliable ground-level surveys but also a strategy that resonated with voters.'

Kejriwal formed a small team, led by Raghav Chadha, to initiate discussions with Kishor and I-PAC. By May 2019, the talks had progressed, and an agreement was finalized. Kishor's team understood the unique challenge: the AAP had pioneered path-breaking policies in education and healthcare but faced dwindling support among key voter segments, including women and Dalits.

A former I-PAC member involved in the campaign recalled, 'It was an exciting assignment. AAP had strong policies, but we found gaps in voter outreach. Women and Dalits were critical for the party's success, and there was room for targeted intervention.'

Before starting full-fledged work, I-PAC conducted a pilot survey across Delhi constituencies to identify strengths, weaknesses and opportunities for the AAP. The findings were eye-opening, and have been added below:

- **Education and Healthcare as Strengths**: Kejriwal's work in these sectors was universally acknowledged, cutting across economic categories.
- **Modi's Popularity in Delhi**: Despite the AAP's local governance record, PM Narendra Modi remained a highly influential figure among voters.
- **Lack of Women-Centric Policies**: A significant gap emerged in this sector, as women were not direct beneficiaries of the AAP's schemes, creating a disconnect with this key demographic.
- **Economic Strata Favouring Modi**: Voters from lower economic backgrounds believed that Modi's welfare schemes directly benefited them and would improve their lives.
- **Accessibility Issues**: Many voters felt that Kejriwal and the AAP MLAs were not accessible outside of election cycles, creating an impression of aloofness.

These findings shaped the AAP's approach to the 2020 elections. The party realized it needed to address its perceived inaccessibility, craft women-centric policies and counter Modi's welfare narrative among economically disadvantaged voters.

The party also took a hard look at its MLAs. Learning from past mistakes in Punjab, Kejriwal emphasized thorough performance reviews. An AAP insider revealed, 'MLAs who were not connecting with people or delivering results would not get tickets.' To regain the trust of women voters, the AAP introduced targeted schemes such as free bus rides for women in public transport and enhanced safety measures. These initiatives were designed to create a direct and tangible impact on women's daily lives, bridging the gap identified in the surveys. Simultaneously, the AAP worked to reinforce its message on education and healthcare, ensuring these achievements were communicated effectively to counter Modi's popularity.

After these findings, Kishor's team made a pivotal recommendation – to introduce a scheme that would directly and tangibly benefit women. This scheme needed to be both empowering and financially advantageous for its beneficiaries. However, there was an additional nuance to the suggestion: the policy should *not* stem from the realms of education or healthcare. A senior AAP leader involved in these discussions explained, 'The rationale was that if we introduced a scheme from education or healthcare, it would dilute the impact of our already successful work in those sectors. Given the limited number of departments under the Delhi government's jurisdiction, the process required intense brainstorming involving the government, party leaders and Prashant Kishor's team.'

Among the sectors overseen by the Delhi government, power and water were key focus areas. However, Kishor's team recognized limitations here. Most electricity and water meters in Delhi, as in many other cities, are registered in men's names, making it challenging to introduce a women-centric scheme through these departments. This led the discussions to focus on other domains, such as social welfare, scheduled castes/schedule tribe (SC/ST) welfare and public transport.

The senior leader elaborated:

> Social welfare and SC/ST welfare departments, while significant, primarily cater to specific communities. If the goal was to benefit women across all economic and social categories, a policy centred on these departments would have limited reach. This realization led to the idea of providing free bus and Metro travel for women, a proposal that could universally empower women while ensuring broad visibility and impact.

Another parallel concern was the need to regain the trust of Dalit voters, a key constituency for the AAP since its inception.

However, any scheme exclusively targeting Dalits risked alienating lower-income voters from other communities. To address this, the AAP government decided on initiatives like free coaching for Dalit students preparing for competitive exams. Still, the need for a broader, more inclusive policy persisted. This led to the conceptualization of the free electricity scheme, capped at 200 units.

'Arvind Kejriwal and Prashant Kishor both recognized the appeal of such a policy,' the senior leader shared. 'Free electricity up to 200 units would primarily benefit lower-income households but also resonate with middle-income and even affluent families, particularly during Delhi's prolonged winters when electricity usage naturally declines. The scheme was designed to be equitable, ensuring benefits across economic strata while retaining a pro-poor narrative.'

A former member of I-PAC who worked on the AAP's campaign strategy recounted:

> While our team contributed to brainstorming and refining these ideas, the ultimate decisions rested with the government and party leadership. Our primary role lay in reshaping AAP's political approach for the upcoming Delhi Assembly election. PK [Prashant Kishor] is deeply data-driven. He presented evidence showing that Prime Minister Narendra Modi's popularity in Delhi was formidable, often surpassing that of Kejriwal. This prompted a strategic pivot: AAP needed to avoid a direct, aggressive anti-Modi stance, as it could alienate floating voters critical to the election outcome.

The recalibrated strategy emphasized governance and grassroots outreach. Kejriwal was advised to focus on showcasing his government's achievements and policies, using hard data to connect with voters. Departments were instructed to compile detailed beneficiary data, which would form the crux of the campaign narrative. '*Kaam ki rajneeti* (work-centred politics)' became the cornerstone of the AAP's new political narrative. This approach sought to highlight tangible outcomes over ideological or divisive rhetoric.

'Prashant Kishor wanted to position AAP as a governance-focused party,' the former I-PAC member added. 'He strongly recommended steering clear of broader national issues like constitutional threats, communal divides or polarized politics. The focus had to remain on hyperlocal issues where the party's track record and policies could shine.'

This shift also marked the birth of a hyperlocal election campaign, a relatively novel concept at the time. The strategy revolved around localized, constituency-specific issues rather than grand national narratives. 'By then, we knew the BJP would base its campaign on nationalism, polarization and other macro-level issues. Our recommendation was for AAP to counter this with a hyperlocal, data-backed campaign focusing on governance and service delivery,' the I-PAC member explained.

This strategy – blending governance with targeted outreach – not only redefined the AAP's approach to electoral politics but also laid the groundwork for a new model of voter engagement that resonated with Delhi's electorate. The results in the subsequent election would vindicate this data-driven, grassroots-focused approach.

Free Electricity

As discussed previously, the free electricity scheme became a pivotal element of the AAP's 'Guarantee Card', where Kejriwal pledged to provide relief to millions of households by waiving charges for the first 200 units of power consumed.[5] This decision targeted the financial concerns of ordinary people in a city where electricity bills had been a longstanding pain point for families. The scheme also sent a message about Kejriwal's focus on everyday issues. Moreover, this policy helped tackle another pressing issue: power outages. With improved infrastructure and subsidies, Kejriwal framed this scheme as more than just a financial relief programme. It showcased his government's ability to address systemic issues and provide reliable, affordable electricity to all, raising the standard of living of the aam aadmi.

'There may be debates over whether schemes like these are welfare-driven or populist, but the fundamental goal is to reach a broader section of society,' says policy researcher Ambar Kumar Ghosh. 'The beauty of such initiatives is that they transcend economic boundaries, offering benefits to all.' Ghosh then emphasized how these policies exemplify tactical governance by delivering tangible advantages to both lower-income groups and the middle class. This broader appeal explains their effectiveness in strengthening Kejriwal's voter base, which spans across socio-economic classes.

Contrary to popular belief, the AAP's support isn't confined to the economically disadvantaged. A notable segment of the middle class and upper-middle class also benefit, which has cemented their loyalty to Kejriwal. His appeal has broadened far beyond conventional expectations.

Aurangzeb Naqshbandi noted that these schemes reinforced Kejriwal's core voter base: 'Kejriwal has strengthened his support among the lower and middle classes because his schemes benefit everyone in some way. It's why his popularity surged.' Naqshbandi further emphasized that the success of these initiatives influenced other political parties, including the BJP and the Opposition, to propose similar schemes. This imitation from rivals underscores how impactful these policies were in shaping the political narrative leading up to the elections.

Today, the model of providing free electricity has gained significant traction and become highly popular across several states. In Karnataka and Telangana, under the Congress government, free electricity is now provided up to 200 units.[6] In Rajasthan, the initiative to offer free electricity up to 100 units was launched by former Congress CM Ashok Gehlot, and the current BJP government has chosen to continue the scheme. Similarly, Tamil Nadu, under the DMK (Dravida Munnetra Kazhagam) government, has introduced a policy granting 100 units of free electricity to every domestic consumer. This approach reflects the growing appeal of such welfare measures across party lines and regions.

The strategy, thus, was clear – address immediate public concerns and create policies that touch lives across economic backgrounds. By doing so, Kejriwal and the AAP not only expanded their base but also set a benchmark for inclusive governance.

Free Bus Rides and Other Populist Measures

By making Delhi Transport Corporation (DTC) buses free for women, Kejriwal not only addressed economic disparity but also enhanced women's access to essential services. The programme made it easier for women to travel to work, attend school or seek healthcare without worrying about the cost of transportation. For many women, especially those from marginalized communities, the scheme represented an opportunity for greater independence and financial savings.

This initiative was also framed as a step towards improving women's safety in public spaces, a critical concern in a city like Delhi. The perception of safety through increased public visibility, along with the tangible benefit of free rides, endeared the policy to many families. Women's rights groups and various social organizations lauded the move as a step towards gender equality, positioning the AAP as a progressive, pro-women party.

'I don't consider these initiatives as mere freebies because they've genuinely empowered people,' says Aurangzeb Naqshbandi. He continued:

> The free bus travel scheme for women has enabled thousands of women to travel long distances without worrying about the cost. In a city like Delhi, where commuting can be expensive for the poor, this scheme has been transformative. Personally, I've seen house helps from far-off areas now being able to work in upscale neighbourhoods – something that was previously difficult due to travel costs.

Naqshbandi's reflection speaks to the broader impact of the scheme, demonstrating how it has not only eased financial burdens but also expanded opportunities for women from lower economic strata. The simple act of removing a fare barrier has brought about a shift in mobility and accessibility, enhancing women's participation in the workforce and their ability to traverse the vast city of Delhi without hesitation. He highlights how this shift is not just a theoretical one, but something visible in everyday life, as these women were now more integrated into the city's economic fabric – a phenomenon made possible by a thoughtful policy intervention.

Rather than being seen as handouts, such schemes were investments in the practical empowerment of Delhi's residents, fostering independence and expanding access to opportunities. They are rooted in real-world challenges, addressing the day-to-day struggles of urban survival for many.

These schemes weren't just election strategies but emblematic of Kejriwal's brand of governance. By directly addressing issues that resonated with the masses, Kejriwal was able to build an emotional and practical connection with voters. This strategic use of populist policies not only shaped the election but cemented Kejriwal's role as a leader who prioritizes the immediate needs of the people.

11

Shaheen Bagh to Welfare: 2020 Delhi Assembly Elections

The 2020 Delhi Assembly elections were a high-stakes political drama. For the AAP, it was a do-or-die battle, especially after their dismal performance in the 2019 Lok Sabha elections. For the BJP, it was a referendum on the ongoing anti-CAA (Citizenship Amendment Act) protests, particularly the Shaheen Bagh sit-in, which had become a symbol of resistance (more on that later).

To better understand the 2020 Delhi elections, it's crucial to look at the broader political landscape. The 2019 Lok Sabha elections were a monumental victory for the BJP, signalling that the party would take bold steps in terms of policies and their socio-cultural agenda. One of the most significant moves was the abrogation of Article 370, which had always been seen as an issue of nationalism. The RSS had been demanding the abrogation of Article 370 since India's Independence. This article granted special status to the state of Jammu and Kashmir. Shyama Prasad Mukherjee, a founding member of the Bharatiya Jana Sangh, had famously declared, '*Ek desh me do vidhan, do nishan aur do pradhan nahi ho sakte* (There cannot be two constitutions, two signs and two heads in one country).'[1] In 1953, the RSS had passed a resolution calling for the abrogation of Article 370, making it a key agenda item for the organization.

When Atal Bihari Vajpayee's government came to power, it was a coalition government, making it difficult to implement the RSS's agenda. However, Modi had the courage, decisiveness and mandate to do so. After returning to power in 2019, within months, in August, the Modi government abrogated Article 370 in an authoritarian fashion, transforming Jammu and Kashmir into a Union territory. The entire Opposition was kept in the dark about this decision. Jammu and Kashmir was sealed off with heavy security deployment, and all mainstream political leaders and separatist leaders were either put under house arrest or jailed. The state was under President's rule, so there was no Legislative Assembly, and the people's mandate was completely unknown or deemed unimportant by the government.

This move was a major boost for the BJP and its core voter base, not only because it was a long-standing demand of the RSS but also because it was seen as part of the nationalistic sentiment and wave that the BJP had created. The BJP presented the abrogation of Article 370 as a measure to ensure India's national security, a crucial issue in the 2019 Lok Sabha elections. Politically, this decision gave the BJP significant momentum.

Interestingly, Delhi CM Kejriwal, who had been demanding full statehood for Delhi just a few months earlier, was the first opposition leader to support the government's decision on the abrogation of Article 370.[2] When I reached out to a senior AAP leader to understand why Kejriwal supported this move, she explained, 'At that time, we did not want to get into any controversy. We did not want to divert our attention from the welfare works going on in Delhi. On an issue related to national security, we thought it best to support the union government.'

This was a well-planned strategy by the AAP. They did not want the BJP to paint Kejriwal as someone against a sensitive issue like the abrogation of Article 370. A senior journalist told me, 'Kejriwal was playing it safe because such national issues would not have helped him in the Delhi Assembly elections. He knew that the welfare schemes would work, so he strategically sided with the central government.'

After the abrogation of Article 370, another bold move by the BJP to fulfil its ideological promise, weaving nationalism and Hindutva into the fabric of its governance, was the passage of the controversial CAA in December 2019. This was a legislative feather in the party's Hindutva crown.

The CAA was unprecedented in its religious specificity. It promised a pathway to Indian citizenship for religiously persecuted minorities – Hindus, Sikhs, Buddhists, Jains, Parsis and Christians – from Pakistan, Bangladesh and Afghanistan, while notably excluding Muslims. On paper, the Act did not strip anyone of citizenship. Yet, it created a stark division. A message had been sent, deliberate or not: some faiths were prioritized over others.

Adding fuel to the fire, then BJP president and now Union Home Minister Amit Shah's infamous speech reverberated across the nation: 'Understand the chronology. First, the Citizenship Amendment Bill (CAB) will come, then the National Register of Citizens (NRC).'[3] Shah's words, laden with intent, invoked fear within India's Muslim minority. Though the NRC remained a distant spectre – never formally introduced on a national scale – the mere thought of it, paired with the CAA, stoked existential dread. A countrywide NRC, many feared, could become a weapon to question and strip citizenship under the guise of documentation, leaving Muslims especially vulnerable.

This fear birthed resistance. While opposition parties raised legal and constitutional concerns, their voices were scattered and lacked coherence. The real outcry, the heartbeat of dissent, came from the streets. Across India, citizens – Muslims, students, activists and everyday people – took to protests. Opposition-ruled states like West Bengal and Rajasthan passed resolutions against implementing the CAA, and leaders like Mamata Banerjee led rallies against the perceived divisiveness of the Act.

In Delhi, the epicentre of this resistance was Shaheen Bagh. What began as a small sit-in by Muslim women soon swelled into a massive, iconic protest. Women draped in hijabs sat defiantly on the streets, wielding the tricolour and copies of the Constitution, their voices carrying slogans of unity and resistance. Children recited poetry, artists painted hope on walls and the streets became a tapestry of democracy's raw essence. Shaheen Bagh was not just a protest – it was a movement, a declaration that voices of dissent would not be silenced.

Yet, even as Delhi burned with passion, the political stage was being set for the 2020 Delhi Assembly elections. The BJP, emboldened by its ideological triumphs, crafted its campaign as a referendum on the CAA and Article 370's abrogation. It wasn't just an election; it was a battle for ideological supremacy. The streets of Delhi became the theatre of a polarizing narrative, where one side thundered about protecting India's unity while the other cried for justice and inclusion.

Polarization vs Welfare

The BJP faced two fundamental challenges in Delhi when it came to competing against the AAP and Kejriwal. Despite winning all parliamentary seats in Delhi during both the 2014 and 2019 Lok Sabha elections, the BJP's organizational structure in the capital was weak, and it lacked a credible, locally rooted face to counter Kejriwal's popularity. These weaknesses significantly hampered the BJP's ability to mount an effective challenge in the 2020 Delhi Assembly elections.

At the heart of the BJP's struggles was the absence of a development or governance narrative that could rival Kejriwal's widely praised Delhi Model. While the BJP leaned on PM Narendra Modi's towering national appeal, Kejriwal focused on showcasing the tangible results of his administration's policies – improved schools, subsidized electricity, free water and quality healthcare. This created a sharp contrast. The BJP's reliance on a broader, Hindutva-driven agenda left it struggling to address local issues that mattered most to Delhi voters.

The BJP's Delhi unit was also handicapped by a lack of prominent leaders who could match Kejriwal's credibility. Manoj Tiwari, an MP (member of Parliament) and the party's most visible face in Delhi, held sway among the Purvanchali community but failed to resonate with the city's diverse electorate. As a result, the BJP's campaign became heavily dependent on its central leadership, particularly PM Modi, Home Minister Amit Shah, and Uttar Pradesh CM Yogi Adityanath.

Instead of focusing on local concerns, the BJP anchored its campaign on polarizing issues like Hindutva nationalism, the Shaheen Bagh protests and Pakistan. Senior journalist Aurangzeb Naqshbandi told me, 'The BJP believed that large-scale polarization would be enough to secure victory in Delhi because of the party's core voter base.' To this end, the BJP deployed an arsenal of leaders, from CMs to MPs and MLAs from other states, in a blitzkrieg-style campaign. The tone of the campaign was divisive, with Shaheen Bagh becoming a focal point.

Prime Minister Modi and Home Minister Shah spearheaded this narrative, framing the BJP as the protector of national security and branding the Shaheen Bagh protests as 'anti-national'. Shah, during a rally in Babarpur, declared, 'Your vote to BJP candidate will make Delhi and the country safe and prevent thousands of incidents like Shaheen Bagh.'[4] He urged voters to press the electronic voting machine (EVM) button with such force that the 'current' would be felt at Shaheen Bagh.[5] This rhetoric set the tone for the BJP's campaign: Shaheen Bagh was not merely a protest site but a symbol of everything the party stood against.

Yogi Adityanath's speeches further amplified this polarization. In several places, including Rohini and Karawal Nagar, he accused Shaheen Bagh protesters of being sympathetic to terrorists and accused the AAP government of 'supplying biryani' to the demonstrators. He linked the protests to an alleged agenda to undermine India's rise, saying, 'The protests happening at various places in Delhi are not because of the Citizenship Amendment Act. They are happening because these people want to prevent India from becoming a global power.' His statements were laced with references to Article 370 and the Ram Mandir, invoking BJP's broader ideological triumphs.[6]

The rhetoric often veered into outright provocation. Then Minister of State for Finance Anurag Thakur, during a rally, led the crowd in chanting the infamous slogan, '*Desh ke gaddaron ko, goli maaro saalon ko* (Shoot the traitors of the country).'[7] This chant became emblematic of the incendiary tone of the BJP's campaign. Kapil Mishra, a BJP candidate, tweeted inflammatory remarks, describing Shaheen Bagh as 'mini Pakistan' and claiming that 'Pakistani hooligans' had taken over Delhi streets.[8] Member of Parliament Parvesh Verma went so far as to compare Kejriwal to a terrorist, saying, 'I don't understand if we should fight terrorists in Kashmir or Kejriwal in Delhi.'[9]

These statements underscored the BJP's strategy of painting the Delhi election as a battle between nationalist forces and so-called anti-national elements. The party sought to equate the protests at Shaheen Bagh with a threat to India's integrity, portraying the AAP as complicit in this alleged conspiracy.

However, in this polarizing atmosphere Kejriwal and the AAP walked a tightrope, carefully sidestepping the explosive debate over the CAA protests. While the BJP leaned heavily on the Shaheen Bagh sit-in as a symbol of alleged anti-national sentiments, Kejriwal chose to tread a different path: he refused to engage.

Kejriwal's approach was calculated. He avoided commenting on the Shaheen Bagh protests and dodged direct attacks on the BJP's CAA policy. Instead, he redirected attention to his administration's welfare achievements. Simultaneously, he embraced a 'soft' Hindutva stance, invoking Hindu cultural symbols to blunt the BJP's attacks. From reciting the Hanuman Chalisa to visiting temples, Kejriwal subtly courted Hindu voters without alienating others. As one senior AAP leader told me, 'If we talk about Shaheen Bagh, BJP will paint us as anti-national. This election is about Delhi's welfare, and that's our focus.'

Yet, Kejriwal's positioning was not without friction. His deputy, Sisodia, inadvertently sparked controversy when he expressed solidarity with Shaheen Bagh protesters during a TV interview.[10] The BJP seized the moment, using Sisodia's comment to attack the AAP as being aligned with 'anti-national elements'.

However, Kejriwal deftly avoided being ensnared, doubling down on his narrative of governance over divisive issues.

As discussed, Prashant Kishor played a crucial role in shaping this communication strategy. Under his guidance, Kejriwal conducted over 10 town halls in collaboration with media outlets, engaging directly with voters. These events highlighted his government's achievements and his vision for Delhi's future, keeping the conversation firmly rooted in local governance rather than national controversies.

Central to this campaign was Kejriwal's 'report card', a detailed account of promises made in 2015 and their fulfilment. Coupled with this was the 'Kejriwal Guarantee Card', a 10-point manifesto for the future. The card was a masterstroke of simplicity and pragmatism, outlining specific commitments that resonated with Delhi's voters:

- **Uninterrupted power and free electricity:** Up to 200 units free electricity and underground cabling for a wire-free Delhi.
- **Clean water access:** 24-hour pure piped water, with 20,000 litres free for every household.
- **World-class education:** Expansion of existing facilities to ensure every child in Delhi receives quality education.
- **Enhanced healthcare:** Strengthening the network of mohalla clinics and government hospitals.
- **Affordable transport:** Free bus travel for students, building on the free rides already offered to women.
- **Tackling pollution:** Pledges to reduce air pollution by planting 2 crore trees and cleaning the Yamuna.
- **Women's safety:** Deployment of 'mohalla marshals' to enhance safety in neighbourhoods.
- **Development of unauthorized colonies:** Providing roads, water, sewers and clinics in unauthorized colonies.
- **Waste management:** Making Delhi garbage-free in five years.
- **Housing for slum dwellers:** Implementation of the 'Jahan Jhuggi Wahin Makaan' (Where there is a slum, there will be a home) scheme to replace slums with permanent housing.

This clear and relatable agenda, coupled with Kejriwal's strategic silence on divisive issues, proved to be a formidable electoral strategy. While BJP leaders like Parvesh Verma ramped up rhetoric, calling Kejriwal anti-national and even a terrorist, Kejriwal turned the attack into an opportunity. With calm defiance, he responded saying that if you think I'm a terrorist, vote for the BJP, and you think I've worked for Delhi, vote for the AAP. This victim card resonated with voters, portraying him as a leader under unfair attack.[11]

The AAP campaign also sought to draw contrasts between the BJP's governance in the MCD and the AAP's governance model. Kejriwal highlighted inefficiencies and corruption in the BJP-controlled MCDs, contrasting them with the AAP's achievements in health, education and public utilities.

When the results were declared, the AAP's strategy had delivered a resounding victory. The party secured 62 out of 70 seats, leaving the BJP with just 8. It was not only a personal triumph for Kejriwal but also a categorical rejection of the BJP's polarizing rhetoric. The mandate was clear: Delhi wanted governance rooted in tangible outcomes, not divisive politics.

Post-election surveys revealed key insights. Women voters played a crucial role, rallying behind the AAP in large numbers. Young voters, too, saw Kejriwal as a pragmatic leader delivering on promises. Support from Dalits and economically weaker sections reinforced the notion that the AAP's welfare policies had struck a chord.[12]

The 2020 Delhi Assembly elections were a lesson in political agility. In the face of an intensely polarizing national environment, Kejriwal and the AAP chose a path of quiet resilience, focused on governance and inclusivity. By refusing to be baited by the BJP's divisive agenda and instead doubling down on welfare promises, they secured not just an electoral win but a mandate for progressive governance. This triumph marked the consolidation of the AAP's unique brand of politics, rooted in pragmatism, communication and the belief that at the heart of every election lie the everyday aspirations of the people.

Part 3

Shifting Ideology

12

Janta-ism or Opportunism: The Ideology Question

Growing up in Kolkata, the ideological capital of Left politics, my understanding of politics was always rooted in theory and doctrine. In my formative years, West Bengal was a hotbed of leftist movements, where ideology wasn't just academic but lived and breathed in the streets, in debates and in governance. It shaped not only my worldview but also the lens through which I, as a journalist, began to interpret politics. So, when I started covering the AAP full-time in 2017, the first question I grappled with was: *What is the ideology of this party?*

Back then, my friends in Kolkata often argued that the AAP was a Left-of-Centre party, leaning towards socialism. Meanwhile, in Delhi, the narrative I encountered suggested that the AAP was a Right-of-Centre entity, even accused of flirting with soft Hindutva. Yet, my own observations placed the AAP somewhere in the nebulous realm of centrism. Frankly, I was confused. I needed clarity.

In a candid conversation with a former advisor to the Delhi government and a close confidant of Kejriwal, I posed the question directly: 'What is AAP's ideology?' The answer I received was succinct and puzzling: 'We are neither Left nor Right nor Centre. Our ideology is Janta-ism. That's it.'

Kejriwal himself has often elaborated on this philosophy. 'We don't get involved in ideologies,' he once said. 'Our model is Janta ka model. If people face a problem, we address it. We find solutions that benefit the people, not a select few. *Hamara Jantanomics hai* [Ours is Jantanomics].'[1]

At its core, the AAP's approach seems to reject the rigidity of established political frameworks. Unlike the BJP, which aligns itself with Right-wing Hindutva ideology, or the Congress, which oscillates between centrist pragmatism and ideological opportunism, the AAP operates in a space that is both novel and amorphous. It is a welfare-centric party that defines itself not by doctrine but by pragmatism.

The AAP's governance model is rooted in hyperlocal, individual-centric welfare schemes. From subsidized electricity and water to the transformation of public schools and mohalla clinics, its focus has always been on addressing specific, tangible needs of citizens. This emphasis on individual solutions contrasts with the Left's collectivist ideology, which champions broader structural change over targeted personal relief.

Leftist politics, deeply rooted in Marxist traditions, advocates for systemic changes that uplift entire classes or communities. The AAP, by contrast, approaches governance like a meticulous repairperson: identifying immediate problems and fixing them. Its vision is not revolutionary but service-oriented, which is why labelling it as Left-of-Centre feels inadequate.

Similarly, the AAP's inclusivity in governance stands in contrast to the BJP's majoritarian tendencies. The BJP openly espouses a brand of nationalism intertwined with religious identity, which forms the backbone of its Right-wing politics. The AAP, however, refrains from such overt ideological posturing. It does not champion hyper-nationalism or religious majoritarianism, nor does it embrace the Congress-style centrism, which has historically adapted and evolved to suit the times.

This lack of a clear ideological anchor often perplexes political analysts. As senior journalist R. Prasannan observed:

> The AAP has no 'ism'. If it has an 'ism', it is simply 'citizen-ism', something no political pundit has yet defined in ideological terms. To that extent, the AAP is not a 'political' party, but a 'civic' party. It practices not politics, but civics – especially the civics of what citizens ought to get from the state, and ought to give the state.[2]

Indeed, the AAP's focus on civics over politics distinguishes it from India's traditional political landscape. It avoids grandstanding on national issues unless they directly intersect with Delhi's governance. For example, during the anti-CAA protests, the AAP refrained from championing Shaheen Bagh, nor did it openly endorse the controversial citizenship law. This strategic ambiguity allowed the AAP to avoid alienating either its minority voters or its Hindu supporters, reflecting its calculated, pragmatic approach to contentious issues.

Despite its inclusive governance model, the AAP has faced accusations of dabbling in soft Hindutva. Critics point to instances like Kejriwal's public recitation of the Hanuman Chalisa during the 2020 Delhi elections or his party's silence during polarizing moments. Such moves are often interpreted as attempts to avoid antagonizing Delhi's Hindu majority. Whether these gestures are tactical or ideological is debatable, but they have fuelled scepticism about the AAP's ideological purity. I will delve deeper into this aspect in the later chapters.

In Kejriwal's own words, the party's ideology rests on three pillars: hardcore patriotism, diehard honesty and humanity.[3] While these principles may seem broad, they encapsulate the AAP's brand of politics – a mix of nationalism, transparency and welfare that appeals to the urban middle class as much as the underprivileged.

Ultimately, the AAP's ideology – or lack thereof – defies traditional political classifications. Its 'Janta-ism' or 'Citizen-ism' is a reflection of its origins as a movement born out of frustration with systemic corruption and inefficiency. By focusing on immediate, localized problems rather than grand ideological battles, the AAP has carved out a unique space in Indian politics.

Whether this approach will evolve into a coherent doctrine or remain a pragmatic, issue-based strategy is yet to be seen. For now, the AAP's identity is as fluid as the needs of the people it claims to serve – a party that practices the politics of service over the politics of ideology. And perhaps, in a country as diverse and complex as India, that in itself is a revolutionary idea.

The AAP has often been lauded for this ideological fluidity, which sets it apart in Indian politics. However, this same adaptability has increasingly painted the AAP as an opportunistic force that prioritizes expediency over principles.

As mentioned earlier, the AAP claims to eschew caste-based or religion-centric politics, projecting itself as a party of governance and welfarism. But some of its actions often tell a different story. In Goa's 2021 Assembly elections, the AAP promised to appoint a CM from the Bhandari community – a dominant caste in the state – and a Deputy CM from the Christian community. To cement this pledge, the party named Amit Palekar, an OBC leader from the Bhandari community, as its chief ministerial candidate.[4]

Similarly, during Punjab's 2022 Assembly elections, Kejriwal explicitly stated that the AAP's chief ministerial candidate would be a Sikh, proclaiming, 'It is the right of the Sikh community. The face of the chief minister will be discussed later, but whosoever he will be, Punjab will be proud of that person.' Such calculated caste and religion-based assurances seem at odds with the AAP's self-declared ethos of transcending identity politics.[5]

Then came the troubling silence during one of Delhi's darkest hours – the 2020 riots in North East Delhi. Following his landslide third-term victory, Kejriwal faced his sternest test as CM when communal violence erupted in the capital. Houses, mosques and lives were consumed by the flames of hatred. Yet, Kejriwal largely remained a passive observer. Beyond issuing perfunctory appeals for peace, he avoided visiting riot-affected areas or meeting victims. His conspicuous absence was stark, especially when other leaders, including Congress's Rahul Gandhi, made their way to the devastated neighbourhoods.

This recurring pattern – emphasizing welfarism while sidestepping deeper ideological commitments – raises uncomfortable questions about the AAP's political identity. While it continues to deliver on promises like subsidized electricity and healthcare in Delhi, its actions outside these governance priorities often reflect an inclination towards political expediency over principle.

A senior AAP leader, when asked about these contradictions, defended the party's approach. He said:

> We are not opportunistic but practical. When we fought the Punjab Assembly election in 2017, we didn't have a CM face, and that decision cost us the election. In 2022, announcing a Sikh CM was a practical choice, as Sikhism is the dominant religion there. Similarly, during the Delhi riots, law and order was not under our jurisdiction. We provided relief camps and food, but visiting the riot-hit areas would have been politicized as a photo op.

This justification does highlight the AAP's reliance on pragmatism to navigate the complexities of Indian politics. Yet, it also underscores how this pragmatism often blurs into opportunism, particularly when it comes to preserving the party's broader political interests.

The success of this approach, particularly in Delhi, and to some extent in Punjab, is undeniable. Unlike the Congress or the TMC, the AAP has managed to avoid being branded as a party that panders excessively to minorities. The BJP's narrative of 'Muslim appeasement' – a weaponized term in contemporary Indian politics – has not stuck to the AAP, despite its targeted welfarism and secular posturing. This balancing act has allowed the AAP to sustain its core voter base without alienating either Hindus or Muslims in a politically polarized landscape.

Yet, as the AAP expands its footprint beyond Delhi, its opportunistic streak could become a double-edged sword. By promising caste- or religion-based representation in states like Goa and Punjab, the AAP risks alienating voters who initially supported its claim of being 'above identity politics'. Similarly, its muted stance on issues like the Delhi riots, though strategically calculated, leaves a troubling vacuum in its moral positioning.

The larger question here is one of sustainability. Can a party, however welfarist in its approach, survive in Indian politics without a strong ideological backbone? While flexibility and pragmatism can be advantageous in navigating electoral complexities, an overt reliance on opportunism may eventually erode public trust.

If the AAP's core philosophy is genuinely centred on governance and people's welfare, why does it selectively engage in identity politics during elections? If it truly stands for all citizens, why did Kejriwal refrain from meeting the victims of the Delhi riots? These are not just rhetorical questions – they are fundamental contradictions that the party must reckon with if it seeks to cement its place as a credible national alternative.

A major issue with the AAP's approach lies in its political opportunism, particularly its reluctance to take definitive stands. Consider the BJP's strategy in Uttar Pradesh elections Despite the state's significant Muslim population, the BJP does not field Muslim candidates, clearly signalling that it does not count on Muslim votes and sees no electoral advantage in such representation. Whether one supports or opposes this stance, it reflects a firm political position – a clarity of intent that cannot be ignored.

Contrast this with the AAP's strategy in Delhi. In seven assembly constituencies with majority Muslim population – Okhla, Ballimaran, Matiamahal, Seelampur, Babarpur, Chandni Chowk and Mustafabad – the party fields Muslim candidates to secure community support. Only two of these constituencies—Chandni Chowk and Babarpur—elected Hindu MLAs in the 2025 Delhi Assembly election: Punardeep Singh Sawhney and Gopal Rai, respectively. While this indicates the AAP's strategic candidate selection to win Muslim-majority seats, it falls short when it comes to advocating for the community's rights. The party's silence on critical issues concerning its Muslim voter base reflects a calculated but glaring opportunism, a pattern that risks undermining its credibility.

This lack of consistency and conviction in the AAP's political ethos stands in stark contrast to parties that, irrespective of agreement, are unambiguous in their positions. For the AAP, such ambivalence raises questions about whether its actions align with its professed values or are merely tactical moves to secure votes.

The AAP's defeat in the 2025 elections has underscored a critical political truth: opportunism without ideological clarity rarely succeeds on the ground. The AAP's attempt to position itself as a centrist alternative ultimately alienated its base. The disconnect between its public posturing and its actual ideological stand became too obvious for voters to ignore. Significantly, the party's ambivalent stance towards Muslims and Dalits – especially its visible distancing from the Muslim electorate – proved costly. In many Muslim-dominated constituencies, candidates unaffiliated with the AAP performed far better, signalling a clear rejection of the AAP's political evasiveness. Meanwhile, its core Hindu vote base began to erode, not just because of its shifting alignments, but also due to the party's failure to deliver on its foundational promise: governance rooted in performance. In Delhi, the very city where it rose to prominence, the AAP's credibility suffered due to administrative stagnation and unmet expectations. The 2025 loss is not just electoral – it is a moment of reckoning for a party that once claimed to redefine Indian politics. Opportunism, while often effective in the short term, cannot be the sole compass for a party seeking long-term relevance in a deeply ideological and polarized political landscape.

The AAP's evolution offers a fascinating study in Indian politics – a party born from an anti-corruption movement, now grappling with the very compromises it once railed against. Whether it can sustain its balancing act without tipping into irrelevance or losing its moral compass will define its future, both in Delhi and beyond.

13

Kaam Ki Rajneeti vs Hanuman Chalisa

It was a crisp evening on 5 October 2022 when thousands of people converged at Ambedkar Bhavan in Karol Bagh. The occasion was Ashoka Vijayadashami, a sacred day for Dalits and Buddhists across India. For many, it is also a day of transformation, marked as Buddhist Conversion Day, when Dalits take the 22 vows (popularized by Babasaheb Ambedkar himself) and embrace Buddhism, rejecting the social inequities embedded in Hindu orthodoxy. The event that year was organized by the Buddhist Society of India and Mission Jai Bhim, under the stewardship of Rajendra Pal Gautam, a cabinet minister in Delhi's government, a noted Dalit activist and then MLA from Seemapuri.

This was no official Delhi government event. Gautam, a staunch Ambedkarite, presided over the ceremony in his individual capacity. Nearly 10,000 attendees pledged to follow the principles of Buddhism. The vows famously include a renunciation of Hindu deities such as Brahma, Vishnu and Mahesh. It was a continuation of a legacy Ambedkar began in 1956 at Deekshabhumi, Nagpur – a moment etched in history as one of resistance and empowerment.

However, a week later, trouble brewed. A selectively edited video of the pledge went viral, with a singular focus on the vow that rejects faith in Hindu gods. The BJP seized the opportunity, accusing the AAP of being 'anti-Hindu'. The timing couldn't have been worse for Kejriwal, who was then deeply engrossed in the Gujarat Assembly elections. Under mounting pressure and a full-throated campaign by the BJP, Gautam was forced to resign from his ministerial position. He complied quietly, without defiance or bitterness, choosing loyalty over spectacle.[1]

Gautam's resignation was met with silence from the AAP. No one in the party publicly defended him – not even Kejriwal, who had once styled himself as a champion of Ambedkar's ideals. Gautam eventually joined the Congress in 2024 but remained gracious, refusing to criticize the AAP despite being left out in the cold during the controversy.

It is worth recalling that during the 2022 Punjab Assembly elections, Kejriwal had declared that portraits of B.R. Ambedkar and Bhagat Singh would adorn the offices of all AAP functionaries, including ministers and CMs, as a tribute to their legacies. It was a calculated attempt to appropriate icons of resistance and social justice.

And yet, when Gautam followed Ambedkar's example – something intrinsic to the very essence of the man the AAP claimed to revere – he was unceremoniously cast aside. Kejriwal's decision was not about ideology, it was about optics. He didn't want to give the BJP ammunition to paint him as anti-Hindu, even at the cost of abandoning a colleague who stood firmly on the principles of Ambedkar.

This is the quintessential Kejriwal paradox: to claim the moral high ground of revolutionary ideals while also ensuring that nothing disrupts his carefully curated image. He wants to be seen as a torchbearer of Ambedkar's vision but won't defend someone living that vision when it risks political fallout. It is like a self-proclaimed Gandhian distancing himself from non-violence to avoid alienating those who endorse force.

By pushing Gautam to resign, Kejriwal sent a clear message: the party's political calculus would always outweigh individual conviction. For all his claims of progressivism and inclusivity, Kejriwal chose pragmatism over principle. His silence during the controversy spoke louder than words. It revealed a leader more concerned with keeping his electoral path smooth than standing firm for the ideals his party professes to uphold.

The Gautam episode is a stark reminder of the tightrope Kejriwal walks – a balancing act where every step is calculated, and every move aims to placate both progressives and conservatives. But as history has shown, walking the middle path too often risks alienating both.

After the drubbing in the 2019 Lok Sabha elections, Kejriwal and his AAP underwent a significant ideological pivot. While freebies – or 'revdis' as critics call them – continued to dominate his policy arsenal, Kejriwal simultaneously began weaving Hindutva elements into his political narrative. Some analysts term this as 'soft Hindutva', but it is perhaps more accurate to call it the 'Kejriwal model of Hindutva' – a calibrated blend of cultural symbolism and strategic appropriation to counter the BJP on its own turf.

This model is reminiscent of the RSS's historical strategy of appropriation. Social scientist Badri Narayan wrote in his book *Republic of Hindutva*, 'Resistance and appropriation are two tactics that work in the domain of power, as both provide space for political expansion. Hindu politics works on the strategic process of appropriation very effectively.' Narayan noted how the BJP and RSS extended their influence by co-opting groups like Dalits, tribals and women – communities traditionally outside their ideological fold. Similarly, Kejriwal appears to have appropriated Hindutva not from conviction but as a tactical response to the BJP's dominance.[2]

As we know, the AAP, from its inception, has championed a secular political ethos. Kejriwal had no qualms about associating with liberal causes, often aligning with Leftist and Congress leaders. In 2016, he stood in solidarity with students at Jawaharlal Nehru University[3] during protests over the disappearance of Najeeb Ahmed. The Kejriwal of that time was unabashedly liberal, a leader comfortable opposing the BJP's nationalist and Hindutva rhetoric.

Post-2019, however, a new Kejriwal emerged. Facing the BJP's juggernaut, he recalibrated his strategy, leaning into Hindutva symbolism to safeguard his political relevance. Temples and gods became fixtures in his speeches. Visits to Hanuman temples and recitations of the Hanuman Chalisa became staples of his public image. This wasn't merely soft Hindutva but an audacious attempt to counter the BJP's rhetoric by offering a parallel narrative.

Aurangzeb Naqshbandi put it succinctly: 'AAP is not engaging in soft Hindutva; it is countering the BJP using the same Hindutva rhetoric. When the BJP references Ram, AAP mentions Hanuman. AAP's stance on Hindutva is clear and straightforward – it is competitive.'

To understand Kejriwal's strategy, one must examine Delhi's electoral dynamics. The BJP commands a robust core vote share of 35 per cent in the capital, while the Congress and the AAP hover around 20 per cent and 18 per cent, respectively. During Lok Sabha elections, the BJP's vote share soars to around 54 per cent, thanks to a swing of floating voters.[4] Conversely, in Assembly elections, the AAP absorbs Congress' votes and captures the same swing voters, raising its vote share to similar levels.

As mentioned previously, this fluid 10–15 per cent of floating voters often shift allegiance between Lok Sabha and Assembly elections, voting for the BJP at the national level but choosing the AAP locally. Recognizing this pattern, Kejriwal understood that maintaining this bloc's support would require a delicate balance: counter the BJP without alienating its ideological sympathizers.

Naqshbandi elaborated: 'In Delhi, some voters support AAP in Assembly elections but choose BJP in Lok Sabha elections. The BJP's ideological presence is robust. AAP's strategy is to avoid opposing this core ideology to retain those voters.'

Kejriwal's pivot to Hindutva was also driven by the AAP's national ambitions. By 2019, the AAP had set its sights on expanding beyond Delhi into states like Gujarat, Haryana, Uttar Pradesh and Punjab. Unlike cosmopolitan Delhi, these regions are deeply entrenched in Hindutva politics. Kejriwal likely realized that without embracing some form of Hindutva, it would be nearly impossible to breach the BJP's strongholds.

However, this approach has yielded mixed results. In states where the AAP has gained ground (Punjab being a notable example) it has largely done so at the expense of the Congress, not the BJP. Kejriwal's strategy of Hindutva appropriation may have neutralized some BJP rhetoric, but it has yet to erode the saffron party's core support base in any meaningful way.

The Kejriwal model of Hindutva is an experiment in countering an entrenched narrative with a carefully curated alternative. Whether this strategy will sustain the AAP's momentum or falter under its inherent contradictions remains an open question. In the labyrinth of Indian politics, where ideologies are fluid and narratives endlessly contested, Kejriwal's journey is a testament to the art of political survival and reinvention.

In the aftermath of the AAP's resounding defeat in the 2025 Delhi Assembly elections, one truth stands out starkly: Kejriwal's experiment with soft Hindutva failed to take root. Despite calibrated attempts to appropriate religious symbolism and appeal to the Hindu vote bank, the AAP could not breach the ideological fortress that the BJP and the RSS have long cultivated in Delhi. Their deep-rooted grassroots machinery, cultural entrenchment and narrative control ensured that Kejriwal's overtures appeared both tactical and unconvincing to the core Hindutva electorate. The gamble to mirror the BJP's identity politics only exposed the AAP's limitations in navigating a terrain already firmly held by its chief political adversary.

Appropriation of Hanuman

In his victory speech following the AAP's decisive win in the 2020 Delhi Assembly elections, Kejriwal struck a surprising chord: 'This is the day of Lord Hanuman who has blessed the people of Delhi. We pray that Hanuman ji keeps showing us the right path so that we can continue to serve people for the next five years.'[5]

Kejriwal's invocation of Lord Hanuman wasn't just a spiritual acknowledgment – it was a masterstroke of appropriation politics. In a political landscape where the BJP has long dominated Hindu-centric narratives, Kejriwal strategically chose to shift the focus from Lord Ram to Hanuman, a figure with universal appeal across caste and regional lines.

The BJP, particularly during the 2019 Lok Sabha elections, had centred its narrative on Ram-centric politics, reinvigorated by the momentum surrounding the Ram Mandir issue. By contrast, Kejriwal's Hanuman-centric approach was both a cultural pivot and a political counterbalance. Hanuman, as historian Devdutt Pattanaik notes, is a figure who transcends caste, class and geography. 'We all want to see Hanuman according to our fantasies,' writes Pattanaik, pointing out how different communities have historically embraced Hanuman in ways that reflect their identities. For example, some see him as a Brahmin scholar, others as a Dalit subaltern, a Dravidian hero or even an Adivasi figure.[6]

Pattanaik's observations highlight why Hanuman is such a politically safe and inclusive figure. His Sanskrit fluency and elite demeanour from the Ramayana coexist with his humility and service, endearing him to both the upper and lower castes. For Kejriwal, this universality was critical. By invoking Hanuman, he avoided alienating his core voter base – predominantly lower castes and classes – while appealing to a broader Hindu sentiment.

The AAP's message was clear: Hinduism isn't the BJP's sole domain. By appropriating Hanuman, Kejriwal signalled a form of Hinduism that was inclusive, grounded and focused on service – a stark contrast to the BJP's more exclusive, Ram-centric nationalism.

An AAP leader, speaking anonymously, explained the party's nuanced stance: 'We are not against Ram. In fact, we celebrated the Ram Mandir's inauguration. During the Gujarat elections, we even promised free pilgrimages to Ayodhya for every citizen. But the BJP behaves as though they alone have the right to Ram. Our Hinduism is broader – it's about inclusivity, not ownership.'

This narrative reorientation wasn't without risks. In a deeply polarized political environment, where the BJP leaders often portray opponents as anti-Hindu, the AAP's embrace of Hanuman was a clever sidestep. By positioning Hanuman as their spiritual lodestar, the AAP avoided the pitfalls of directly contesting Ram's symbolism while resonating with diverse Hindu communities.

Kejriwal's Hanuman strategy underscored a larger lesson in modern Indian politics: the battle for narratives is not won through rejection but by redefining the symbols themselves. With Hanuman as his chosen emblem, Kejriwal not only countered the BJP's dominance but also broadened the spectrum of what Hindu identity could mean in contemporary politics.

Appropriation of Babasaheb and Shaheed Bhagat Singh

In contemporary Indian politics, legacies are more than just markers of the past – they are strategic tools for constructing a political future. The BJP has long demonstrated mastery over this craft, rooting its ideological moorings in the legacy of the RSS and icons like Veer Savarkar, while simultaneously attempting to appropriate figures like Subhas Chandra Bose, who stood for secularism. The Congress, on the other hand, draws from the institutional legacy of stalwarts such as Mahatma Gandhi and Jawaharlal Nehru. Socialists like Ram Manohar Lohia continue to influence India's Left-leaning socialist politics.

But what about the AAP? Founded in the crucible of the IAC movement, the AAP emerged without an ideological inheritance. This void, however, became an opportunity for Kejriwal, who has skilfully stitched together a tapestry of appropriated legacies to create a narrative that suits the party's ambitions.

Kejriwal's choice of icons – Babasaheb Ambedkar and Shaheed Bhagat Singh – is as calculated as it is evocative. Both figures carry immense pan-Indian appeal, transcending regional, caste and religious divides. Ambedkar, the architect of the Indian Constitution and champion of Dalit rights, embodies the fight against systemic oppression. Bhagat Singh, the revolutionary martyr, symbolizes fearless defiance against colonial rule. Together, they form a duo that represents justice and resistance, ideals central to the AAP's self-styled image as a party for the common man.

But why Ambedkar and Bhagat Singh? The answer lies in the emotional and political resonance these figures command. Unlike Gandhi (whose legacy is often associated with non-violence and patience) or Nehru (tied to elitist intellectualism), Ambedkar and Bhagat Singh represent action, urgency and rebellion – qualities Kejriwal believes align with the AAP's narrative of change.

However, Kejriwal's strategy reveals its contradictions when examined closely. For instance, while Ambedkar's legacy is deeply intertwined with his critique of Hinduism and its caste-based inequalities, the AAP has simultaneously courted Hindu symbolism, as discussed previously.

This duality – celebrating Ambedkar's call for caste annihilation while invoking Hindu religious traditions – exposes the limits of the AAP's ideological coherence. Ambedkar himself was unequivocal in his critique of Hinduism, stating, 'Hinduism is the greatest obstacle to Hindu unity.'[7] His rejection of Hinduism culminated in his conversion to Buddhism. It showed a profound repudiation of a faith he believed perpetuated social inequities. How, then, can a party reconcile his vision with its own forays into Hindu symbolism?

Similarly, Bhagat Singh's legacy poses challenges for the AAP. A staunch atheist, Bhagat Singh mocked religious dogma and the caste system, critiquing both Hinduism and other organized religions. His writings, including *Why I Am an Atheist*, leave no room for doubt about his rejection of faith-based nationalism. Yet, Kejriwal's AAP often juxtaposes Bhagat Singh's radical ethos with religious practices like invoking Hanuman, creating a contradictory narrative that feels more opportunistic than authentic.

Critics have not missed these contradictions. Political scientist Ashutosh Kumar of Panjab University points out that the AAP's appropriation of Bhagat Singh and Ambedkar is a matter of 'political expedience'. He observes that while both icons are revered across India, their philosophies clash with the religious nationalism that the AAP seems increasingly eager to co-opt in its quest for power.[8]

Former AAP leader and journalist Ashutosh also critiques the party's shallow engagement with these legacies. He notes that while the AAP glorifies Bhagat Singh's defiance against British rule, it neglects his ideological depth, particularly his commitment to socialism and atheism. Writing for the *Indian Express*, he asks pointedly, '[...]How come Hanuman and Bhagat Singh are walking together?'[9] This rhetorical question underscores the inherent contradiction in the AAP's ideological cocktail – an uneasy blend of aggressive nationalism, secularism and religious symbolism.

If the BJP's Hindutva agenda seeks to glorify traditional Hindu structures, Ambedkar's life work was about dismantling them. His scathing critique of the caste system and his insistence on equality were direct challenges to the Hindu orthodoxy. His assertion, 'People are not wrong in observing caste. In my view, what is wrong is their religion, which has inculcated this notion of caste', is a stark reminder of his uncompromising stance.[10]

Thus, any attempt to align Ambedkar with religious nationalism – whether by the AAP or the BJP – feels disingenuous. His legacy is not just a symbol to be celebrated, it is a mission to be understood and acted upon. Co-opting Ambedkar while ignoring the transformative social justice he stood for risks reducing his contributions to mere political branding.

Similarly, Bhagat Singh's radical vision extended far beyond his revolutionary acts. His atheism, commitment to socialism and critique of imperialism placed him in stark contrast to the religious and capitalist narratives dominating today's politics. Appropriating his legacy while ignoring these dimensions diminishes his stature and reduces him to a caricature of rebellion.

At the heart of Kejriwal's strategy lies a simple yet potent goal: to position the AAP as a counterbalance to the BJP's ideological dominance. His rhetoric – such as declaring that we are sons of Bhagat Singh and not Savarkar – seeks to create a moral and political distinction between his party and the BJP. Yet this approach, steeped in selective appropriation, raises questions about authenticity.[11]

By blending Ambedkar, Bhagat Singh and Hanuman into a single narrative, Kejriwal is crafting what journalist Ashutosh describes as 'an ideological cocktail'. This concoction may yield short-term electoral gains, but it risks alienating those who see through its inconsistencies. As Ashutosh aptly puts it, '[..]Who is worried about ideology when winning elections? Let's not forget that opportunism is also an ideology.'[12]

Other Aspects of the Kejriwal Model of Hindutva: Symbolism and Policy Decisions

Apart from the details offered previously, there are a few more aspects to the Kejriwal Model of Hindutva. As time progressed, the Hindu symbolism became even more aggressive, to the point where the party urged the central government to include images of Ganesha and Lakshmi on currency notes. More examples of this symbolism have been discussed below. The Hindu symbolism is evident in actions such as reciting the Hanuman Chalisa, drawing parallels between Delhi's governance and Ram Rajya, visiting Hanuman and other temples, and urging the central government to include images of Ganesha and Lakshmi on currency notes. These gestures serve as a symbolic counter-narrative to the BJP's approach.

The party's launch of the 'AAP ka Ram Rajya' website during the 2024 Lok Sabha campaign on Ram Navami.[13] The imagery on the site was striking – a silhouette of Lord Ram with bow and arrow, juxtaposed with a picture of Kejriwal holding the tricolour. The website, adorned in the AAP's signature blue and yellow, sought to link Kejriwal's governance model to the ideals of 'Ram Rajya' – a just and equitable society as envisioned in Hindu tradition. A key feature of the site was a video of Kejriwal's speech in the Delhi Assembly explaining his concept of 'AAP's Ram Rajya'. Sanjay Singh, an AAP Rajya Sabha MP, echoed the sentiment during the launch, stating, 'This is the Ram Rajya that was discussed and fulfilled by Lord Shri Ram. Mahatma Gandhi wanted to implement it to bring equality. To fulfil the dreams of Ram Rajya, Kejriwal has done tremendous work in Delhi in the last 10 years.'[14]

This wasn't an isolated instance. Days after the consecration ceremony at the Ram Temple in Ayodhya, Kejriwal invoked the ideals of Lord Ram to highlight his governance philosophy. Seamlessly merging religious symbolism with welfare policies, he said[15]:

> Inspired by 'Ram rajya', our government gives good education and health for all. Lord Ram never discriminated on the lines of caste and religion, but society has been divided on the same lines. [...] Running an administration with inspiration from 'Ram rajya' also includes providing 24/7 power supply. It also means respecting the elderly and we have been doing that by increasing their pension and arranging free pilgrimages for them.

Even more striking was the symbolism employed by Atishi upon taking over as acting CM in Kejriwal's absence in 2024. In a poignant gesture, she placed an empty chair beside her, likening it to the rule of Bharat, who governed Ayodhya in Lord Ram's absence by placing his sandals on the throne. She declared that just as Bharat ruled with Lord Ram's 'khadaun', she would run the Delhi government during Kejriwal's absence – weaving mythology into contemporary politics in a manner that resonated with many.[16]

What is clear now is that Hindu symbolism has become an integral part of the AAP's evolving political identity. Whether it is Kejriwal's invocation of Lord Ram to underscore the values of equity and welfare or Atishi's dramatic evocation of Bharat's devotion, the party has embraced these narratives with finesse. In doing so, it positions itself as a party that respects tradition while delivering modern governance – a strategy that may well redefine the contours of its politics in the years to come.

Now let us look at the policy aspect of the Kejriwal Model of Hindutva. Here I will discuss two policies of the Delhi government: one about patriotism and another about pilgrimage.

The Tirth Yatra Scheme: Soft Hindutva and Cultural Outreach

A populist measure that reflected the AAP's evolving strategy was the Tirth Yatra Scheme (Mukhyamantri Tirth Yatra Yojana) introduced by Kejriwal in 2019. Under this scheme, the Delhi government offered to bear the cost of pilgrimage for senior citizens to various religious sites across India. This initiative was framed as an effort to honour the cultural and religious traditions of Delhi's residents, providing them with an opportunity to undertake spiritual journeys that they might not otherwise be able to afford. The scheme covers all expenses related to travel, food and accommodation, making it accessible to economically weaker sections.[17] The packages in the scheme include round-trips such as (not exhaustive)[18]:

- Delhi–Mathura–Vrindavan–Agra–Fatehpur Sikri–Delhi
- Delhi–Haridwar–Rishikesh–Neelkanth–Delhi
- Delhi–Ajmer–Pushkar–Delhi
- Delhi–Amritsar–Wagah border–Anandpur Sahib–Delhi
- Delhi–Vaishno Devi–Jammu–Delhi
- Delhi–Ayodhya–Delhi

The inclusion of predominantly Hindu pilgrimage sites in the scheme led to speculation about the AAP's intentions. The Mukhyamantri Tirth Yatra Yojana is a prime example of how the AAP navigated the complex terrain of Indian politics. By promoting religious tourism, the party appealed to Hindu voters without overtly aligning with the more aggressive Hindutva agenda. This strategy allowed the AAP to maintain its focus on governance and welfare while subtly engaging with religious sentiments. Whether this approach will pay off in the long run remains to be seen, but it certainly adds an interesting dimension to the party's political strategy.

The Desh Bhakti Curriculum

One of the most notable outcomes of the AAP's shift towards nationalism was the introduction of the Desh Bhakti Curriculum in Delhi's schools.[19]

The Desh Bhakti Curriculum, introduced in 2020, was designed to instil a sense of patriotism and national pride among students. It emphasized the values of sacrifice, courage and love for the country, aligning with the broader nationalist narrative that had become increasingly prominent in Indian politics. This move was seen as an attempt by the AAP to co-opt the nationalism narrative, ensuring that the BJP did not have a monopoly on this powerful political theme.

Shailendra Sharma, former principal advisor to the Directorate of Education of the Delhi government, has denied claims that this curriculum was influenced by the BJP. He explained, 'The Deshbhakti curriculum focuses on how individuals see themselves as citizens and the role they can play at different stages of their lives to contribute to the nation's development. The primary aim is to teach students about participating in nation-building. It is not affiliated with any particular ideology and aligns with the values of the Constitution.'

However, this shift did not go unnoticed. Many observers noted that the AAP's embrace of nationalism was a significant departure from its earlier secular and reform-oriented stance. Critics argued that the introduction of the Desh Bhakti Curriculum was a calculated move to curry favour with the electorate that had been swayed by the BJP's brand of politics. They also pointed out that this shift towards nationalism and Hindutva risked alienating the AAP's traditional voter base, particularly minorities and secular-minded citizens.

14

Muslim Vote Matters But...

In the previous chapters on the AAP's Hindutva overtures, I have touched upon its nuanced relationship with Delhi's Muslim voters, but not in detail. It is time to delve deeper into it. Understanding this dynamic requires some context. Delhi's Muslim population, pegged at 12 per cent in the 2011 census, is now estimated to have grown to 15–18 per cent. This demographic is pivotal, influencing electoral outcomes significantly.

Traditionally, the AAP has enjoyed robust Muslim support, bolstered by its focus on governance and welfare. However, the Congress also commands a share of this vote bank during Lok Sabha elections, creating a competitive tussle for loyalty. The tide, however, has been shifting. Since 2020, Kejriwal's calculated silence on issues central to Muslims – be it the anti-CAA protests or communal clashes – has sparked disillusionment. This disenchantment was evident in the 2022 MCD elections, where a section of Muslim voters pivoted back to the Congress, signalling a crack in the AAP's base.

The 2024 Lok Sabha elections, where the AAP and the Congress joined forces, blurred voting patterns, making it hard to gauge where the Muslim vote landed. In the 2025 elections, the Aam Aadmi Party (AAP) garnered around 51 per cent of the vote in constituencies where Muslims make up more than 25 per cent of the population. While this indicates continued strong support, it also reflects a notable drop of 10.8 percentage points from its performance in 2020. The data highlights a consistent pattern—the AAP's vote share tends to rise in direct correlation with the percentage of Muslim residents in a constituency. In Delhi's political history, the Congress had long held sway over the city's Muslim community. This trend persisted until the 2013 Assembly elections, where a nascent AAP disrupted the status quo slightly but failed to secure a majority, largely due to the still enduring Muslim support left for Congress. Of the eight seats Congress won that year, four came from Muslim-dominated constituencies, underscoring the community's pivotal role in the city's political calculus.[1]

The 2015 Delhi Assembly elections marked a turning point. For the first time, the Muslim vote shifted decisively to the AAP. Around 77 per cent of Muslim voters backed the AAP, enabling them to win 9 out of 10 constituencies with over 30 per cent Muslim population by staggering margins. For instance, Amanatullah Khan of the AAP clinched the Okhla seat with a victory margin of nearly 65,000 votes.[2]

This overwhelming support stemmed from the AAP's secular positioning and grassroots focus, which resonated deeply with the community. However, by 2020, the political narrative began to evolve. Despite the AAP's subtle shift towards Hindutva posturing following its 2019 Lok Sabha election defeat, 69 per cent of Muslims still backed the party in the 2020 Assembly polls, while Congress managed only 15 per cent.[3]

The reason for this enduring support lies in the unique circumstances of that election. Having observed the 2020 campaign closely as a research fellow at the Delhi Assembly Research Centre, I found that the BJP's aggressive Hindutva rhetoric had profoundly unsettled the Muslim community. In this climate, the AAP was seen not as a perfect ally but as the most viable opponent to the BJP's rise in Delhi.

Sabir Ahmed, a shopkeeper in Shaheen Bagh, shared his perspective during the anti-CAA protests: 'I understand that AAP is not openly supporting us, but their MLA, Amanatullah Khan, has stood with us, providing logistical help. This election is about defeating the BJP, and AAP is our best bet. Congress is a finished party – they can't even manage their own house.'

Ahmed's sentiment reflects a pragmatic choice rather than unwavering loyalty. While the AAP's Hindutva tilt did not go unnoticed, the Muslim community viewed it as a necessary evil in a polarized environment. However, the equation is far from static.

The AAP's approach to issues concerning Muslims can be categorized into three distinct strategies: maintaining silence, staying vague while diverting focus and engaging in victim-shaming.

Remaining Silent

Among the many contradictions in Indian politics, Arvind Kejriwal's strategy of silence on Muslim issues stands out starkly. Unlike most opposition leaders and parties with a long-standing secular stance, Kejriwal's AAP has adopted an ambiguous position that raises eyebrows. While other opposition parties openly defend minority rights, driven by historical commitments and the significance of minority votes, the AAP's approach is markedly different, rooted in electoral caution and political ambition.

The underlying reason for the AAP's silence lies in its fear of alienating Hindu voters. The AAP strategists believe that an overtly pro-Muslim stance could push away the floating Hindu vote bank, which might then gravitate towards the BJP. This concern is particularly acute in Delhi, where the AAP's dominance hinges on its ability to appeal across communities. The party calculates that any significant shift among Hindu voters could lead to electoral setbacks, especially in Assembly elections.

Kejriwal's ambition also plays a crucial role in shaping this approach. Like PM Narendra Modi, Kejriwal has his eyes on the future and a broader national stage. In a candid conversation, a senior AAP leader revealed: 'The BJP's aggressive Hindutva has a shelf life. Over time, voters will tire of this rhetoric and seek a moderate Hindutva alternative – one that champions Hindus but also emphasizes development. Congress, Samajwadi Party or Trinamool Congress can never occupy that space. But we can.'

This perspective shed light on the AAP's broader strategy. Kejriwal seeks to position himself as a development-oriented leader who appeals to Hindus without openly embracing Hindutva, thereby creating a unique political identity. His model closely mirrors Modi's trajectory during his tenure as Gujarat CM. Modi also built his reputation on a mix of Hindutva symbolism and a strong development narrative. On the national stage, Modi's initial slogan, '*Sabka Saath, Sabka Vikas* (Together with All, Development for All)', helped him craft an image that extended beyond sectarian politics. It was not until the 2024 general election campaign that Modi's rhetoric took a distinctly anti-Muslim turn.

Kejriwal, in a way, follows a similar playbook. His governance model emphasizes welfare policies and development schemes designed to appeal across religious lines, but his silence on Muslim rights and issues of communal justice has been deafening. This selective approach underscores a calculated bid to appear as a centrist leader who avoids the polarizing extremes of overt secularism or aggressive Hindutva.

However, Kejriwal's silence has not gone unnoticed. Senior journalist Nistula Hebbar, political editor of *The Hindu*, reflects: 'From the time of the India Against Corruption movement, it was clear that Kejriwal had proximity to the Sangh's ideology. In my view, his political stand has remained consistent – firmly Right of Centre, but in his unique way.'

This ideological undercurrent explains the AAP's reluctance to take a firm stand on contentious Muslim issues, even during crises like the anti-CAA protests or the Delhi riots. While other opposition parties rallied around minority voices, the AAP chose strategic silence, prioritizing broader electoral calculations over minority rights.

2020 Delhi Riots

In the 2025 Delhi Assembly elections, the AAP experienced a notable decline in support among Muslim voters in constituencies where Muslims constitute over 25 per cent of the population.

Despite retaining dominance in six of seven such seats, the AAP's vote share dropped significantly, from 53.57 per cent in 2020 to 43.55 per cent in 2025.[4] This erosion was particularly evident in Mustafabad, where the AAP's vote share plummeted from 53 per cent to 33 per cent, enabling the BJP to secure the seat with a 17,578-vote margin. The shift was not primarily to the BJP, which maintained a steady 42 per cent vote share, but to the All India Majlis-e-Ittehadul Muslimeen (AIMIM) and, to a lesser extent, Congress.[5] The All India Majlis-e-Ittehadul Muslimeen's candidate, Tahir Hussain, a former AAP councillor accused in the 2020 Delhi riots, garnered 33,474 votes (16.6 per cent) in Mustafabad, finishing third. His performance, despite legal controversies, underscores a growing appeal of the AIMIM's narrative of Muslim representation, resonating with voters frustrated by the AAP's perceived silence on atrocities against Muslims and its occasional adoption of Hindutva rhetoric to counter the BJP's narrative.[6]

In Okhla, another Muslim-majority seat, the AIMIM's candidate secured 27.1 per cent of the vote, further splitting the AAP's traditional Muslim vote base. This division of votes highlights a strategic challenge for the AAP, as smaller parties like the AIMIM capitalized on community discontent, while the Congress saw marginal gains. The significance of Hussain's vote share lies in its indication of a potential realignment of Muslim voters towards parties explicitly addressing their concerns, particularly in riot-affected areas like Mustafabad. The North East Delhi riots in February 2020, which left over 50 people dead, primarily Muslims, serve as a dark reminder of the community's grievances with Kejriwal and his party. The AAP's silence and inability to address the violence – blamed on its lack of control over Delhi Police – fuelled further resentment. In the 2022 MCD elections, this frustration translated into electoral defeats for the AAP in key Muslim-majority wards. While the AAP retained its hold over constituencies in Old Delhi, where anti-CAA protests did not occur, Muslim-majority areas that had witnessed unrest, such as Seelampur and Shaheen Bagh, shifted their allegiance to the Congress.

In Mustafabad, Brijpuri and other riot-hit areas (which had long been AAP strongholds), Congress gained a foothold, winning seven of the nine seats it captured in Muslim-dominated wards. Despite having sitting AAP MLAs such as Amanatullah Khan (Okhla), Haji Yunus (Mustafabad) and Abdul Rehman (Seelampur), the party failed to secure municipal wins even in these constituencies.

The AAP's Calculated Gamble on the Bilkis Bano Case

When the Gujarat government in 2022 controversially released 11 convicts serving life sentences for the gang rape of Bilkis Bano and the murder of her family during the 2002 post-Godhra riots, condemnation poured in from across the political spectrum. Opposition parties – usually fragmented in their strategies – came together to denounce the decision. The Congress, TMC, BSP and Left parties unequivocally criticized the BJP-led Gujarat government and PM Narendra Modi for what they called an affront to justice and morality.

Yet, amidst this unified opposition outcry, one party conspicuously chose silence: the AAP. At the time, Gujarat was in the throes of its Assembly elections, and the AAP, a new entrant in the state's political arena, opted to steer clear of the controversy. When the Deputy CM Manish Sisodia was asked to comment on the remission, his response was telling: 'हम लोग शिक्षा पर चल रहे हैं, स्कूल-अस्पताल पर चल रहे हैं, नौकरियों पर चल रहे हैं... हमको इससे मतलब है. जिसको जिससे मतलब है वो उस पर बात कर रहा है [We are on the track of education, schools, hospitals and jobs. These things matter to us. People speak about what matters to them].'[7]

The response – or lack thereof – shows that the party was seeking to establish itself as a serious contender in Gujarat by prioritizing its developmental narrative while avoiding issues that could be perceived as polarizing. Months later, after the Supreme Court revoked the remission order, the AAP's Gujarat leader Gopal Italia briefly remarked that 'those convicted by the courts of law in cases of rape should not be granted pardon under any constitutional law'.[8] But this statement, made after the elections, lacked the forcefulness expected of an opposition party.

This calculated reticence invites scrutiny. Political observers, such as Sanjay Kumar of the CSDS, argue that the AAP's silence reflects its electoral pragmatism. 'For the AAP, there is an immense amount of risk in this. Taking an aggressive stand on the matter could create a perception that the party is indulging in Muslim appeasement, potentially alienating Hindu voters,' Kumar noted in a media interview.[9]

This strategy speaks to a larger challenge facing the AAP as it seeks to expand beyond its Delhi stronghold. The party has positioned itself as a development-centric alternative, steering clear of the entrenched communal narratives that dominate Indian politics. However, this approach also means avoiding contentious issues, even those with clear moral imperatives, to prevent backlash from the Hindu electorate.

Silence on Anti-Muslim Hatemongering

In August 2021, the heart of the nation's capital, Jantar Mantar, turned into a chilling stage for genocidal slogans against Muslims. A mob of Hindutva supporters gathered, brazenly chanting calls for violence and hatred. Among the slogans were incendiary lines, such as:

> '*Jab mulle kaate jayenge, wo Ram Ram chillayenge* (When Muslims will be slain, they will chant Lord Ram's name).'
>
> '*Suaron ki karo vidai, Hindu Hindu bhai bhai* (Farewell to the pigs/Muslims, Hindus are brothers).'
>
> 'Hindustan mein rehna hoga, to Jai Shri Ram kehna hoga (If you want to live in India, you must say Hail Lord Ram).'[10]

This horrifying spectacle came barely a year after the communal violence in North East Delhi, where mobs unleashed devastation that left 53 people dead – three-fourths of them Muslims – alongside the destruction of mosques, shrines, businesses and property worth hundreds of crores, primarily owned by Muslims. The hostility did not end there. In Dwarka, hundreds protested the construction of a Haj house, while in Uttam Nagar, Right-wing mobs targeted Muslim fruit vendors, labelling them as Rohingya infiltrators. Dozens were attacked, boycotted and forcibly evicted. Among the victims was Rizwan, a street vendor beaten so severely by a mob chanting 'Jai Shri Ram' that his injuries required immediate medical attention.[11]

Amidst these rising tensions, one political leader remained conspicuously silent – then Delhi CM Kejriwal. The AAP leadership, often vocal on governance and development issues, chose to sidestep these communal flashpoints. Their reasoning? Law and order in Delhi fell under the purview of the central government and Delhi Police, not the state government.

But this justification rings hollow in the face of moral responsibility. For a party that came to power promising a new brand of politics, the AAP's silence during these dark moments raises uncomfortable questions. Can the commitment to secularism and justice be sacrificed at the altar of electoral calculations?

The silence becomes even more significant when juxtaposed with the AAP's carefully crafted image of inclusivity. In Delhi's electoral landscape, where Muslims constitute a significant voting bloc as mentioned before, this calculated neutrality could be seen as an effort to avoid alienating Hindu voters while hoping to retain minority support through governance initiatives. But silence in the face of hate speech and communal violence isn't neutrality – it is complicity by omission.

In Delhi, Kejriwal appears to operate on the assumption that Muslims, faced with a weakened Congress, have little choice but to vote for the AAP. This belief is not without merit; electoral data from the 2015 and 2020 Assembly elections suggest a significant shift of Muslim votes from the Congress to the AAP. However, the assumption that loyalty is guaranteed risks reducing the community's concerns to mere electoral calculations.

Unlike the BJP, Kejriwal has shown no hesitation in fielding Muslim candidates from constituencies with significant Muslim populations, signalling a willingness to offer some political representation. For instance, leaders like Amanatullah Khan have consistently been given platforms to contest elections and represent Muslim-majority constituency like Okhla. Yet, this calculated inclusion stops short of genuine advocacy.

This balancing act, however, raises questions about the AAP's ideological core. By failing to champion the constitutional rights of Muslims while still seeking their votes, Kejriwal risks positioning his party as one that is secular in rhetoric but evasive in action. His strategy may be rooted in pragmatism, but it chips away at the moral foundation the AAP claims to uphold. The political space Kejriwal offers Muslims, while notable compared to the BJP's overt marginalization, is transactional at best. It stops short of addressing systemic issues or protecting the community from targeted violence and discrimination. This hollow representation underscores the opportunism embedded in the AAP's political calculus.

The silence of Kejriwal and the AAP on issues concerning Muslims cannot be dismissed as neutrality. It is a deliberate strategy to secure votes without rocking the boat of communal harmony – a strategy that prioritizes electoral gains over justice. For a party that emerged as a symbol of clean politics and progressive governance, this approach risks alienating not just Muslims but also those who once believed in the AAP as a force for real change. Kejriwal's strategy may yield short-term electoral dividends, but it risks undermining the long-term credibility of the AAP as a party capable of standing up for all sections of society. Silence, after all, can be as telling as words – and in this case, it speaks volumes about the compromises the AAP is willing to make in the pursuit of power.

Remaining Vague: Issue of the Shaheen Bagh Protest

Kejriwal's approach to issues concerning Muslims often involves vagueness and calculated diversions. By doing so, Kejriwal crafts a narrative that projects governance and development as his priorities, subtly implying that contentious issues like those affecting Muslims are distractions unworthy of his attention.

The AAP's ambiguous stance on the CAA and the Shaheen Bagh protests serves as a case study of this strategy. When the protests captured national attention in early 2020, Kejriwal tread a fine line. At a *News18* event in February, he criticized the BJP for not clearing the road where the protests were held, simultaneously affirming citizens' right to protest while suggesting he would have opened the blocked road within two hours if Delhi Police were under his government.

This duality is classic Kejriwal. He avoided addressing the core issue – whether the protest against the CAA was justified – instead redirecting attention to administrative control over the Delhi Police. This deliberate evasion allowed him to avoid alienating Hindu voters while keeping the Muslim electorate from feeling entirely abandoned.

During the 2020 Delhi Assembly elections campaign, Kejriwal shifted the narrative further by framing the CAA as a law that could harm Hindus. 'We don't need this law; it is unnecessary,' he remarked, adding, 'Where will we accommodate two crore Hindus from Pakistan?' 'This is not a Hindu-Muslim issue,' he asserted in another interview. 'Through this Bill, both Hindus and Muslims will be evicted. Hindus must arrange identity proofs for themselves and their parents.'[12]

Behind the scenes, however, the story was different. The AAP insiders suggest that Kejriwal instructed local MLA Amanatullah Khan to maintain close ties with Shaheen Bagh protest organizers. This tactical engagement allowed the AAP to retain its foothold in Muslim-majority areas like Okhla (which includes Shaheen Bagh). During the 2020 elections, the AAP won the Okhla seat with a significant majority, underscoring the effectiveness of this two-faced strategy. However, this strategy comes at a cost. It exposes Kejriwal's unwillingness to take a firm stand on fundamental rights, leaving questions about his commitment to secular values.

For the Muslim community, his calculated silence and shifting narratives may secure short-term electoral gains but it also erodes trust in his willingness to defend their rights in the long term.

As Kejriwal balances his ambitions of national expansion with the demands of Delhi's complex electorate, his ambiguous stance on issues like the CAA and Shaheen Bagh protests reflects the tightrope he continues to walk – a strategy that is pragmatic but ultimately risks undermining the AAP's credibility as a party of principled governance.

The AAP's Dangerous Playbook: Demonizing Muslims for Electoral Gains

As the 2025 Delhi Assembly election campaign unfolded, a disturbing pattern emerged in the AAP's rhetoric – a strategy that subtly shifted blame onto the Muslim community through victim-shaming and demonization. This approach not only mirrored the divisive tactics employed by the BJP but also raised troubling questions about the party's political ethics.

Take, for instance, Kejriwal's accusations during the campaign. He blamed the BJP for settling Rohingyas in Delhi, portraying it as part of a larger political conspiracy. On the surface, this might seem like an attempt to corner the BJP. However, such statements have a more insidious consequence – they stigmatize a community and fan the flames of communal animosity.

This was not an isolated incident. The Jahangirpuri riots in April 2022 were a stark reminder of the communal tensions simmering in Delhi under the Kejriwal government. The violence erupted during a Hanuman Jayanti procession organized by the Bajrang Dal, a Right-wing Hindu nationalist group. The procession, which included participants brandishing swords and pistols, halted near a mosque where Muslims were holding Ramadan prayers. The loud music and provocative slogans led to a clash between the two communities, resulting in stone-pelting and arson.[13]

The AAP's response to the violence was marked by a troubling silence, followed by victim-blaming and demonization of the Muslim community. Initially, the AAP's leadership, including

Kejriwal, maintained a conspicuous silence as the violence unfolded. This silence was seen as a strategic move to avoid alienating Hindu voters, especially with the then upcoming MCD elections. However, this inaction left the Muslim community feeling abandoned and vulnerable.

As the situation escalated, the AAP shifted its stance to victim-blaming. Party leaders, including Atishi, accused the BJP of orchestrating the violence and claimed that the main accused, Ansar, had links to the BJP. This narrative diverted attention from the real issues and painted Muslims as the instigators of the violence. The party's reluctance to acknowledge the grievances of the Muslim community further alienated them.

Adding to the controversy, the BJP-led North Delhi Municipal Corporation launched a bulldozer drive to demolish 'illegal encroachments' in Jahangirpuri, targeting structures associated with Muslims. Despite a Supreme Court order to halt the demolitions, the bulldozers continued their work, razing homes and shops.[14] The AAP's response to this action was not to condemn the bulldozer drive but to blame the BJP for taking bribes and settling illegal immigrants including Bangladeshis and Rohingyas in the area. The then AAP MLA Atishi claimed, 'The BJP leaders have settled Bangladeshis and Rohingyas across the country to cause riots everywhere.'[15] While the statement sought to attack the BJP, it ended up demonizing an entire section of the population. Jahangirpuri, like many areas in Delhi, has had Muslim settlements for decades. Yet, the blanket tagging of all Muslims in these areas as 'Bangladeshis' or 'Rohingyas' reeks of the same divisive narrative often deployed by the BJP.

This BJP followed a similar tactic during the 2024 Jharkhand Assembly elections, where opposition parties were branded as pro-illegal migrants or *ghuspetiya*s. The similarities between the two parties' playbooks are striking, revealing the AAP's growing alignment with the BJP's polarizing strategies.

The AAP's handling of the Jahangirpuri riots highlights a troubling trend of political expediency over principled leadership. By remaining silent, engaging in victim-blaming and demonizing Muslims, the AAP failed to uphold its commitment to secularism and inclusivity. This approach not only undermined the party's credibility but also deepened the communal fault lines in Delhi. As the AAP continues to navigate the complex terrain of Indian politics, it must prioritize justice and inclusivity over short-term political gains.

In another example, the AAP's handling of the Tablighi Jamaat issue during the COVID-19 pandemic is another glaring example of the party's victim-shaming attitude towards Muslims and its role in demonizing the community. The Tablighi Jamaat congregation at the Nizamuddin Markaz in Delhi, held in March 2020, was quickly labelled a 'super-spreader' event, and the attendees were vilified by the media and political leaders alike. The AAP's response to the incident was marked by a troubling silence and a lack of support for the Muslim community. Instead of defending the Jamaat members or calling for a balanced and fair investigation, the AAP leaders, including Kejriwal, chose to remain silent, allowing the narrative of blame to take root.[16]

Adding to the controversy, the AAP leaders blamed the Tablighi Jamaat for spreading the virus and demanded strict action against them. The Delhi government asked the police to file FIRs against the Jamaat members for violating lockdown norms and endangering public health. This move further stigmatized the Muslim community and reinforced the narrative of blame.

The demonization of the Tablighi Jamaat members was further exacerbated by the spread of misinformation and conspiracy theories. Media outlets and political leaders accused the Jamaat of deliberately spreading the virus, dubbing it 'corona jihad'. This narrative was not only baseless but also dangerous, as it fuelled communal tensions and led to a spike in hate crimes against Muslims.[17]

The AAP's failure to counter this narrative and its active role in blaming the Tablighi Jamaat members highlighted a pattern of victim-shaming. By not condemning the vilification of the Jamaat members and instead demanding legal action against them, the AAP tacitly endorsed the demonization of Muslims, further marginalizing an already vulnerable community.

During a visit to North East Delhi on September 2024 where the riots of 2020 left a lasting scar, conversations with residents revealed simmering dissatisfaction with the AAP. Zaffar Sheikh, a grocery shop owner from Seelampur, voiced his disappointment: 'AAP worked for education and healthcare, but those efforts seem to have stalled. What troubles us more is how Arvind Kejriwal increasingly mirrors BJP leaders in shaming Muslims.'

Similarly, Abdul Hassan Karim, an auto driver from Karawal Nagar, shared his loss of faith in the AAP: 'We believed in Arvind Kejriwal, but today he seems like the RSS's B-team. Congress is the only party standing against the BJP's divisive politics and can protect us.'

If the AAP continues down this path, it risks losing its identity as a party that once championed inclusivity and good governance. Kejriwal's calculated silence on communal issues, coupled with a narrative that blames and demonizes Muslims, paints a troubling picture of a leader prioritizing political expediency over principles.

The real cost of this will be felt in the long run. While Kejriwal may win over sections of the electorate by pandering to anti-Muslim sentiments, such politics will ultimately alienate the very communities the AAP once relied upon for its rise. By adopting a playbook that echoes the BJP's, the AAP risks undermining its claim of being a progressive alternative, exposing the contradictions at the heart of its politics. Whatever the AAP could become tomorrow is not known but it cannot be a political national alternative with such hypocritic politics. Senior journalist Aakash Joshi writes:

> Most importantly, a national party needs a national vision that also articulates who it wants us to be as a people and what it stands for beyond service delivery. Even if the AAP ever manages to achieve its utopia – a "No. 1 India" where the state provides quality healthcare, education, employment and ensures farmers' welfare and gender equality – it will be tarnished by an outlook that looks at refugees as rioters, and demolitions as sacred.[18]

The 2025 Delhi Assembly elections are critical for the AAP's political trajectory. If the dissatisfaction of the Muslim community persists, it could signal a deeper erosion of trust, one that even Kejriwal's much-touted welfare schemes may not be able to repair. While the Congress' resurgence in Muslim-majority areas has been slow but steady, the AAP must recalibrate its strategy to avoid further alienating this crucial voter base.

For the AAP, the stakes are high, and the road ahead demands a careful balancing act between retaining its appeal among Delhi's diverse electorate while addressing the legitimate grievances of its Muslim supporters. Will Kejriwal rise to the challenge or lose the community's trust for good? Only the upcoming elections will reveal the answer.

Part 4

One-Man Show

15

Arvind Kejriwal-Centric AAP

During my journalism days covering the Delhi government, my mentor was the inimitable Roushan Ali, a senior journalist whose wit and wisdom was legendary. COVID-19's second wave cruelly took away the always-smiling Roushan ji, whose one-liners were, as we fondly called them, 'killer'. Once, Roushan ji remarked about the AAP, saying, 'There is only one post [read Kejriwal] and others are lamp-posts.' This succinctly captured the essence of the AAP – a political entity orbiting around the gravitational pull of Kejriwal.

The AAP's initial promise was to be a party of the people, for the people and by the people, echoing the principles of direct democracy, transparency and accountability. As we now know, in its nascent days, the party adhered to these ideals, striving to uphold the notion that governance should be a shared responsibility.

However, over the years, the AAP's vision of decentralization has morphed dramatically. At the heart of this transformation is Kejriwal, whose leadership style has increasingly centralized the party's power around him. Today, the once-prominent idea of decentralization seems more like an illusion, as Kejriwal's influence over the party has overshadowed its founding principles. The AAP's metamorphosis from a collective force to a personality-driven party has become glaringly apparent, with Kejriwal emerging as the sole power centre.

'Everything in AAP happens under the instruction of Arvind Kejriwal, and no other leader really matters,' says Ashutosh. His words paint a stark picture of a party where internal democracy has eroded, and the space for dissent or discussion has dwindled. He added, 'There is no internal democracy whatsoever within the party because every person there tries their best to obey Kejriwal and his instructions. Any person who wants to question the decisions of Kejriwal is being sidelined.'

According to sources and in my personal experience what I have witnessed, every morning, a small group of top AAP leaders, advisors and government officials gather in a closed-door meeting where Kejriwal sets the agenda for the day. These meetings are not open; the number of attendees is limited to fewer than 10 people. In these daily briefings, Kejriwal outlines the key messaging and strategy the party should follow, after which a series of press conferences and public statements are held by the AAP leaders, all echoing the same carefully crafted narrative. The repetition of the same talking points across multiple platforms helps reinforce Kejriwal's message, making it the dominant narrative of the day. The underlying belief, as I came to understand, is that setting the public discourse requires relentless focus on a singular message – repeated consistently – until it becomes ingrained in public consciousness.

During the 2020 Delhi Assembly election campaign, I was part of a team tasked with preparing a detailed report card on the MCD, which was under the control of the BJP. The report was full of data, graphs and a meticulous analysis of the MCD's functioning, highlighting its various failures. The idea was to provide a robust, fact-based counter to the Opposition's narrative during the election campaign. After weeks of hard work, the report was finalized and approved by then Deputy CM Manish Sisodia. Just a few days back, with the help of I-PAC, Kejriwal had presented the report card of the Delhi government, so this was nothing but a contrast between the Delhi government's model and MCD's model.

When the MCD report was presented to Kejriwal, he swiftly dismissed the idea of focusing on detailed data and its analysis. Instead, he chose to attack the BJP's governance of the MCD with one sharp, sweeping statement and two data points (from an over 200-page report). Then he instructed Sisodia to address the press focused on rhetoric and not data. The entire report, despite the effort and expertise that had gone into its preparation, was sidelined. Not a single person in the room dared to question this decision. It was clear that Kejriwal's political instincts would drive the campaign's messaging. This experience highlighted the reality of how the AAP operates: Kejriwal's word is final and all other opinions, no matter how well-reasoned or researched, are secondary.

Arvind Kejriwal, during the press conference where he released the report card, said, 'People of Delhi will have to choose between two models of governance during the polls on February 8.' Then he added two data points:

> He then highlighted the contrasting performance of the Municipal Corporation of Delhi (MCD) and the Delhi government in education and healthcare. He noted that over the past nine years, the MCD closed 109 schools, with student enrollment dropping from nearly 9.85 lakh in 2011–12 to 7.32 lakh by 2018–19. In contrast, the Delhi government added 20,000 new classrooms in five years, equipping its schools with advanced facilities like swimming pools, elevators, sports fields, and complexes, surpassing many private schools in infrastructure quality. In healthcare, Kejriwal pointed out that the MCD failed to establish any new dispensaries and added only one hospital in seven years, with existing facilities often poorly maintained. Meanwhile, the Delhi government introduced 450 mohalla clinics and 26 polyclinics in five years, increased hospital beds from 7,200 to around 10,000, and is close to completing three new government hospitals.[1]

After Kejriwal, Sisodia presided over the press conference. He said, 'I want to challenge the BJP to show me one positive programme they have designed for the development of education which has received a positive response from every section of the society or other states and countries. When we launch our programmes, people from across the world take notice and praise our model of education.'[2]

Frustrated by the decision, I approached one of Kejriwal's senior advisors to understand why no one had raised concerns about discarding the report. With a knowing smile, he said, '*Raajniti mein har samay intelligent neta banna zaroori nahi hota hai, kabhi kabhi yes man banna zyada zaroori hota hai* (In politics, it is not always necessary to be an intelligent leader; sometimes it is more important to be a yes man).' This response meant that loyalty to Kejriwal outweighed independent thought and challenging his authority was seen as unnecessary, even counterproductive.

Another major consequence of the AAP's centralization is the lack of leadership growth within the party. Ashutosh gave the example of Sisodia, who despite being a capable and respected leader, has remained in the same position – both literally and figuratively – since the party's inception. Sisodia has always been Kejriwal's second-in-command. His loyalty is unwavering, but his role has not evolved. Ashutosh said, 'There is no growth because it is all about Arvind and nobody else. So people with lesser ambition remain in AAP today.'

The only leader who has managed to carve out a somewhat independent identity within the AAP is Rajya Sabha MP Sanjay Singh, according to Ashutosh. His pragmatic approach, dynamic public speaking skills and willingness to engage in national politics have allowed him to rise within the party ranks. Yet, even his stature pales in comparison to that of Kejriwal, whose authority remains unchallenged.

The story of the AAP's journey from decentralization to centralization illustrates the nature of political power.

Here, as the AAP is now a one-person-centric political party, the pertinent question is what's wrong with a political party revolving around one individual, given that the history of Indian politics is replete with such examples? The BJP orbits Narendra

Modi, the Congress is almost inseparable from the Gandhis and most regional parties are anchored to a prominent figure. Yet, as former AAP leader Ashutosh pointed out, the problem with AAP is not merely that it is led by one man. It is that the party lacks a durable institutional structure beyond Kejriwal. There exists no independent organization, no institutional memory – only Kejriwal.

In other political setups, while the dominance of one leader is evident, there remains a cadre of influential personalities who carve their own niches. The BJP, for example, boasts of figures like Nitin Gadkari, Rajnath Singh and Shivraj Singh Chouhan, each commanding individual respect and influence. The Congress, despite the shadow of the Gandhis, has leaders like Mallikarjun Kharge, Ashok Gehlot and Bhupesh Baghel who enjoy their own spheres of power. These leaders contribute to their party's diversity and strength, offering alternative perspectives and a robust institutional backbone. The AAP, however, is so Kejriwal-centric that no other leader has been allowed to evolve similarly.

Aurangzeb Naqshbandi summed up this dynamic sharply: 'There is no leadership in AAP beyond Kejriwal. Standing today in 2024 the Chief Minister of Delhi, Atishi, runs her office while keeping an empty chair for Kejriwal. It's humiliating for her, as it underscores her dependency on him.' This dependency extends across the party's operations, manifesting in troubling ways. During an interaction with an AAP MLA who had walked out of a meeting at the party headquarters, his frustration was evident. 'Arvind ji never listens to anyone,' he confided, emphasizing how those working at the grassroots often find their voices stifled. This MLA, who didn't secure a ticket for the 2020 elections, encapsulated the growing discontent within the ranks.

The erosion of internal democracy within the AAP is one of its starkest realities. Former MLA Alka Lamba, who eventually left the AAP to join the Congress, publicly criticized Kejriwal for sidelining the party's elected representatives.[3] Ashutosh echoed this sentiment, stating, 'The problem is that the leadership in AAP is so focused on one person that no one else is allowed to rise. Whoever is needed at a particular time is given prominence, but they are soon sidelined when Kejriwal no longer needs them.' This strategy of elevating individuals temporarily and then relegating them to the background has created a vacuum in leadership.

The centralization of control extends to the operational dynamics of the party across states. In Punjab, where the AAP governs, Bhagwant Mann is the sole prominent figure. Beyond him, no leader has been allowed to take the stage. During the Goa elections, Kejriwal entrusted Atishi and with the campaign's management, while in Punjab and Gujarat, figures like Raghav Chadha, Jarnail Singh and Sandeep Pathak took the reins, respectively.[4] Yet, even here, the strings were pulled from Delhi. A senior leader from Gujarat shared insights into this process, revealing how decisions on candidates and campaign strategies were often made without any meaningful consultation, highlighting the top-down approach that defines the AAP.

This trend isn't new. I recall covering the 2019 Lok Sabha elections when the AAP engaged in seat-sharing negotiations with the Congress in Delhi. Sanjay Singh was spearheading the discussions, with Sharad Pawar mediating between the parties. While a tentative arrangement had been reached, Kejriwal's sudden public denial of these talks at a rally shocked everyone.[5] Insiders later revealed that the move stemmed from Kejriwal's discomfort with others, like Singh or Pawar, gaining visibility for brokering the deal. Such instances underscore his unease with sharing the limelight, an approach that restricts the party's ability to cultivate diverse leadership.

Perhaps, the most glaring example of Kejriwal's unyielding control came in the aftermath of allegations by Rajya Sabha MP Swati Maliwal against Kejriwal's then private secretary Bibhav Kumar. Sanjay Singh initially held a press conference condemning the incident, but the party's stance was reversed within a day.[6] Sources indicated that Kejriwal was displeased with the initial condemnation and directed the party to adopt a hardline position against Maliwal. This incident reflects how Kejriwal's influence pervades even the minutest of decisions, reinforcing the narrative of the AAP being a one-man show.

As we delve into how the AAP has increasingly become a Kejriwal-centric political entity, it's crucial to highlight a pivotal moment: Kejriwal's arrest by the Enforcement Directorate (ED) for his alleged involvement in the Delhi liquor policy scam. This event dramatically shifted the party's narrative, centring it even more around Kejriwal.

In a later chapter, I will explore in detail the AAP's campaign strategy post-Kejriwal's arrest and the 2025 Delhi Assembly election campaign as well. However, it's important to note that when the Supreme Court granted Kejriwal interim bail to campaign for the 2024 general elections, his efforts were relentless in Delhi and Punjab. Yet, the campaign was less about the Delhi government or AAP's achievements and more about Kejriwal's arrest. This shift in focus was evident as the AAP lost all seven seats in Delhi to the BJP in the 2024 general elections.

As the 2025 election campaign began, following the Supreme Court's bail decision, Kejriwal's first move was to resign as CM and appoint Atishi in his place. This strategic resignation set the tone for the entire 2025 Delhi Assembly election narrative, which then revolved around the goal of reinstating Kejriwal as CM. The campaign was no longer about government policies or achievements but solely about Kejriwal.

This transformation underscores the extent to which the AAP has become synonymous with Kejriwal. The party's identity, strategy and future are inextricably linked to his persona, highlighting a significant shift from its original vision of collective leadership and decentralization. Today, the AAP's political narrative is a testament to the centralization of power around a single individual, reflecting a broader trend in Indian politics where personality often overshadows policy.

Arvind Kejriwal's centrality to the AAP is undeniable, but the party's evolution into a formidable political force was not a solo endeavuor. Like any leader who becomes the fulcrum of a party's politics, Kejriwal relied on a carefully curated inner circle of trusted lieutenants, strategists and loyalists. This coterie, composed of individuals with specialized skills and unwavering loyalty, played a pivotal role in shaping the AAP's governance model, national ambitions and organizational machinery, while ensuring Kejriwal remained the unchallenged face of the party.

Kejriwal recognized early on that the AAP could fill the vacuum left by a declining Congress in India's opposition landscape. To realize this vision, he nurtured a team tailored to specific roles, each member chosen not only for their competence but also for their inability to overshadow him. In governance, leaders like Manish Sisodia, Satyendar Jain and Atishi were instrumental in establishing the AAP's signature model – the Kejriwal model of governance centred on education and health reforms. Sisodia and Jain, with their administrative acumen, and Atishi, with her intellectual rigor, became the architects of policies that defined the AAP's Delhi success.

For the AAP's national expansion, Kejriwal needed a different breed of leaders – those with street-fighting grit and political acceptability. Sanjay Singh emerged as the ideal fit, blending negotiation skills with a public persona that resonated beyond Delhi. On the ground, political strategists like Raghav Chadha and Sandeep Pathak, with their sharp political instincts, were entrusted with crafting the AAP's state-level strategies, ensuring the party's footprint extended beyond the capital.

Kejriwal also understood the importance of communication, fundraising and networking in modern politics. Vijay Nair, with his extensive corporate connections and expertise in social media, became the linchpin for managing celebrity outreach, business ties and the AAP's public narrative. For policy innovation, Kejriwal tapped Jasmine Shah, whose scholarly background and experience at institutions like the Abdul Latif Jameel Poverty Action Lab (J-PAL), founded by Nobel laureates Abhijit Banerjee and Esther Duflo, lent credibility and depth to the AAP's policy framework.

To manage the party's day-to-day operations, Kejriwal relied on loyalists like Bibhav Kumar and Aswathi Muralidharan, who executed tasks with unquestioning dedication. This carefully constructed ecosystem allowed Kejriwal to maintain control while delegating critical functions to capable hands. Each member of this inner circle was chosen not just for their skills but for their alignment with Kejriwal's vision, ensuring that their ambitions remained subordinate to his leadership.

To understand the AAP's Kejriwal-centric model, one must look beyond the man himself and examine the roles of these key figures. Their contributions, while vital to the party's rise, were orchestrated to reinforce Kejriwal's dominance, creating a delicate balance between collective effort and singular leadership.

16

Manish Sisodia: The Constant Deputy

The announcement of the AAP's second list of candidates for the 2025 Delhi Assembly elections sparked significant interest, particularly the decision to field former Deputy CM Sisodia from Jangpura instead of his long-held Patparganj constituency. This change raises questions about the internal dynamics of the AAP and its leadership strategies. Sisodia, a political heavyweight and the architect of Delhi's education reforms, was moved to what is perceived as a 'safe' seat, while Patparganj has been allocated to Avadh Ojha, a recent AAP entrant and popular UPSC tutor.

Why did the AAP shift Sisodia, who has won Patparganj three times? What does this reveal about Sisodia's political standing within the party and the challenges the AAP faced in retaining its stronghold in Delhi?

The roots of this decision can be traced back to the 2020 Assembly elections. Despite the AAP's landslide victory, Sisodia's win from Patparganj was a close shave – he managed to scrape through with a margin of just around 3,000 votes, one of the narrowest among the AAP candidates. On the day of the counting, while the party's headquarters was abuzz with celebrations, there was palpable tension over Sisodia's performance.

During interactions with voters in Patparganj in 2020, a complex narrative emerged. Some supporters felt there was a lack of robust campaigning by Kejriwal for Sisodia. Others speculated about internal sabotage. Rishi Singh, a labourer and AAP supporter, observed, 'Kejriwal didn't campaign much for Sisodia. We felt it was only the grassroots workers holding the campaign together.'

Beyond the campaign strategies, there were signs of growing anti-incumbency against Sisodia. The constituency, with its diverse voter base – Uttarakhandis (22 per cent), Purvanchalis (15 per cent) and Brahmins (15 per cent), among others – showed discontent with his local engagement.[1]

Rachna, a schoolteacher, pointed out, 'Sisodia was always busy with higher political work. While schools were built, basic local issues remained unaddressed. Kejriwal's absence from the constituency further hurt trust in Sisodia's leadership.'

Sisodia's controversial statement during the Shaheen Bagh anti-CAA protests further complicated matters. As mentioned before, breaking party lines, he expressed solidarity with the protesters, a move that invited fierce BJP criticism and reportedly demoralized the AAP cadres in Patparganj. A party supporter, speaking anonymously, said, 'There were strict instructions to avoid commenting on Shaheen Bagh. When Sisodia broke ranks, Kejriwal distanced himself to protect the larger campaign. This alienated some booth-level workers.'

The perception of internal rifts and lack of solidarity within the party may explain Sisodia's reassignment to Jangpura. The AAP leadership might have decided to shield Sisodia from a potentially tough battle in Patparganj, opting instead to leverage his stature in a constituency with stronger support.

A senior AAP leader defended the move, stating, 'The BJP's targeted campaign against Sisodia in 2020 had long-lasting effects. Moving him to a safer seat is about ensuring his victory, not undermining his role. Kejriwal's support has always been steadfast, but strategic decisions sometimes require hard calls.'

This development underscores the shifting dynamics within the AAP. The party, once hailed for its collective ethos, appears increasingly reliant on a few key figures. While Kejriwal continues to dominate the narrative, Sisodia's trajectory illustrates the challenges of balancing individual prominence with organizational cohesion. The decision to allocate Patparganj to Avadh Ojha also signals a calculated gamble. They believed that bringing a new face to a high-profile constituency could rejuvenate the party's image. However, it also risked alienating Sisodia's loyal voter base. In this chapter, we go through Sisodia's journey in the AAP and with Kejriwal, to better understand the pitfalls of a centralized political party."

The Unbreakable Bond

When the AAP began its journey in the bustling heart of Delhi, amidst the cacophony of politics and the relentless pursuit of change, two men emerged as the architects of a new political narrative. Kejriwal and Sisodia, the dynamic duo of the AAP, share a bond that transcends the usual political alliances. Their relationship was forged in the crucible of activism, tempered by the trials of governance and solidified by a shared vision for a better India.

The story of Kejriwal and Sisodia began long before the formation of the AAP. Both men were deeply entrenched in the world of social activism. Kejriwal, an IIT graduate and former IRS officer, had already made a name for himself as an anti-corruption crusader. His work with the Parivartan movement and the RTI Act had earned him national recognition. Sisodia, a former journalist, was equally passionate about social change. His work with the NGO Kabir, which focused on promoting transparency and accountability in governance, brought him into Kejriwal's orbit.

Their paths crossed during the IAC movement. When the AAP came to power in Delhi in 2015, Kejriwal entrusted Sisodia with a record number of portfolios, making him the deputy CM and head of critical departments like education, finance, public works and urban development. Sisodia's versatility and work ethic became the backbone of AAP's governance.

Sisodia as Finance Minister

Manish Sisodia's tenure as the finance minister of Delhi was marked by a blend of innovative policies and pragmatic governance. His approach to managing the capital's finances was both visionary and grounded, reflecting his deep understanding of the socio-economic fabric of Delhi.

One of Sisodia's most notable achievements was the transformation of Delhi's education system. As finance minister, he allocated substantial funds to revamp government schools, introducing initiatives like the Happiness Curriculum and the Entrepreneurship Mindset Curriculum. These programmes, as discussed previously, aimed to foster holistic development and entrepreneurial skills among students, setting a new benchmark for public education in India.

Sisodia's budgetary allocations consistently prioritized health and education, sectors he believed were fundamental to the city's growth. Under his stewardship, the Delhi government significantly increased spending on healthcare, leading to the establishment of mohalla clinics and the expansion of hospital infrastructure. These initiatives made healthcare more accessible and affordable for Delhi's residents, earning widespread acclaim. He was also the brain behind the making of the outcome budget report, which he published every time before the budget to let people know what work has been done with the help of the last budget.

In addition to his focus on social sectors, Sisodia was also instrumental in promoting fiscal discipline and transparency. His budgets emphasized efficient resource allocation and robust financial management, ensuring that public funds were utilized effectively. He championed the cause of participatory budgeting, encouraging citizen involvement in the budget-making process to ensure that the government's financial decisions reflected the needs and aspirations of the people.

In an earlier chapter, I have discussed in detail the work of the Delhi government on the education sector and Sisodia was the key person behind the education revolution as the AAP calls it.

Punjab Crisis: Sisodia the Troubleshooter

As Kejriwal's most-trusted lieutenant, Sisodia consistently demonstrated his prowess beyond his government portfolios, emerging as one of the AAP's most prominent troubleshooters and strategists. Whenever the party faced turmoil, Kejriwal entrusted Sisodia with full autonomy to navigate the crisis. A prime example of Sisodia's crisis management skills can be seen in the aftermath of the 2017 Punjab Assembly elections.

Following the AAP's disappointing performance in the 2017 Punjab Assembly elections, where the party secured only 20 seats despite being a strong contender, internal fractures within the Punjab unit threatened its survival. The election loss intensified grievances among the leadership and cadres, leading to a period of significant turmoil. In response, Sisodia was appointed as the Punjab in-charge, tasked with addressing these challenges.

One of the major crises during this period was the rebellion led by Sukhpal Singh Khaira, then leader of the Opposition in the Punjab Assembly. Khaira criticized the central leadership for excessive interference and demanded greater autonomy for the Punjab unit. He was vocal about the Delhi leadership's failure to address Punjab-specific concerns, which he believed contributed to the electoral defeat. This conflict culminated in Khaira forming a rebel faction and establishing an alternative PAC to challenge the AAP's official decision-making.[2]

Sisodia's approach to resolving this rebellion showcased his role as a troubleshooter. He initiated dialogues with Khaira and other dissenters, but remained firm in upholding the party's core structure and decisions. Despite his efforts, Khaira's stance hardened, leading to his removal as the leader of opposition in 2018 – a decision that further escalated tensions. Khaira ultimately quit the party and formed his own outfit, the Punjab Ekta Party, in 2019.

While the rebellion posed a significant setback, Sisodia worked tirelessly to restore discipline and morale within the Punjab unit. He held multiple meetings with Punjab leaders and volunteers, emphasizing grassroots engagement and organizational restructuring. This period tested his crisis-management skills and, while not all conflicts were resolved, his leadership helped stabilize the party and lay the groundwork for its future resurgence in Punjab politics.

Sisodia's tenure as Punjab in-charge underscored his reputation as a troubleshooter and a leader capable of steering the party through turbulent times. His ability to manage crises, implement innovative policies and maintain the party's stability during challenging periods has been instrumental in the AAP's journey. Sisodia's role in navigating the Punjab crisis is a testament to his strategic acumen and unwavering commitment to the party's vision.

Sisodia as Mentor and Strategist

As mentioned previously, Sisodia's role in the AAP extends far beyond his administrative and political duties. He has been a pivotal mentor to many emerging leaders within the party, fostering a culture of innovation and inclusivity. Among those he has mentored are Atishi and Jasmine Shah, both of whom have made significant contributions to the party and the governance of Delhi.

Atishi, who served as CM of Delhi from September 2024 to February 2025, owes much of her political journey to Sisodia. Recognizing her potential and impressive background as a Rhodes Scholar, Sisodia brought her into the AAP and entrusted her with the critical task of transforming Delhi's education system. Atishi graduated with a Bachelor of Arts in history from St Stephen's College, Delhi, and went on to complete her master's degree at the University of Oxford as a Rhodes Scholar. Her academic excellence and dedication to social work made her an ideal candidate for the role. Under Sisodia's guidance, Atishi played a crucial role in implementing groundbreaking reforms that revitalized government schools in Delhi. Together, they introduced initiatives like the Happiness Curriculum and the Entrepreneurship Mindset Curriculum, which set new standards for public education in India.

Jasmine Shah, who served as the vice chairperson of the Dialogue and Development Commission of Delhi (DDCD), also benefited from Sisodia's mentorship. Shah holds a BTech and MTech in mechanical engineering from IIT Madras, as well as a master's in public administration from Columbia University. His academic background and passion for public policy made him a valuable asset to the AAP. Shah's work in shaping the Delhi Model of Governance, which emphasizes human capital development and equitable service delivery, has been instrumental in redefining public administration in the capital. Sisodia's support and encouragement allowed Shah to implement innovative policies in areas such as education, healthcare and transport, further solidifying the AAP's reputation for progressive governance.

Sisodia's ability to identify and nurture talent has been a cornerstone of the AAP's success. By empowering leaders like Atishi and Jasmine Shah, he has ensured that the party remains dynamic and forward-thinking. His mentorship has not only strengthened the party's leadership but also contributed to the overall development and governance of Delhi.

Could Manish Sisodia Have Been Delhi's CM?

In the corridors of the AAP, there was a time when speculation buzzed about Manish Sisodia ascending as the CM of Delhi. Post the sweeping victory in the 2015 Delhi Assembly elections, Sisodia emerged as the face of the government. While Kejriwal, the party supremo, held no portfolios, Sisodia managed significant ones, including education, finance and urban development, further cementing his prominence within the administration.

The chatter gained momentum during the 2017 Punjab Assembly elections. Rumours swirled that if the AAP won in Punjab and Kejriwal assumed the CM's role there, Sisodia would lead Delhi. This narrative picked up steam after Sisodia, in an election rally at Mohali, urged voters to 'vote as if you're voting for Kejriwal as Punjab CM', a strategic statement designed to capitalize on Kejriwal's popularity.[3]

The move, however, invited backlash. Critics like the Congress and Shiromani Akali Dal accused the AAP of betraying Delhi's voters and plotting to impose Kejriwal on Punjab. Sukhbir Singh Badal, former deputy CM of Punjab, labelled it a conspiracy to transfer Delhi's leadership to Punjab. Kejriwal refuted these claims, asserting at a Patiala rally, 'How can I be Punjab CM when I'm Delhi's CM? Punjab's CM will be from Punjab.'[4] According to sources, when Manish Sisodia suggested that Arvind Kejriwal could become the chief minister of Punjab, it was not in sync with Kejriwal's own political strategy. Those close to him viewed it as an overstep, as the leadership never seriously considered Kejriwal relocating to Punjab. Nor was there any discussion within the party about Sisodia stepping in as Delhi's CM if Kejriwal moved.

The AAP has always been centred around Kejriwal, and he swiftly dismissed the idea. Internally, he reasserted that abandoning Delhi would be a mistake and made it clear he had no intention of doing so, quickly regaining control of the narrative.

At the time, the AAP lacked the political depth to cultivate or project an alternative leadership in Punjab. The campaign continued to hinge entirely on Kejriwal's image and the party deliberately avoided naming a local face for the chief minister. Any such projection risked elevating someone to a stature that could rival Kejriwal's own within the party.

Despite these clarifications, the internal dynamics hinted otherwise. A senior journalist covering the AAP at the time revealed that in some East Delhi areas, posters featuring Sisodia – without Kejriwal – surfaced, signalling ambitions for Delhi's top post. 'While AAP leaders denied these were official, the mood suggested Sisodia's aspirations,' the journalist observed.

However, the AAP's lacklustre performance in Punjab squashed these prospects. The party's inability to clinch Punjab confirmed Kejriwal's indispensability in Delhi politics, leaving Sisodia to continue in his pivotal but secondary role within the party. These speculations, however short-lived, reflected Sisodia's stature and the shifting dynamics within the AAP's leadership at the time.

17

Entry of Sunita Kejriwal

It was December 2019 at the CM's residence in Delhi, during an intimate gathering of journalists, the AAP cabinet ministers and leaders, that I first observed Sunita Kejriwal's quiet yet striking presence. Draped in a simple blue sari, paired with a black sweater and grey shawl, she radiated warmth as she ensured everyone was well-served with tea and snacks. Despite the flurry of questions from journalists, she deftly dodged them, responding with humour and grace. When asked if she would ever join politics, she quipped in Hindi, 'Then who will take care of the house?'

Fast forward to February 2024, the scene at the same residence was starkly different. According to sources, Kejriwal convened a high-stakes meeting with top AAP leaders. As the ED intensified its investigation and Kejriwal anticipated his imminent arrest, the party faced a looming crisis. To counter the turbulence, Kejriwal laid out a comprehensive plan.

Cabinet ministers would manage governance – Atishi and Saurabh Bhardwaj were tasked with alliance-building and Congress negotiations, while veterans like Gopal Rai and Sandeep Pathak would strategize campaigns and coordinate with state units. But the most intriguing decision was Kejriwal's suggestion for Sunita to take a more public role, emerging as his messenger to rally the party workers and connect with the grassroots.

An IRS officer since 1993, Sunita had taken voluntary retirement in 2016, a decade after Kejriwal left government service. Known for her administrative acumen, she had refrained from formally joining the AAP, adhering to the party's rule against family members of leaders holding membership.

On 21 March 2024, Kejriwal was arrested by the ED in connection with the alleged liquor policy scam. While the leadership grappled with panic, Sunita's role became pivotal. Her emergence as a political force underscored the party's resilience, demonstrating her ability to navigate crises and inspire solidarity in turbulent times.

His arrest in the liquor policy scam sent shockwaves through the nation. As the investigation unfolded, a new narrative began to form. Suddenly, the AAP's political machinery converged upon one entity – Kejriwal and, by extension, his family.

Instead of rallying behind the numerous senior leaders within its ranks, the AAP made an unexpected choice: they launched Sunita as the face of their campaign during the general elections and the Haryana elections.

The decision to bring Sunita to the forefront was both surprising and revealing. The question was not one of capability – she may well have the potential to be an effective leader – but of sheer symbolism. In a party that had, until then, prided itself on being a platform for the common citizen, why had the leadership mantle been placed on someone who had never campaigned for it before? Sunita was suddenly thrust into the spotlight, representing not only her husband but the entire party.

When Kejriwal was arrested, there was a crisis of leadership because Rajya Sabha MP Sanjay Singh, former Deputy CM Manish Sisodia and former Health Minister Satyendar Jain were all in jail. But there were others who could have become frontline leaders, but that did not happen.

One cannot help but draw comparisons between the AAP and other family-centric political parties in India. The Samajwadi Party, the DMK and, of course, the Congress have long been criticized for their reliance on political dynasties. The AAP sought to break away from this tradition initially, offering a new kind of politics that was supposed to be free from nepotism and political inheritance. Yet in 2024, it too seemed to go the dynastic way, made starker by the fact that Sunita was not even a member of the party's top decision-making body.

Here it is important to look into two cases.

Rabri Devi

In the annals of Indian politics, the appointment of Rabri Devi as the CM of Bihar in 1997 stands out as a dramatic and unexpected turn of events. This decision was necessitated by the legal troubles of her husband, Lalu Prasad Yadav, the chief of Rashtriya Janata Dal, who was embroiled in the infamous fodder scam. The scam, which involved the embezzlement of approximately ₹950 crore from the Bihar state treasury under the guise of purchasing fodder for livestock, had far-reaching political ramifications.

On 25 July 1997, an arrest warrant was issued against Lalu Prasad Yadav, compelling him to step down as the CM of Bihar. In a strategic move to retain control over the state's political machinery, Lalu appointed his wife as his successor. This decision was met with widespread astonishment and scepticism, given Rabri Devi's lack of political experience. However, it allowed Lalu to maintain his influence over the state's governance from behind the scenes.

Rabri Devi's tenure as CM was marked by significant challenges, including managing the state's administration amidst ongoing legal battles and political opposition. Despite the initial doubts about her capabilities, she managed to hold the office for three terms, becoming the first and only woman to serve as the CM of Bihar.

Champai Soren

Another important example is that of Jharkhand CM Hemant Soren, who was arrested by the ED for an alleged money laundering scam in 2024. Unlike Lalu, Soren did not appoint his wife, Kalpana, as the CM. Instead, he chose senior leader of

Jharkhand Mukti Morcha (JMM), Champai Soren, to take on the role. However, Kalpana led the election campaign of the JMM both nationally and in the state, resulting in the party winning 5 out of 14 Lok Sabha seats. In 2024, after Hemant Soren's release, he resumed his position as CM. During the subsequent Jharkhand Assembly elections, Kalpana not only contested but also campaigned vigorously for the party, leading to the JMM forming the government once again.

Coming back to the AAP, it is now time for the party to grapple with its own identity. Is it still a party of change, driven by the common citizen, or has it become yet another player in India's political game?

To repeat the obvious: the AAP of today is no longer the AAP of the IAC movement. It is no longer a party of ideals but one of personalities. 'When we created AAP, we were clear about not letting two family members lead the party,' noted Ashutosh, 'but now those principles are gone.'

A senior AAP leader, speaking under the condition of anonymity, said, 'It's easy to label Sunita Kejriwal's involvement as dynastic politics, but that misses the context.' He said that her role was not to pursue personal ambition but to stand as a voice for her husband's political vision as well as to highlight his alleged mistreatment. 'Only she, as his wife, could convey the depth of his dreams and the unfairness of his arrest,' the leader added.

Also, with parties like the Nationalist Congress Party (NCP) and Shiv Sena suffering fractures due to the BJP's political manoeuvring, many in the AAP perhaps correctly feared a similar fate. Her presence was considered crucial to keep the party united in a time of crisis. 'She was seen as the only one who could connect with both the masses and the party leadership to prevent a potential collapse,' the leader noted. A senior journalist echoed this, saying that when Kejriwal was arrested, the AAP felt vulnerable and feared that its members could be lured by the BJP. Sunita's involvement was meant to rally the party together, deliver her husband's messages to the public and offer a symbol of continuity. Her emergence as the face of the party during this turbulent time was no coincidence but rather a calculated decision by the AAP to ensure stability, emotional resonance and organizational coherence.

However, after Arvind Kejriwal secured interim bail and was released from jail, there was another subtle shift in the AAP's internal strategy. It could be called 'course correction' due to the BJP starting a narrative around the AAP's seeming turn to dynastic politics. When Kejriwal decided to resign from his position as Delhi's CM, despite speculation that Sunita might succeed him, he chose to appoint Atishi to the role. This was seen as a conscious effort to distance the AAP from the accusation of dynastic politics.

In an interview taken during 2024, Nakshbandi told me, 'The 2025 Delhi election is critical for AAP, and the last thing Arvind Kejriwal wants is to fuel the BJP's narrative of dynastic politics. He knows it would only strengthen the BJP's position and contradict the founding principles of AAP, which appeared in opposition to political dynasties. Appointing Atishi as the chief minister over Sunita reflects this awareness.'

The impact of Sunita's role has been mixed. The AAP did not fracture under pressure, unlike the NCP and Shiv Sena, although it remains unclear whether this was because of Sunita's presence. It also failed to fully harness her emotional appeal, given the outcomes of both the general elections and the Haryana Assembly elections.

Another primary reason for Sunita's elevation was the emotional appeal her leadership brought to the narrative. The party sought to project the arrest of Kejriwal as a politically motivated act by the BJP, aimed at undermining the AAP ahead of the 2024 general elections. While party leaders vocally criticized the alleged targeting, Sunita's personal narrative as a wife fighting for justice struck a deeper chord. She emphasized not only her family's victimhood but also framed the arrest as an affront to the people of Delhi, whose mandate had been undermined. This humanized the party's position and widened its appeal.

Additionally, Sunita's leadership quelled potential power struggles within the party. With Kejriwal behind bars and several senior leaders under investigation, there was a real risk of multiple power centres emerging. By positioning Sunita as Kejriwal's emissary, the party maintained its hierarchical structure, ensuring all decisions flowed to the jailed leader through her. This move reinforced Kejriwal's undisputed authority within the party and prevented any internal fragmentation.

Sunita also played a pivotal role in managing the AAP's alignment with the opposition INDIA (Indian National Developmental Inclusive Alliance) bloc. As a trusted representative, she facilitated seamless communication between the bloc's leaders and the party. Her meetings with prominent figures like Sonia Gandhi, Rahul Gandhi and Kalpana Soren underscored her strategic importance. Her ability to articulate the AAP's stance and carry directives from Kejriwal ensured unity within the bloc and streamlined campaign coordination.

Critics have argued that Sunita's rise marked the AAP's full transition into a Kejriwal family-centric party. However, this narrative overlooks the strategic brilliance of the move. By leveraging her position, the AAP maintained internal stability, avoided significant defections (except for cabinet minister Rajkumar Anand, who later joined the BJP) and sustained its momentum during a critical election season.

In hindsight, Sunita's leadership was not merely a stopgap measure but a testament to the AAP's adaptability under pressure. Her role exemplified a strategic response to adversity, enabling the party to navigate one of its most challenging phases with resilience and coherence.

18

Vijay Nair: 'The Blue-Eyed Boy of Arvind ji'

Vijay Nair is a name shrouded in intrigue within the AAP. A college dropout turned entrepreneur, Nair's journey from founding an entertainment empire to becoming a pivotal figure in the AAP's communication and strategy landscape is both unconventional and revealing. This account explores his enigmatic role within the AAP, the controversies that followed him and his eventual political and legal entanglements.

My first encounter with Nair was over a phone call during my tenure at the DARC. My routine included monitoring media narratives about the Delhi government. On one occasion, I flagged a news article published in a reputed English daily for their positive assessment of the government's work, despite noting certain gaps. Minutes after submitting my report, I received a call from one of the government's media coordinators. 'Vijay ji is on the line,' the advisor said, handing over the conversation to Nair.

Nair's voice – husky yet composed – offered a direct critique: 'Please correct it and submit a fresh report.' When I later questioned why he, an outsider to my reporting hierarchy, wielded such authority, I learned from the media coordinators that he was the CMO's de facto power broker in communication and media strategy.

It became evident that Nair controlled an elaborate network within the AAP, managing everything from advertisements to social media and consultancy services. He worked with a core team, often comprising individuals not officially part of the government or party but hired through third-party companies. These consultants reportedly earned substantial salaries from party funds, illustrating Nair's wide-reaching influence over the AAP's communication apparatus.

When I raised questions about Nair's authority with a senior AAP leader, their response was telling: 'He's the blue-eyed boy of Arvind ji.' This endorsement further explained Nair's commanding position within the AAP despite not holding a formal government title.

Nair had formally joined the AAP in 2014 itself. He had reportedly donated to the party before the 2014 Lok Sabha elections and was deeply involved in its social media campaigns and event organization. By 2018, he was promoted to the party's communication in-charge, a role that positioned him at the nexus of strategy and execution.

One of his significant contributions to the AAP was orchestrating its transition from an insurgent political outfit to a mainstream force with a sharp focus on branding and public relations. His team's ability to harness social media to shape narratives gave the AAP an edge over traditional parties, especially in urban centres.

Nair's influence extended to managing the AAP's public messaging, advertising and social media narratives. He was also instrumental in strategizing events and fundraising. The AAP's public communication became synonymous with targeted campaigns, thanks in part to his efforts.

Nair's proximity to power came under scrutiny in September 2022 when he was arrested by the CBI in connection with the alleged liquor policy scam. The AAP officially acknowledged his role for the first time, describing him as the 'communication in-charge'. Kejriwal later downplayed his significance, calling him a '*chhota sa karyakarta* (a small worker)'. However, the scale of

Nair's operations and his residence in a bungalow assigned to a cabinet minister belied such modest descriptions.

This arrest cast a shadow over the AAP's governance narrative. The liquor policy scam, which involved allegations of irregularities in liquor distribution licences, was a major embarrassment. Nair's arrest highlighted not only the party's vulnerability to corruption charges but also the risks of relying on unelected figures for key decisions.

Before entering politics, Nair was a force in India's entertainment industry. As the founder of Only Much Louder (OML), he shaped the independent music and comedy scene. Only Much Louder managed bands like Pentagram and organized prominent events like the NH7 Weekender. Under Nair's leadership, OML gained recognition for introducing Indian audiences to global music icons like David Guetta. Nair even earned a spot in *Fortune India's* 40 Under 40 list in 2016.

However, his entertainment career was not without controversy. During India's MeToo Movement in 2018, multiple allegations of sexual harassment surfaced against Nair (which he denied). It tarnished his reputation in the media and creative industries (more on this later).[1]

Nair's story raises larger questions about the role of backroom operators in politics. While his strategies helped the AAP consolidate power, his arrest in 2022 underscored the dangers of concentrating influence in unelected individuals. Critics argue that this reliance compromises transparency and accountability, eroding public trust in governance. Moreover, the allegations of sexual misconduct against Nair remain a stain on his legacy, bringing to light the ethical challenges of blending politics with private enterprise.

Nair's journey from managing rock bands to shaping the AAP's communication machinery is emblematic of the blurred lines between creativity and political strategy. This reflects the growing influence of unelected strategists in Indian politics, a trend that has redefined public engagement but also introduced ethical complexities.

While his contributions to the AAP's rise are undeniable, his involvement in controversies illustrates the precarious nature of wielding influence from the shadows. As the AAP moves forward, the lessons from Nair's ascent and fall will likely influence how the party navigates its reliance on behind-the-scenes operators in its pursuit of political dominance.

The AAP's former social media head Ankit Lal told me:

> I was handling the day-to-day work of social media, but at the same time, I wanted to pursue my interest in political consultancy. I told Arvind about my plans to move on and he requested me that time to be there till 2020 Assembly elections. I was working with my team and I was also desperately looking for a person to whom I can give this job, and stay away in peace.

He added that Nair was not new in AAP politics and that Maharashtra AAP leader Preeti Sharma Menon (the president of the party in Mumbai and a National Executive member) had brought Nair and Vishal Dadlani to the party's fold.

He said, 'Nair and Dadlani, as I have known were childhood friends and from 2014 onwards, they were part of the AAP and supporting the party from the backstage. It is important to remember that Nair came from a corporate background. He was very popular in the Bombay corporate circles and has successfully led a company.'

Lal further added:

> During the 2019 [Lok] Sabha election, I suddenly bumped into Vijay Nair at Atishi's Lok Sabha campaign office, which was located in Geeta colony. I was surprised to see Nair because I knew that he was very busy man, so I asked him about how come he is there and he told me that he was managing the campaign of Atishi and helping her. What I gathered is that by that time he was transferring

> all the roles of his company to his brother because prior to that, there was some controversies regarding MeToo and related issues. I was very happy to see him because I knew that if he has plans to be full time part of the AAP, then he would be the best person to handle the social media and IT cell of the party.

According to him, from him to Nair, the transfer of the social media and IT cell happened organically. He said, 'During 2020 Assembly elections, we both worked together with the team and it was a successful campaign in terms of social media, and there is no doubt that he indeed changed several things on the social media campaign or the strategy of the AAP, because he was from the corporate background and I was from an engineering background, so our outlook and expertise were different.'

Sexual Harassment Allegations

As a journalist and during my time working with the DARC, I came across numerous accounts that painted a complex and troubling picture of Nair's presence in professional and political circles. Known for his sharp communication strategies and formidable influence within the AAP, Nair's reputation was shadowed by allegations of misconduct that raised serious questions about the party's internal ethics and accountability.

Many women who worked closely with Nair confided in me about their discomfort. His overzealous involvement in every task, coupled with an intimidating demeanour, often created an uneasy work environment. Some women outright refused to work with him, citing his alleged past misconduct during his tenure at OML.

The investigative report by *The Caravan* in November 2018 brought these allegations into sharp focus.[2] The exposé detailed first-hand accounts from multiple women accusing Nair of inappropriate behaviour, including unsolicited advances and creating a hostile workspace. These revelations shocked the entertainment industry but didn't seem to impede his association with the AAP.

As part of a Delhi government initiative to organize the 'Delhi ki Diwali' event, I was tasked with inviting editors and senior journalists. While on my way to meet *The Caravan's* Editor-in-Chief Anant Nath, I received a call from a senior AAP functionary who questioned my actions. The functionary's concern was not about the invitation itself but about the ongoing investigative story *The Caravan* was preparing, which implicated Nair and raised questions about other party leaders.

This interaction highlighted Nair's controversial standing even within the party. Despite the damaging allegations, Nair continued to operate in significant capacities, underscoring a dichotomy between his professional utility and the party's ethical dilemmas. The MeToo allegations against Nair revealed a stark gap in how political and professional institutions address sexual harassment. *The Caravan's* report was comprehensive, detailing inappropriate conduct that included sending unsolicited explicit content and exploiting his position of power.

According to the report, when the journalist questioned Atishi about the allegations of sexual harassment against Nair in 2019, she stated that she had no knowledge of the matter. The report further noted that the reporter later shared the details of the allegations along with follow-up questions but Atishi did not respond. Atishi later confirmed Nair's involvement with the party but stated she was unaware of the allegations This revelation highlighted systemic oversights in the AAP's vetting processes, raising broader questions about the party's commitment to maintaining a safe and ethical work environment.

The report brings unsettling attention to the AAP's internal mechanisms for addressing sexual harassment complaints. The report states that the party has an Internal Complaints Committee (ICC), helmed by senior leader Atishi at one point. Ironically, this is the same Atishi whose 2019 Lok Sabha campaign was reportedly managed by Nair. This juxtaposition raises troubling questions about accountability and ethical consistency within the party.[3]

The timing and nature of this overlap are too significant to ignore. Did the party knowingly overlook the allegations against Nair for the sake of political expediency? Was Atishi's campaign strategy prioritized over her leadership of the ICC, which exists to ensure a safe and equitable environment? The possibility of quid pro quo looms uncomfortably over these revelations.

The AAP, a party that stormed into power with promises of clean politics and a fresh approach, seems to have betrayed its foundational ideals. Its willingness to engage Nair, despite well-documented accusations, showcases the often hypocritical nature of political pragmatism. People like Nair, with their strategic expertise, may be seen as indispensable, but this comes at the cost of undermining the party's moral authority.

Former AAP leader Ashutosh's remark resonates here: 'When a party is surrounded by people like Nair, how can you expect clean politics?' His critique underscores a broader truth about Indian politics – where lofty promises of reform often crumble under the weight of ambition and convenience.

The AAP's handling of the Nair episode serves as a stark reminder of the compromises political organizations make, even those claiming to be alternative forces of change. It is a lesson in vigilance for voters and a call for accountability that transcends the rhetoric of reform.

19

The Curious Case of Raghav Chadha: From Prominence to Absence

When Kejriwal was arrested, the entire AAP machinery was out on the streets of Delhi. Protests erupted not just in the capital but also in Punjab, Gujarat, Goa and beyond. Every prominent leader of the AAP was vocally opposing Kejriwal's arrest. Yet, amidst this sea of defiance, one notable figure was conspicuously absent: Raghav Chadha.

Raghav Chadha, a name that has become synonymous with the AAP, has been a prominent figure in Indian politics. Born on 11 November 1987, in New Delhi, Chadha's journey from a chartered accountant to a Rajya Sabha MP is a testament to his political acumen and dedication.

His political career took a significant leap when he contested the 2019 Lok Sabha elections from the South Delhi constituency. Despite his efforts and the support of the AAP, he lost to BJP's Ramesh Bidhuri by a substantial margin. This defeat, however, did not deter him. Instead, it fuelled his determination to make a mark in Indian politics.

In March 2020, Chadha was appointed as the vice chairman of the Delhi Jal Board (DJB). His tenure was marked by ambitious projects aimed at improving Delhi's water supply and cleaning the Yamuna. Chadha's leadership in DJB showcased his ability to handle significant responsibilities and implement impactful policies. His political journey saw another milestone when he was elected as the MLA from the Rajinder Nagar constituency in the 2020 Delhi elections. His victory was a testament to his growing popularity and the trust people had in his leadership. As an MLA, he continued to work on various developmental projects and remained a vocal spokesperson for the AAP.

In December 2020, Chadha was appointed as the co-in charge of the AAP's Punjab unit ahead of the 2022 Punjab elections. His strategic planning and campaigning played a crucial role in the AAP's landslide victory in Punjab, where the party won 92 out of 117 seats. This victory solidified Chadha's position as a key player in the party.

Following the AAP's victory in Punjab, Chadha was appointed as the chief advisor to Punjab CM Bhagwant Mann. In this role, he was responsible for overseeing the implementation of pro-people initiatives and advising the government on financial matters. His appointment, however, drew criticism and allegations of him being the 'super CM' of Punjab (as described by the Akali Dal leader Daljit Singh Cheema). Chadha dismissed these allegations, emphasizing his role as an advisor and his commitment to serving the people of Punjab.[1]

Chadha's personal life also became a topic of public scrutiny when he married Bollywood actress Parineeti Chopra in September 2023. The couple's lavish wedding in Udaipur drew significant media attention and trolling. Critics questioned the extravagant expenses, with allegations that Chadha bore all the costs. Parineeti Chopra addressed these rumours, clarifying that the wedding was held at a five-star hotel and was not as extravagant as portrayed. She highlighted the double standards faced due to Chadha's political career, noting that if she had married an actor or businessman, the narrative would have been different.

As mentioned earlier, the Rajya Sabha MP, once one of Kejriwal's closest lieutenants, was nowhere to be seen during one of the toughest phases for the AAP in 2024, following Kejriwal's arrest. This absence did not go unnoticed, and it raised questions about Chadha's political activity, which had drastically diminished.

Speculation has been rife about Chadha's absence. Some even suggested he might be on the verge of joining the BJP, but that did not materialize. The reality, however, is more mundane. Chadha was in London when Kejriwal was arrested, and he had also undergone eye surgery. Despite these reasons, the drastic reduction in his political activity remains unexplained.

According to some AAP insiders, Chadha's retreat from active politics coincided with his marriage to Parineeti Chopra. There are whispers that Chadha's involvement in the Delhi liquor policy scam might have influenced his decision to step back. Insiders believe that if Chadha had been arrested, it could have impacted the careers of both Parineeti Chopra and her cousin, Priyanka Chopra, who as we all know is married to Nick Jonas. The potential fallout from such an arrest might have prompted Chadha to adopt a low profile.

In a TV interview, Chadha addressed the rumours, saying:

> Let me tell you the truth. The fact is, I had a lecture scheduled at the London School of Economics in the first week of March. Then I had to undergo preventive eye surgery to fix some retina spots … After I recovered, I returned and spent the month of May campaigning for our party in Delhi and Punjab. By levelling false allegations against me, people were trying to end my 13-year-old political journey … I can only say, 'Do not strive to make your presence felt, make your absence felt.'[2]

In an interview, Ankit Lal offered another perspective.

> In politics, we have a different kind of lifestyle which is 24×7 involvement. From such a background, when you get married to a Bollywood star, it is indeed important

> to acknowledge that balancing between political life and personal life at that level will take some time. After getting married to Parineeti Chopra, Raghav indeed faced several kinds of online trolling because political people do not understand that the lifestyle of a Bollywood celebrity is different from that of a full-time political worker. Raghav has been trying to balance these two, which is why I believe he took a back seat in active politics.

Lal also emphasized that Chadha remains active in politics, albeit away from the media limelight. He said, 'There are several reasons behind it. One is indeed the marriage, and the other is that there were some controversies because of his media statements in Punjab, which might have put the party in a difficult position. That's why he is avoiding media attention.'

However, former AAP leader Ashutosh has a different take. He believes that Chadha's importance within the party has waned, leading to his sidelining by Kejriwal. He said, 'Arvind Kejriwal believes in a use-and-throw policy. Raghav Chadha was an important man in the party till he was delivering. When his work was done, as the AAP won Punjab, he was sidelined because Kejriwal did not need him anymore.'

The whispers in Punjab's political corridors tell a compelling story. Several AAP leaders from the state have expressed discomfort with what they perceive as Delhi's overreach through Chadha. 'He's viewed as a Delhi outsider who swooped in during elections and started making pronouncements about Punjab politics without proper consultation,' confided a senior AAP leader from the state. The sentiment reflects a deeper tension between regional autonomy and central control, a classic challenge in Indian political parties.

Chadha, for his part, has attempted to deflect these criticisms with characteristic political finesse. In a recent television appearance, he cleverly reframed the 'remote control' narrative, asserting that Punjab's true remote control lies with its people. His self-designation as *supersevaar* (super servant) of Punjab, rather than the 'super chief minister', demonstrates his effort to project humility while maintaining his connection to the state.[3]

The parallel trajectories of Chadha and Atishi, who entered AAP politics simultaneously, offer fascinating insights into the party's internal dynamics. Both faced similar electoral setbacks in the 2019 Lok Sabha elections before winning Assembly seats in 2020. However, their paths have diverged significantly since then. While Atishi ascended to the chief ministership of Delhi in 2024, Chadha's public profile has notably diminished, with his visibility largely restricted to Rajya Sabha appearances.

This shift is particularly striking given Chadha's former omnipresence in the AAP's media strategy. 'There was a time when Raghav was the go-to spokesperson for every issue,' notes a veteran political journalist, 'His current absence from major party communications is conspicuous.' This transformation hints at subtle but significant changes in the AAP's power structure.

As mentioned before, party insiders offer various explanations for this apparent retreat. Some point to controversies stemming from his statements about Punjab politics (although no one clarifies what statements created this discord), while others suggest his recent marriage has prompted a desire to maintain a lower profile. The official party line, however, maintains that there's no deliberate sidelining, with Kejriwal's trust in Chadha reportedly unchanged.

A more nuanced interpretation emerges from those who cite that Chadha's absence during Kejriwal's arrest may have caused some friction. However, some developments suggest a possible recalibration of his role. His presence alongside Kejriwal at opposition rallies indicates he remains within the party's inner circle, albeit in a modified capacity.

The evolving saga of Raghav Chadha within the AAP reflects broader themes in Indian politics: the delicate balance between central and state leadership, the rise and repositioning of young leaders, and the complex interplay of personal and political factors in shaping political careers. As the AAP continues to evolve, the trajectory of leaders like Chadha will remain a telling indicator of the party's internal dynamics and future direction.

20

Kejriwal's Coterie

It is an unwritten rule in politics that around every autocratic leader, there grows a coterie. Indira Gandhi had one, Narendra Modi has one and so does Arvind Kejriwal.

A seasoned AAP member once confided in me that every significant decision within the party is orchestrated by this coterie. Kejriwal, he noted, tends to weave his personal touches into their ideas, yet it is evident that this inner circle runs everything.

During my tenure at the DARC, a senior AAP leader convened a press conference at the party office. I was tasked with drafting the press release for it. I did so and submitted it for approval, expecting a straightforward review process. However, shortly thereafter, I received a call from the CMO. The voice on the line exuded authority, a confident individual who had assumed a pivotal role in media communications.

To my astonishment, I was instructed to change the entire narrative of the press conference and was given specific directives on how to do so. My curiosity piqued, and I couldn't help but inquire about the rationale behind this abrupt change. In a measured yet firm tone, I was informed that this alteration was not merely a suggestion but a *mandate* from the CMO.

This might be a minor example but it does show how a coterie around Kejriwal wields significant control over the AAP's political narrative, shaping not only the party's internal discussions but also its public communications. Decisions of substantial consequence, be it in governance or media strategy, seemed to flow from this group, reinforcing the notion that the power within the AAP was concentrated in the hands of a few.

There are many implications of this sort of opaque decision-making. The ability of this select group to steer the party's narrative raises questions about the intra-party democracy. What was once envisioned as a movement of the people appears to have evolved into an organization where the voices of a select few overshadow the collective wisdom of the party.

Kejriwal's coterie includes political leaders and also backstage workers of the party who operate outside public view. This centralization of power is not just a reflection of his authoritative style, it is a strategic necessity. Given the choppy waters the AAP often finds itself in, there are issues and events that demand swift and decisive action. Kejriwal's coterie functions as an efficient and cohesive unit, enabling the AAP to respond promptly to emerging challenges and opportunities.

I have already discussed about Sisodia and Nair, who are an integral part of the core team of Kejriwal. There are also other members of Kejriwal's coterie, like Atishi, who have been discussed in later chapters.

In this chapter, I will look into the other important members, but before that, it is important to acknowledge that because the Delhi government does not have full control over the bureaucracy, with time, the AAP tried to establish a kind of bureaucratic structure with the help of highly educated middle class young men and women who would work within or outside the government in their personal capacities, but at the end of the day would work as a bureaucrat who would help the government. It is well known that a government cannot function without a strong bureaucracy, which is why Kejriwal decided on this kind of external power structure – a government within a government.

For example, in February 2015, the Delhi cabinet passed a proposal to set up DDCD under the leadership of the then AAP member and former journalist, Ashish Khetan. Initially it was a nine-member panel and the key goal of the DDCD was to implement the AAP government's vision for the city.[1]

The DDCD was to create a platform that fosters sustainable solutions to the complex problems facing Delhi by involving voices from outside the government – common citizens, academia, industry and civil society. This inclusive approach aimed to ensure that policymaking was not just top-down but also reflective of the needs and aspirations of the people.

The DDCD was envisioned to nurture dialogue between the people of Delhi and their government, facilitating effective formulation and implementation of policies. The Commission's objectives included promoting innovation, guiding spending by Corporate Social Responsibility (CSR) and philanthropic initiatives into high-impact areas, and creating a conducive environment for attracting cutting-edge technology, talent, skills and best management practices.

One of the key initiatives under the DDCD's vision was the Delhi@2047 platform, which aimed to make Delhi an equitable, modern and sustainable city by the 100th year of India's independence in 2047. This initiative sought to foster partnerships with the private sector, CSR initiatives and philanthropic organizations to achieve ambitious goals such as providing clean air and water to all residents, transitioning to 100 per cent electric vehicles and building world-class infrastructure.

In summary, the DDCD was formed with the vision of creating a collaborative and inclusive platform that leverages the expertise and resources of various stakeholders to address Delhi's developmental challenges to build a better future for its residents.

In 2018, Jasmine Shah became the vice-chairperson of DDCD. While the work continued, the DDCD allegedly started to become a place to give settlements to the coterie members of Kejriwal. It is important to note that DDCD vice-chairperson is a cabinet equivalent post with all the similar perks like house, car, free electricity and so on. The members used to get the perks and salary equivalent to any secretary of the Delhi government.

The DDCD included members like Sisodia, Satyendar Jain, Gopal Mohan, Aswathi Muralidharan and Vijaya Chandra Vupputuri. Gopal Mohan and Aswathi Muralidharan are considered key figures in Arvind Kejriwal's inner circle. Jasmine Shah, who was reappointed in 2020, retained the same set of members during his second tenure.[2]

From 2022 onwards, the DDCD has been engulfed in controversy, culminating in its temporary dissolution by Delhi LG Vinai Kumar Saxena. Allegations of nepotism, favouritism and arbitrary appointments have raised questions about the Commission's integrity and efficiency.

The LG's office alleged that the AAP government misused the Commission to provide financial benefits and political patronage to preferred individuals. What were initially honorary roles were transformed into highly paid positions without adhering to a transparent selection process. For instance, the high status granted to the vice-chairperson and the salaries of non-official members being at par with secretaries to the government (as mentioned earlier).

Critics argue that this practice lacked merit and accountability.

Moreover, the LG pointed out that no clear work allocation was provided to these members, undermining their purpose. These developments not only highlight lapses in governance but also reflect the political tussle between the Delhi government and the LG's office. As the controversy unfolded, it cast a shadow on the DDCD's role as a facilitator of progressive policies.[3]

Now, we get into the details of the members of Kejriwal's coterie, apart from the ones discussed already.

Gopal Mohan

Gopal Mohan, a prominent figure in the AAP and a key advisor to Kejriwal, was instrumental in shaping and implementing the Delhi Model of Governance. His portfolio focuses primarily on anti-corruption measures and governance reforms, making him one of Kejriwal's closest confidants. Mohan's technical background and strategic acumen have allowed him to influence the AAP's policies, particularly in areas like public service delivery and technology-driven solutions.

In Delhi, Mohan has played a pivotal role in advancing initiatives such as grievance redressal mechanisms and community-driven governance reforms. His innovative approaches aligned with the AAP's vision of transparent and accountable administration. This trust and collaboration stemmed from his longstanding association with Kejriwal during the IAC movement, where he was involved in mobilizing grassroots support for systemic change.

Following the AAP's historic victory in Punjab in 2022, Mohan expanded his role by working closely with the newly formed AAP government in the state. His primary responsibility has been to adapt the Delhi Model – focusing on education, healthcare and public-service efficiency – to Punjab's unique socio-economic challenges. This includes overseeing initiatives like improving government schools, establishing mohalla clinics and ensuring subsidized electricity and water for residents. His expertise has been crucial in aligning Punjab's governance structure with the AAP's broader policy goals, helping to replicate Delhi's success in a full-fledged state with its own fiscal and administrative complexities.

Mohan's involvement in Punjab underlines his strategic importance within AAP's leadership. His ability to translate governance models across different regions showcases his role as both a policy innovator and an implementer. This dual capacity ensures his continued influence in the AAP's state-level and national ambitions.

Aswathi Muralidharan

Aswathi Muralidharan, a prominent figure within the AAP, has been at the centre of several controversies regarding her appointments and roles within the Delhi government. Her association with the AAP began with her appointment as a joint secretary in the CMO. This role, which came with a substantial salary, equivalent to that of an under-secretary to the Government of India, was seen by many as a significant leap for someone relatively new to the political scene.[4] Critics argued that her appointment was a clear case of favouritism, given her close ties with key AAP leaders, including Kejriwal.

The controversy surrounding her appointment was further fuelled by the lack of a transparent selection process. The Delhi government's services department highlighted that such high-paying positions are typically reserved for officers with decades of experience in the IAS. The decision to appoint Muralidharan to this role without a competitive selection process was seen as an undue favour, raising questions about the integrity of the appointment.

In 2020, Muralidharan was appointed as a non-official member of the DDCD. This move was part of a broader strategy to leverage her expertise and close association with the CM to drive key policy initiatives. However, her appointment to the DDCD did not come without controversy.

Muralidharan's role within the DDCD was to contribute to the ideation and implementation of policies, particularly in areas such as health and environment. Despite her contributions, her appointment was criticized for being another instance of favouritism, as it was perceived to be based more on her political connections than on merit.

As a member of the DDCD, Muralidharan was involved in several key initiatives aimed at improving the quality of life in Delhi. One notable project was the Rozgar Bazaar portal, launched to connect job seekers with employers in the aftermath of the COVID-19 lockdown. This initiative was crucial in addressing the employment crisis faced by many residents of Delhi and showcased the DDCD's ability to find innovative solutions to pressing challenges.

Muralidharan was also active in addressing health and environmental issues, working closely with various stakeholders to develop and implement policies that promote sustainable development. Her role in the DDCD was to bridge the gap between the government and the citizens, ensuring that the voices of the common people are reflected in policy decisions.

Muralidharan's journey within the AAP and the Delhi government highlights the complexities and challenges of political appointments. While her contributions to the DDCD and her role in key initiatives cannot be overlooked, the controversies surrounding her appointments raise important questions about transparency and meritocracy in governance.

Bibhav Kumar: The Man Friday

Bibhav Kumar, a name that has become synonymous with controversy within the AAP, was a close aide and personal assistant to Kejriwal. Kumar's association with Kejriwal began during the IAC movement, where he worked as a video journalist, editing videos for the movement's magazine. His dedication and close working relationship with Kejriwal earned him a position as the CM's personal assistant when the AAP formed the government in Delhi in 2015. His role was re-engaged in 2020 when the AAP secured another term in office.

Kumar's influence within the AAP and his proximity to Kejriwal made him a powerful figure. He was involved in various key decisions and has played a significant role in managing the CMO. However, his rise to power has not been without controversy.

Kumar has been embroiled in several controversies, the most notable being his alleged involvement in the Delhi excise policy-linked money laundering probe and irregularities in the DJB. The ED conducted raids at multiple locations connected to Kumar and questioned him regarding the excise policy case. These allegations cast a shadow over his role within the Delhi government.

In April 2024, the Directorate of Vigilance terminated Kumar's services as Kejriwal's personal assistant, citing a pending case against him for obstruction and criminal charges dating back to 2007. The charges included assault or criminal force to deter a public servant from discharging their duty. Despite his termination, Kumar's influence within the AAP remained significant, highlighting the complexities of political power dynamics.[5]

The most recent and perhaps the most serious controversy involving Kumar is the alleged assault on AAP MP Swati Maliwal (as mentioned earlier).[6] On 13 May 2024, Maliwal accused Kumar of assaulting her at Kejriwal's residence. According to Maliwal, Kumar repeatedly slapped her, kicked her in the stomach and pelvic area and used abusive language. The incident allegedly occurred while Maliwal was waiting to meet Kejriwal.

Maliwal's allegations led to Kumar's arrest and subsequent judicial custody. The Delhi Police booked Kumar under stringent sections of the Indian Penal Code, including charges of criminal intimidation, assault and attempt to commit culpable homicide. The case sparked a political storm, with the AAP leaders accusing Maliwal of targeting Kejriwal at the behest of the BJP.[7]

The court proceedings were intense, with Maliwal breaking down in court while recounting the assault. The court denied Kumar's bail plea, citing the seriousness of the allegations and the potential for him to influence witnesses. The case highlighted the deep fissures within the AAP and raised questions about the party's internal dynamics and handling of such serious allegations. However, later he got bail on September 2024.[8]

Sandeep Pathak: The Strategic Mind Behind the AAP's Success

Sandeep Pathak, a prominent figure in the AAP, emerged as a key strategist and close aide to Kejriwal by 2017. His journey from academia to politics is marked by significant contributions to the AAP's electoral successes, particularly in Punjab and Gujarat.

Born in Bataha village in Mungeli, Chhattisgarh, Pathak's academic journey is impressive. He completed his early education in his village and later moved to Bilaspur for further studies. Pathak pursued his master's degree at the Indian Institute of Chemical Technology, Hyderabad, and the National Chemical

Laboratory, Pune. He then went on to earn a PhD in high-temperature superconducting materials from the University of Cambridge. Following his doctoral studies, Pathak engaged in post-doctoral research projects at the University of Oxford and MIT.

In 2016, Pathak joined the faculty of IIT Delhi as an assistant professor, where he worked on the fabrication of perovskite-based photovoltaic devices and its photo-physical properties. Despite his promising academic career, Pathak's passion for public service and policymaking led him to join the AAP in 2017.

Pathak's expertise in building organizational structures and his strategic acumen played a crucial role in the AAP's electoral victories. As the election-in-charge for Punjab and Gujarat in 2022, Pathak was instrumental in devising and implementing strategies that resonated with the electorate.

In Punjab, Pathak's behind-the-scenes work was pivotal in the AAP's landslide victory in the 2022 elections. His approach involved rigorous surveys to understand voter sentiments and issues, which formed the basis for the AAP's campaign design and messaging. Pathak's emphasis on addressing local issues, such as improving healthcare and education, helped the AAP connect with voters and secure a decisive mandate.

Similarly, in Gujarat, Pathak's strategic insights were crucial in the AAP's efforts to make inroads into a BJP stronghold. Although the AAP did not achieve the same level of success as in Punjab, the party managed to win five seats in the 2022 elections, securing a vote share of nearly 13 per cent. This performance earned the AAP the status of a national party and highlighted Pathak's ability to navigate challenging political landscapes.

Pathak's close association with Kejriwal dates back to the early days of the IAC movement. Pathak, who had recently completed his PhD, was drawn to Kejriwal's vision and joined the AAP to contribute to its mission of clean and effective governance. Over the years, Pathak's strategic contributions and loyalty cemented his position as one of Kejriwal's most trusted aides.

In December 2022, the AAP created the position of national general secretary (organization) to strengthen its organizational structure and expand its footprint across India. Pathak was appointed to this role, making him the first person to hold this position. His appointment was a recognition of his strategic prowess and his contributions to the AAP's electoral successes.

As the general secretary (organization), Pathak is responsible for overseeing the AAP's organizational activities and ensuring effective coordination across states. His role involves building robust party structures, formulating strategies for upcoming elections and guiding the AAP's expansion efforts.

Sanjay Singh: The Activist

Sanjay Singh has been a key figure in shaping the AAP's strategies and communications. Singh's journey from a social activist to a Rajya Sabha MP is marked by his dedication to public service and his strategic acumen.

Singh's early life was rooted in social activism. He founded the Azad Samaj Sewa Samiti in Lucknow in 1994, which focused on providing employment opportunities to the poor and advocated for the rights of street vendors. His commitment to social causes led him to work closely with socialist leader Raghu Thakur and participate in various welfare and socialist movements.

Singh's association with Kejriwal began during the RTI campaign in 2006 and the IAC movement. His active involvement in these movements laid the foundation for his role in the formation of the AAP in 2012. Singh quickly rose through the ranks, becoming a founding member of the party and a key strategist.

As a national spokesperson for the AAP, Singh has been instrumental in handling the party's communication with national political parties and other opposition parties. His eloquence and ability to articulate the AAP's positions have made him a prominent voice in Indian politics. Singh's role extends beyond mere communication; he is deeply involved in crafting the party's strategies and ensuring that the AAP's message resonates with the electorate.

Elected to the Rajya Sabha in January 2018, Sanjay Singh has played a crucial role in coordinating the AAP's parliamentary strategy. As a Rajya Sabha MP, he is responsible for floor coordination with other leaders and deciding on the party's stance on various issues. Singh's ability to navigate the complexities of parliamentary procedures and build alliances with other opposition parties has been vital in advancing the AAP's legislative agenda. One of Singh's notable contributions in Parliament has been his advocacy on issues such as child trafficking, stringent punishments for sexual abuse of children and the rights of street vendors. His efforts were recognized by UNICEF India, and he was felicitated with the PGC Award in 2020.[9]

However, Singh's political career has not been without controversies. In October 2023, he was arrested by the ED on allegations of bribery and involvement in the Delhi liquor policy case. After spending six months in custody, Singh was released on bail by the Supreme Court, which criticized the lack of concrete evidence against him. Despite these challenges, Singh has continued to be a vocal critic of the central government and a staunch advocate for the AAP's policies.

While the AAP emerged from a mass movement, it lacked leaders with deep-rooted political experience, especially those shaped by grassroots struggles. Among its ranks, Sanjay Singh stood out as a rare exception. Hailing from Uttar Pradesh and involved in political activism from a young age, Singh brought to the AAP qualities that were otherwise missing – street-level political instinct, powerful oratory, cross-party networking and strong negotiation skills. Unlike Kejriwal, Singh possessed the temperament and tools to operate in the broader national arena. Yet, despite his distinct stature, he remained under Kejriwal's shadow, never fully breaking out on his own – but still carving a unique place for himself within the party.

Part 5

The AAP Under Fire

21

Liquor-gate: Delhi Excise Policy Scam

During the first wave of COVID-19, when the entire country was grappling with the lockdown, I found myself making daily trips to the Delhi Secretariat. My work was directly tied to coordinating hospital services and overseeing stakeholders involved in COVID-19 treatment and hospitalization. It was a time of unprecedented crisis, and while the lockdown affected everyone in different ways, it put a unique strain on the government, particularly in terms of managing public health and economy.

The economic burden on the Delhi government was immense. As the streets emptied and transportation ground to a halt, the state's revenue, much of which came from petrol and diesel taxes, plummeted. Similarly, the closure of liquor shops – another key revenue stream – hit the government hard. Across the board, the usual flow of tax collections dried up, leaving the government in an economic freefall. Yet, while the revenue was shrinking, the government's expenses were skyrocketing, driven by the need to manage the public health crisis. Hospitals required resources, medical staff needed to be compensated and facilities had to be set up to accommodate the growing number of COVID-19 patients. The Delhi government was, quite simply, unprepared for the economic and logistical disaster that was unfolding.

One day, during an informal conversation, a senior official working as an officer on special duty (OSD) confided in me. 'The income of the Delhi government has come to a complete halt,' he said, his tone weary, 'but our spending is increasing exponentially. If the government doesn't take drastic measures to improve revenue, we are headed for a financial disaster.'

This looming crisis extended beyond the government. Political parties were also suffering from severe financial shortages. The AAP found itself in an increasingly precarious situation. Amidst this backdrop, the Delhi government began to work on a new excise or liquor policy. Initially seen as a means to stabilize the government's revenue, this policy quickly became a flashpoint of controversy between the AAP and the central government. What began as a fiscal necessity spiralled into a political showdown.

There are three crucial aspects to consider in understanding the fallout between the AAP and the BJP. First, the AAP did make mistakes in formulating several policies in Delhi. There were loopholes in the system and the party's inexperience in governance showed at times. Second, the BJP was eager to create a narrative that painted the AAP as hypocritical – a party that preached clean governance but was involved in corruption. Lastly, it is essential to acknowledge the unique scrutiny that the Delhi government faces. No government in India is immune to making mistakes or drafting policies that are less than foolproof, but Delhi's power structure means that the AAP's policies were subjected to far more intense scrutiny from the central government than those of other state governments.

The controversies surrounding the AAP and its governance during the pandemic reflect the complexities of navigating politics in a city where power is constantly contested. While the central government has leveraged these controversies to weaken the AAP, the party's grassroots support, built on its track record of service delivery, remained resilient. For many in Delhi, the question was not whether Kejriwal or his party was entirely free of corruption, but whether they were delivering on their promises amidst a crisis. And in this, the AAP held ground.

The Delhi Liquor Policy Controversy

As mentioned before, in response to the financial crisis during COVID-19, the Delhi government introduced a new excise policy in November 2021. The policy aimed to stabilize the government's revenue by privatizing the liquor trade. Under the new policy, the government exited the liquor trade entirely, shutting all government-run liquor stores and handing over the sale of liquor exclusively to private players. The policy was intended to eliminate the liquor mafia, increase revenue for the government and enhance the consumer experience.

The Delhi liquor policy, officially known as the Excise Policy 2021-22, became a major political flashpoint in India, causing significant friction between the AAP and the BJP-led central government. What started as a revenue-generating initiative during the pandemic soon spiralled into a series of corruption allegations, legal battles and political posturing that raised questions about governance, transparency and federal control.

Alcohol sales were a significant source of income for the state government, as liquor taxes made up a considerable portion of Delhi's revenue. In this context, the Delhi government sought to overhaul its liquor distribution system, moving from government control to a privatized model, which, they argued, would increase revenue, reduce corruption and improve customer experience.

Key Features of the Delhi Excise Policy 2021-22

1. **Privatization of Liquor Retail**: The policy shifted liquor retail from government-run shops to private entities. It divided Delhi into 32 zones, each with around 27 retail outlets, totalling approximately 849 private liquor stores. These stores were licensed through a competitive bidding process, aiming to modernize the retail experience with walk-in shops offering better ambiance and customer service.[1]
2. **Increase in License Fees for Revenue Growth**: The policy replaced the previous tax-based system with a license fee model. Retail and wholesale licenses were auctioned, requiring licensees to pay fixed fees, which aimed to boost government revenue. Estimates suggested an increase of ₹3,500 crore in excise revenue by curbing tax evasion and streamlining collections.[2]

3. **Liberalized Licensing and Market Competition**: The policy introduced a liberalized licensing regime, allowing more private players to enter the liquor market. It aimed to break the monopoly of a few suppliers, promote competition and ensure the availability of diverse liquor brands. Wholesalers were also given freedom to offer discounts, fostering a competitive market environment.[3]
4. **Age-Based Retail Regulations**: To regulate alcohol consumption, the policy lowered the legal drinking age to 21 from 25 for certain types of liquor and introduced measures like requiring age verification at retail points. It also allowed bars and restaurants to serve liquor until 3 a.m., extending operating hours to align with nightlife trends and boost hospitality revenue.[4]
5. **Home Delivery and Digital Integration**: The policy permitted home delivery of liquor through mobile apps or online portals, a novel feature aimed at convenience and modernizing sales. It emphasized digitization to track transactions, reduce illegal sales and enhance transparency in the supply chain, aligning with global trends in retail innovation.[5]

Allegation of Kickbacks

The allegations at the heart of the Delhi liquor policy controversy centre around an alleged kickback scheme orchestrated by the AAP leaders. The ED claimed that the new excise policy allowed private entities to obtain wholesale liquor licences with a fixed margin of 12 per cent, in return for a 6 per cent kickback. This kickback, the ED suggested, was funnelled to the AAP leaders to fund their political campaigns. According to the ED, these kickbacks were disguised as legitimate business transactions, making the money trail harder to trace.[6]

In conversations with sources close to central agencies, one insider revealed, 'We have evidence that key individuals involved accepted kickbacks, and the money was used to finance AAP's campaigns during the 2022 Goa and Punjab elections. The funds cannot be recovered because they have already been spent in these elections.'

At the centre of this controversy is Sisodia. Both the CBI and the ED accused Sisodia of playing a major role in the creation and execution of the liquor policy. They allege that he, along with other AAP leaders, received large sums from liquor businesses in exchange for preferential treatment. This included offering discounts, waiving licence fees and providing relief to liquor businesses impacted by the disruptions caused by the COVID-19 pandemic.

According to reports:

> [...]The Chief Secretary of the Delhi government submitted a report alleging 'ulterior motives of monetary gains' on the part of the accused in the implementation of the new policy, which the Delhi government then withdrew. The controversial policy, which was rolled out on November 17, 2021, had privatized and liberalized the liquor trade, with the Aam Aadmi Party (AAP) government projecting a revenue increase of ₹9,500 crore. The report has accused Mr Sisodia of 'deliberate and gross procedural lapses' to give 'undue benefits to liquor licensees' through the policy and receiving kickbacks through clandestine routes [...].[7]

The probe led to numerous raids and arrests, with Sisodia being one of the highest-profile figures apprehended. The CBI conducted searches at 30 locations, seizing documents and evidence related to the case. Meanwhile, the ED's investigation uncovered alleged money laundering through various channels, adding another layer of complexity to the case. The intricate financial trail and the involvement of prominent political figures has made this case a flashpoint in Delhi's political landscape, deepening the rivalry between the AAP and the central government.[8]

Kejriwal stated that the CBI had not approved the report of the chief secretary. He mentioned that the case is based on a narrative suggesting that some liquor companies paid money to other liquor companies. Kejriwal questioned the involvement of the AAP or Sisodia, noting that over 800 officers investigated the AAP leaders but did not find any evidence of a scam.[9]

During a press conference, Kejriwal claimed that over 1,000 raids failed to find evidence of corruption. 'The agencies have searched the houses and lockers of our leaders. They claimed that we spent money on the Goa Assembly election and questioned our vendors. But they found nothing. We had made all payments through cheques,' he said.[10]

The Arrest of AAP Leaders

- **Arvind Kejriwal** was arrested by the ED on 21 March 2024. The ED alleged that Kejriwal was involved in the formulation of the liquor policy, which was designed to benefit certain private entities in exchange for kickbacks.
- **Manish Sisodia** was arrested by the CBI in February 2023. Sisodia was accused of playing a pivotal role in drafting and implementing the policy, allegedly receiving substantial sums of money from liquor businesses for preferential treatment.
- **Sanjay Singh** was arrested by the ED in October 2023. Singh was accused of being a key conspirator in the case, allegedly collecting kickbacks from the liquor scam.
- **Vijay Nair** was arrested by the CBI in November 2021. Nair was accused of conspiring with others to secure undue benefits by circumventing the provisions of the excise policy for the year 2021–22.

To understand the real impact of these controversies, I took to the streets of Delhi, speaking with people from different walks of life to gauge their perspectives. At a small tea shop in Adarsh Nagar, I met Deepak Sharma, a 57-year-old daily-wage worker in 2024. When I asked him about the allegations of corruption against Kejriwal and the AAP, he responded thoughtfully, '*Ghotala sabhi party karti hai, lekin sarkari kaam bandh nahi hona chahiye. Kejriwal ki giraftari ke baad sarkari kaam bandh ho gaya. Yeh nahi hona chahiye tha* (Every party has its share of corruption, but government work should not come to a halt. After Kejriwal's arrest, all government work stopped. That shouldn't have happened).'

His words revealed a deeper truth about public sentiment. While people are aware of the allegations, there is also a pragmatic acceptance that corruption exists in every political party. What truly matters to people like Deepak Sharma is the continuity of government services. The disruption caused by the arrest of Kejriwal hit ordinary citizens hard, especially those who rely on government schemes and services for their livelihoods.

When I pressed Deepak on whether he believed Kejriwal himself was corrupt, he paused before saying, '*Ghotala toh hua hai, par kisne kiya, pata nahi* (Corruption has happened, but who did it, I don't know).' His uncertainty reflects the broader public confusion surrounding the allegations. While the media and political opponents have been quick to paint the AAP as corrupt, many citizens are unsure of the truth. They are caught between the narratives spun by political parties and their own lived experiences of governance.

Involvement of 'South Lobby' and the Larger Debate

The Delhi liquor policy controversy took a significant turn with the emergence of the 'South Lobby' during investigations by the ED and the CBI. This lobby, allegedly connected to the Bharat Rashtra Samithi (BRS) led by former Telangana CM K. Chandrashekar Rao (KCR), added another layer of complexity to the case. The ties between BRS and the AAP have been close politically, with their leaders frequently sharing platforms. Kejriwal and KCR were often seen together, particularly when KCR visited Delhi government-run schools and mohalla clinics, praising the AAP's model of governance.

The narrative around the South Lobby intensified when the ED arrested Kejriwal in connection with the alleged excise policy scam. The ED claimed that Kejriwal had requested a sum of ₹100 crore from the South Group to fund the AAP's Punjab elections. Earlier, in February 2023, the ED had also stated that the South

Group was intricately involved in the Delhi excise policy scam, working in collaboration with the AAP leaders.[11]

The South Group, according to the ED's findings, included several prominent figures such as former YSRCP MP Magunta Sreenivasulu Reddy, his son Magunta Raghava Reddy, BRS MLC (member of Legislative Council) K. Kavitha and businessman Abhishek Boinpally, among others. These individuals allegedly conspired with key officials like Nair and Sameer Mahendru to form a cartel that would benefit from the changes in the excise policy, allowing them to recoup kickbacks paid to the AAP leaders. The allegations suggested a calculated manipulation of the policy to favour specific liquor businesses, leading to a significant windfall for the conspirators.[12]

A CBI probe uncovered digital evidence from the systems at a hotel business centre in Delhi, where members of the South Lobby allegedly met with the AAP's Nair to finalize the details of the excise policy. The CBI officials claimed that the South Lobby aimed to secure exorbitant profits by influencing the policy, particularly through the increase in profit margins for liquor wholesalers.[13]

Further forensic analysis revealed a draft note from the group of ministers (GoM) dated 15 March 2021, which initially proposed a 5 per cent profit margin for wholesalers. However, the final draft of the excise policy, which was submitted just days later, increased this margin to 12 per cent, a key point of contention in the case.[14] The CBI alleged that during this period, Nair had met with the South Lobby members to finalize these favourable changes.

According to reports, on 18 March, Sisodia, who also held the excise portfolio, allegedly called his Secretary C. Arvind to Kejriwal's residence, where he was given a document, which was a draft of the GoM's report on the excise policy, to be put before the council of ministers.

However, the AAP claimed that this revelation by C. Arvind does not mean anything. Former Delhi CM Atishi said:

> Arvind Kejriwal told in the Rouse Avenue court that his arrest is based on just four statements. Among these, the first statement is from Manish Sisodia's secretary, C. Aravind, who simply mentioned that some documents related to the excise policy were handed over to him at the Chief Minister's residence. Nowhere in C. Aravind's statement does it imply that Arvind Kejriwal took money or received any funds from anyone. There's no mention of any financial transactions.[15]

One critical moment in the investigation occurred when the CBI discovered that the number of pages photocopied by the South Lobby members at the hotel's business centre matched the GoM report handed over by Sisodia to his secretary. This report included the controversial 12 per cent profit margin for wholesalers and higher turnover eligibility, aligning with the suggestions discussed by South Lobby members in chat records recovered by the CBI.[16]

As the investigation deepened, the CBI found that the recommendations of an expert committee, which had originally been tasked with revising the excise policy, were disregarded. The committee's October 2020 report did not advocate for the zonal licence system at the retail level or privatization at the wholesale level. Yet, these elements were introduced later, following the GoM's recommendations, under Sisodia's supervision.[17]

The GoM – consisting of Sisodia, Satyendar Jain and Kailash Gahlot – was accused of making decisions favourable to private liquor interests. These decisions, the CBI alleged, were influenced by Nair's meetings with liquor traders and middlemen, including those connected to the South Lobby. The central agencies also claimed that Nair played a pivotal role in soliciting money from liquor traders in exchange for favourable policy terms. These traders, according to the investigation, worked closely with the South Lobby to ensure the policy benefited them disproportionately.[18]

The AAP has vehemently denied the allegations made by the CBI and the ED in the Delhi liquor policy controversy, countering with claims of its own. According to the AAP, the BJP is the one with actual ties to the so-called South Lobby. Former Minister of Health Saurabh Bharadwaj pointed to Magunta Sreenivasulu Reddy, who was arrested by the ED in connection with the case. Bharadwaj highlighted that Sreenivasulu Reddy had been fielded by the BJP's ally, the Telugu Desam Party (TDP), in the 2024 Lok Sabha elections. This, according to the AAP, demonstrated a direct link between the BJP and the South Lobby.[19]

Bharadwaj elaborated on this claim during a press interaction, stating that Sreenivasulu Reddy initially gave two statements in which he explicitly denied any discussions with Kejriwal regarding the excise policy. However, Bharadwaj alleged that after Reddy's son Raghava was arrested, he eventually succumbed to pressure and issued a third statement that contradicted his earlier claims. This new statement implicated Kejriwal, raising questions about the timing and circumstances under which it was made. Similarly, Bharadwaj noted that Raghava himself had not mentioned Kejriwal's name in six earlier statements but later added it in a seventh statement. Bharadwaj suggested that this change in testimony came after Raghava became a government witness, a move that allowed him to secure bail.[20]

Bharadwaj further challenged the integrity of the investigation, calling for scrutiny of Sreenivasulu's and Raghava's association with the BJP. He urged investigative agencies to examine years of phone records between the two parties, asserting that even a preliminary inquiry would expose a 'direct nexus' between the two parties. 'The ED should also investigate Magunta Reddy and Raghav Magunta's direct association with the BJP,' he remarked. Bharadwaj expressed confidence that an honest investigation would reveal the truth, separating 'fact from fiction'.[21]

The AAP has consistently maintained that the charges against its leaders, particularly Kejriwal and Sisodia, are politically motivated. They have accused the BJP of orchestrating these probes as part of a broader effort to tarnish the party's image. This counter-allegation involving the South Lobby is part of the

AAP's narrative that the BJP, not the AAP, is working with questionable entities in the liquor business.

Political Impact

The political fallout from the liquor policy controversy has been one of the most severe blows to the AAP since its inception. The scandal didn't just challenge the party – it struck at the very core of its identity: the promise of clean, corruption-free governance. For a political movement born out of the anti-corruption crusade, allegations of corruption in a policy like the liquor trade, which directly affected public interests, was a devastating turn of events. The magnitude of this crisis cannot be overstated, particularly given that the AAP's brand was built on the moral capital of being a fresh alternative to the corruption-riddled mainstream parties.

Satyendar Jain, Delhi's former health minister, was arrested in a money laundering case, and soon after, Sisodia – widely regarded as the backbone of the Delhi administration – was also apprehended. Sisodia, with his extensive portfolio, managed most of the day-to-day affairs of the Delhi government. Kejriwal, AAP's figurehead, held no official portfolios, leaving Sisodia to handle governance responsibilities directly. With Sisodia and Jain behind bars, the very foundation of the Delhi government's operational structure crumbled.

The arrests led to widespread demoralization, both within the party and among its supporters. On the one hand, the people of Delhi felt the impact as governmental functions came to a standstill. On the other, the AAP's rank and file were left demoralized, grappling with the twin crises of leadership arrests and mounting public dissatisfaction.

Shailendra Sharma, the principal advisor to the Directorate of Education in Delhi, remarked on the impact: 'The work of the Delhi government never stopped, but the arrests made a lot of people demoralized. The central government, through the Lieutenant Governor, always interfered in the good work of AAP, and this situation led to a setback for the government's work indeed.' Sharma's statement underscores the internal and external pressures the AAP faced in continuing its governance amidst legal challenges and central interference.

Meanwhile, the BJP, recognizing its own organizational weaknesses in Delhi, saw an opportunity to strike. Despite ruling India nationally, the BJP had struggled to build a credible, strong face in Delhi who could take on Kejriwal. As discussed, over time, the AAP's dominance in the capital led the BJP to shift strategies, crafting a narrative aimed at undercutting the AAP's moral high ground. The arrest of its key leaders, along with the liquor policy scandal, became the perfect vehicle for this assault.

Nisthula Hebbar explained the BJP's strategy succinctly: 'The BJP's narrative against the AAP is that it is a political party of corrupt people. However, it is true that all the leaders of the AAP are now out on bail in 2025, but the BJP has successfully established this narrative.' Hebbar's analysis reveals how, regardless of judicial outcomes, the damage to the AAP's image is what mattered most to the BJP. By consistently associating the AAP with corruption, the BJP has sought to erode the trust that Kejriwal's party had built over the years.

As for opposition parties, their stance has been more nuanced. In the past, during the 2024 Lok Sabha elections in Delhi and some other states, the AAP and the Congress briefly joined hands to contest Delhi together. Despite ideological differences, the Congress condemned Kejriwal's arrest, offering rhetorical support. Yet, as the scandal grew, the Congress's backing remained superficial. Their endorsement was, at best, half-hearted – an acknowledgment of political alliances but not a defence of the liquor policy itself.

Other opposition parties also took a cautious approach. While they condemned the arrests of the AAP leaders, few publicly dismissed the allegations surrounding the liquor policy. Hebbar compared the response of the AAP to how Kalpana Soren (the wife of JMM Chief and Jharkhand CM Hemant Soren, as mentioned earlier) galvanized support after his arrest. The AAP, she pointed out, failed to muster similar solidarity or mobilization after the arrests of Sisodia and Kejriwal.

A senior AAP leader, speaking anonymously, revealed that the party had tried to rally opposition parties behind Kejriwal. 'We did try to get all the opposition parties to rally behind Kejriwal's arrest. They condemned it, but no one was willing to take on the liquor policy scam head-on,' the leader said. After Kejriwal's arrest, his wife Sunita organized a large rally in Delhi, aiming to show strength and solidarity. While opposition leaders, including those from the Congress, participated, they distanced themselves from making it an outright defence of Kejriwal. 'They were scared,' the senior AAP leader admitted, pointing out the reluctance of the Opposition to be seen as fully endorsing the AAP's narrative.

This political isolation left the AAP vulnerable. The BJP's narrative of corruption, combined with the lack of robust opposition support, has placed the party in a precarious position. What once was its greatest strength – the promise of clean governance – now feels fragile. As the party battles its way through legal and political storms, the fallout from these scandals has reshaped its standing in Delhi and beyond.

Reasons for the Massive Political Impact

In many ways, the AAP never envisioned that a controversy of this scale, involving accusations of financial misconduct, would be aimed at them. The sheer enormity of this crisis seemed to catch the party off guard. While formulating the liquor policy, there were gaps in judgement and a lack of vigilance. In hindsight, it is clear that the Delhi government, in its enthusiasm to reform the liquor trade, let its guard down in crucial areas of transparency and accountability.

Ashutosh, a former AAP leader and now a political columnist, once reflected on the ideological crossroads the party found itself at. He said:

> A political party which came into existence based on its moral capital, if it loses that moral capital, it means you are appropriated by the politics of India itself. If the AAP

> had remained the AAP of 2014 or 2015, maybe this kind of crisis would not have happened. It has faced this crisis because it tried to imitate the conventional political parties of India.

Ashutosh's insight is telling; he suggested that the AAP's drift from its original ideals was not just a deviation but a transformation that led to its vulnerability.

Political analyst Amitabh Tiwari, in an interview for the book, pointed out the BJP's keen understanding of the AAP's potential: 'AAP is the only political party which had the opportunity, ambition and plan of expansion beyond Delhi, and that is why it is natural that the BJP came after it.' Tiwari's observation highlights the broader strategic battle at play. The liquor policy controversy, while ostensibly about a policy misstep, became a symbol of a larger political war aimed at curbing the AAP's rise.

Another significant factor in this crisis is the AAP's internal structure. Despite governing two states, the party has always been centred around its Delhi leadership. The liquor policy investigation, which implicated the top leaders – Kejriwal, Sisodia and Sanjay Singh – left the AAP vulnerable, as there was no established second-tier leadership to step in and manage the crisis. The controversy exposed the party's over-reliance on its top brass and raised questions about its ability to decentralize leadership and groom new faces capable of carrying the AAP's banner at the national level.

During a conversation with Ashutosh, he highlighted this organizational weakness. Unlike larger and more established parties like the Congress or the BJP, the AAP lacked both the institutional memory and organizational resilience to weather a scandal of this magnitude. 'AAP doesn't have the robust institutional framework to deal with a crisis of this order,' Ashutosh said. This lack of organizational depth became glaringly evident as the party struggled to respond cohesively to the allegations, while its leaders were pulled into legal battles and public scrutiny.

A crucial aspect of this saga is how deeply intertwined the AAP's identity is with Kejriwal, as we have discussed before. Over the years, Kejriwal has become synonymous with the party itself, and in doing so, he has never allowed another leader to emerge as a clear second-in-command. This centralization of power worked for the AAP when it was fighting its early battles, but in a crisis like this, it left the party without alternative voices to stabilize the ship. Kejriwal's reluctance to cultivate a broader leadership team means that when he is under attack, so is the entire party's ability to function.

The liquor policy controversy, then, is not just a story about corruption allegations – it is a reflection of deeper structural challenges within the AAP. The party's journey raises uncomfortable questions about how political movements evolve, and the risks they face when they stray from their founding principles. As the investigation continues and the legal battles play out, the long-term impact of this controversy on the AAP's image and prospects remains to be seen.

What is clear, however, is that this episode will be a defining chapter in the AAP's history. The party's response to this crisis, its ability to recover and regain public trust, and its capacity to reinvent its internal structures will determine whether it can continue its journey as a significant political force in India. For now, the liquor policy scandal has cast a long shadow over the AAP's once-untouchable image of integrity and clean governance.

22

Liquor Scam Aftermath: Kejriwal's Second Resignation

As discussed in the previous chapter, Kejriwal's arrest in 2024, months before the Lok Sabha elections, marked a critical juncture for him and for the AAP.

Despite securing bail in the ED case by July 2024, his detention continued due to the CBI charges. It is pertinent to mention that earlier the Delhi High Court had upheld Kejriwal's ED arrest citing substantial evidence and dismissing claims of political vendetta. The court had argued that, as a significant political figure, Kejriwal could influence witnesses, which justified his prolonged detention.[1]

The case saw a dramatic turn when the Supreme Court intervened on 13 September 2024, granting Kejriwal regular bail in the CBI case.[2] However, the relief came with strict conditions, signalling the judiciary's cautious approach. Kejriwal was barred from making public comments on the case, restricted from entering his office or the Delhi Secretariat and was required to attend all court hearings. Even his ability to sign official documents was curtailed, requiring prior approval from the LG, effectively limiting his functional authority as CM.

These restrictions highlight the gravity of the case and its impact on governance in Delhi. Kejriwal's inability to access his office or engage in official duties without clearance left the AAP in a precarious position, raising concerns about the party's leadership dynamics during Kejriwal's legal troubles. While the bail was a relief for the party, the stringent conditions underscore the challenges Kejriwal faced in reclaiming his administrative and political momentum.

Kejriwal's handling of this crisis was crucial for both his personal credibility and the AAP's future. While his supporters argued that the case was politically motivated, critics pointed to the stringent conditions imposed by the judiciary as indicative of the seriousness of the allegations. For the AAP, the road ahead demands a strategic recalibration to rebuild its image and sustain its momentum in Delhi politics.

Kejriwal was Delhi's CM from 2013 to 2024, except for a brief period of Central Rule in 2014-15. A decade-long tenure inevitably brings anti-incumbency challenges. Kejriwal's decision to resign as Delhi's CM for a second time, announced shortly after his release from Tihar Jail, left political observers and the public alike questioning his motives. When I spoke to a senior AAP leader to understand the rationale behind Kejriwal's resignation, the response reflected confusion and dissatisfaction. The leader, who preferred to remain anonymous, remarked, 'I don't think Arvind Kejriwal should resign. It sends the wrong message. Perhaps he is aiming for early elections.' It was believed that by calling for early polls, he hoped to capitalize on public sympathy and the AAP's ability to set the agenda before poll restrictions limit new policy announcements. Further, early elections would also shorten the time available for opposition parties to mobilize and campaign effectively.

The move was a dramatic turn in Delhi's political narrative, coming just months before the 2025 Assembly elections. While Kejriwal framed his resignation as a step towards seeking justice from the people, the underlying motivations appeared more strategic than altruistic.

Legal Restrictions and Governance Efficiency

The restrictions mentioned previously effectively rendered him a CM in name only and severely curtailed his ability to govern. Continuing under such conditions would have exposed his government to criticism for inefficiency and policy paralysis, providing ample fodder for the BJP and other opposition parties to target him.

As mentioned before, many AAP MLAs speculated that Kejriwal's resignation was intended to call for an early election. However, within 24 hours, it became apparent that his plan also included appointing Atishi as the new CM. This decision seemed calculated: Kejriwal and the AAP aimed to finish pending projects before elections were announced. They recognized that once the model code of conduct was in effect, new schemes could only be announced, not implemented, and that would prove an obstacle in securing votes. By stepping aside, they hoped to gain time to formulate impactful policies.

At the same time, the AAP leaders were acutely aware of growing public dissatisfaction. Despite his landslide victory in 2020, Kejriwal's government had failed to deliver on several major promises. For instance, his pledge to clean the Yamuna remained unfulfilled. Similarly, the promise of 24×7 water supply to every household had not materialized, and the fight against pollution stagnated. These unmet promises created a perception of stagnation in governance, exacerbated by Kejriwal's recent legal troubles.

During a conversation with Radheshyam, a 56-year-old vegetable vendor from Mayur Vihar Phase-1 in September 2024, he voiced his frustration, saying, 'Arvind Kejriwal went to jail, and Delhi has been left in a state of neglect because no government work is getting done. Look at the roads – they are in poor condition. There are frequent power cuts and a severe water crisis in many areas, including Mayur Vihar. Why should we vote for Kejriwal?'

This sentiment reflected a broader wave of dissatisfaction among the residents of Delhi. Many felt that the government had been paralysed due to Kejriwal's absence while he was in jail. Concerns about stalled public works, deteriorating infrastructure and basic utility disruptions fuelled resentment, with some questioning his decision to remain CM despite his legal troubles.

Amidst this growing unease, is when Kejriwal sought to shift the narrative by proposing Atishi's appointment as the CM. It was a bid to introduce a fresh face while retaining Kejriwal's influence behind the scenes. It was believed that Atishi, known for her contributions to education reform in Delhi, could help reinvigorate the AAP's image and deflect some of the criticism directed at Kejriwal personally.

This transition also allowed the AAP to highlight its governance record, focusing on achievements rather than the controversies surrounding its leader. With a new CM, the AAP campaigned as a team rather than a one-man show, which has often been a point of criticism against the party.

Public Sympathy and Vendetta Politics

By resigning, Kejriwal also avoided the image of a compromised leader unable to act. Instead, he positioned himself as a victim of 'vendetta politics' by the BJP-led central government. This narrative aligned with the AAP's broader messaging, which often portrayed the party as a crusader against corruption and an underdog fighting a powerful adversary.

Stepping down allowed Kejriwal to frame the then upcoming 2025 elections as a referendum on his leadership and the BJP's alleged misuse of central agencies. It is possible that it was believed that these strategies could galvanize the AAP's base, especially if Kejriwal positioned himself as a leader willing to face the people's judgement rather than cling to power under a cloud of controversy.

The resignation allowed Kejriwal to distance himself from the allegations and reclaim the moral high ground. His narrative of undergoing an '*agnipariksha* (trial by fire)' could resonate with voters, particularly those who remained loyal to the AAP's founding ideals.[3]

Additionally, the resignation might have also been part of a broader strategy to position the AAP as a national player. By framing himself as a victim of central overreach, he strengthened his narrative against the BJP, which could resonate beyond Delhi. This move came at a time when the AAP was eyeing expansion in states like Punjab, Gujarat and Haryana.

Fear of Central Rule

One of the most pressing threats Kejriwal faced at that time was the possibility of central rule being imposed in Delhi. The BJP leaders had vocally criticized his prolonged absence and the alleged governance vacuum it created. Resigning pre-emptively neutralized this threat, as it removed the grounds for the BJP to justify such a move. Additionally, it positioned the AAP to demand elections on its own terms, rather than being at the mercy of central intervention.

While the resignation might seem like a masterstroke, it is not without risks. By stepping down, Kejriwal ceded the immediate reins of power, leaving the AAP's governance record vulnerable to criticism. Moreover, the move could backfire if voters perceive it as a tactic to evade accountability rather than a genuine act of principle.

Additionally, the corruption allegations continue to loom large. Even with a new face like Atishi at the helm, the AAP will need to address these charges convincingly to rebuild trust among sceptical voters. The party also faces the challenge of managing internal dissent, as not all the AAP leaders were reportedly on board with the decision to replace Kejriwal as CM.

Kejriwal's resignation was a high-stakes gamble aimed at turning a crisis into an opportunity. By stepping down, he sought to reframe the narrative around his leadership, neutralize criticism and position the AAP for electoral success. However, the success of this strategy will depend on how effectively AAP can address governance challenges, manage the transition of power and convince voters of its commitment to Delhi's development.

The 2025 Delhi Assembly election marked a turning point for Kejriwal and the AAP culminating in their resounding defeat. In the aftermath, it became evident that Kejriwal's resignation was a grave misstep, one that eroded public trust and fuelled disillusionment. The timing of his decision proved particularly damaging. While Kejriwal's imprisonment could have justified a resignation – potentially seen as a principled stand – his choice to step down only after his release baffled many. During his incarceration, Delhi's government languished without clear leadership, leaving citizens grappling with administrative paralysis. When Kejriwal emerged from jail, the public expected him to seize the opportunity to restore stability and rectify the chaos. Instead, his abrupt resignation raised questions about his intentions, governance and commitment to Delhi's welfare.

For many, the resignation signalled indecision that stalled critical development projects and disrupted essential government functions. Others speculated that mounting allegations of corruption forced his hand, casting a shadow over his leadership. As public frustration grew, the 2025 election transformed into a referendum not on the BJP's merits, but on Kejriwal and the AAP's failures. Disenchanted voters, distancing themselves from AAP, cast their ballots not to crown the BJP, but to reject Kejriwal's faltering vision, sealing the party's electoral fate.

23

Atishi: The New Delhi CM

When Kejriwal returned as Delhi's CM for a third term in 2020, speculation was rife about Atishi's induction into the cabinet. Many within the AAP believed she deserved the role, given her contributions to shaping Delhi's education policies. In the AAP's first cabinet, Rakhi Birla was the sole woman minister, but since then, Kejriwal had avoided appointing women to his council of ministers. Few would have predicted that within a few years, circumstances would compel Atishi not only to join the cabinet but also to rise as Delhi's CM.

Atishi's leadership credentials were built on a track record of relentless work alongside Sisodia, particularly in transforming Delhi's public education system. As an MLA, her administrative and strategic prowess became evident, earning her a reputation as one of AAP's most efficient performers. Her eventual ascent to leadership reflects a combination of merit and political necessity, underscoring her vital role in the party's governance model. Her journey symbolizes not just her individual growth but also the evolving dynamics of the AAP, where leadership and loyalty converge.

Born to professors Tripta Wahi and Vijay Singh, Atishi grew up in an academically inclined household in Delhi. She attended Springdales School before pursuing history at St Stephen's College. Her academic journey then took her to the University of Oxford, where she earned two master's degrees – one through a Chevening Scholarship and another as a Rhodes Scholar, specializing in educational research.

After returning to India, Atishi took an unconventional path. She initially taught at a school, then spent years in rural Madhya Pradesh, focusing on organic farming and progressive education. By 2013, she had joined the fledgling AAP and contributed to the drafting of its maiden manifesto. Her intellectual rigour and commitment to public policy began to take shape as cornerstones of her career.

As we know, when the AAP first came to power in Delhi in 2013, it was for a brief 49 days. During this period, Atishi worked largely behind the scenes. Following the AAP's sweeping 2015 victory, her role became more defined when she was appointed as an advisor to the education minister. However, internal party strife soon engulfed the AAP, with founding members Prashant Bhushan and Yogendra Yadav parting ways. Atishi, initially perceived as being aligned with the dissidents, chose to side with Kejriwal and Sisodia, cementing her loyalty to the party's leadership.

Her contributions to Delhi's education reforms were significant. Atishi was instrumental in launching initiatives like Mission Buniyaad, aimed at strengthening foundational literacy and numeracy, and the much-lauded Happiness Curriculum. These programmes helped redefine public education in Delhi, garnering national and international acclaim.

In the summer of 2018, I vividly recall receiving an urgent call from a journalist friend: 'The BJP has removed Atishi as an advisor to Manish ji. This is a big story. Let's head to the AAP office.' Upon reaching the scene, we learnt that the Union Ministry of

Home Affairs had advised the cancellation of appointments for 10 advisors to Delhi's AAP ministers. But what stood out that day was the fiery response from Sisodia, then Delhi's education minister, who zeroed in on one name: Atishi.

'This orders' actual intention is to remove the adviser to Education Minister, Atishi. Their target is Atishi,' Sisodia declared. 'She is that woman who is working to take the Delhi government's education to new heights. She has studied from the Oxford University, but works as the adviser at a salary of one rupee.'[1]

At the time, Atishi wasn't the household name she is today. Fast forward six years, and her rise to prominence is nothing short of remarkable. In 2023 as Delhi's new education minister, she held an unprecedented 13 portfolios, running the government in the absence of her mentors, Sisodia and Kejriwal, both of whom are embroiled in legal troubles.

The removal of Atishi as an advisor in 2018 was a defining moment. While the controversy underscored the BJP's growing opposition to the AAP's governance model, it also marked Atishi's transition from a backroom strategist to a public figure. Later that year, she was announced as the AAP's candidate for the East Delhi constituency in the 2019 Lok Sabha elections.

This period also saw Atishi recalibrate her public persona. She dropped the second name given by her parents, 'Marlena' – which was a tribute to Marx and Lenin – reportedly to counter the BJP propaganda labelling her as a Christian. The party officially began referring to her simply as 'Atishi'. She also attended a Kshatriya community event where she was referred to as 'Atishi Singh'. However, despite a spirited campaign, she lost the 2019 election.[2]

Atishi's political career took a decisive turn in 2020 when she won the Delhi Assembly elections from the Kalkaji constituency. Over the next few years, she became one of the AAP's most trusted leaders. Her portfolio expanded significantly, and she took charge of crucial initiatives as a cabinet minister. Atishi was increasingly seen as the torchbearer of the AAP's Delhi Model of Governance, characterized by robust education and healthcare reforms.

Atishi's rise began in earnest in March 2023, when she, along with Saurabh Bharadwaj, was inducted into the Delhi cabinet following the arrests of Sisodia and Satyendar Jain. Taking charge of key portfolios like education, finance, PWD and law, she showcased remarkable efficiency in navigating governance challenges during one of the AAP's most turbulent periods.[3] Despite being a first-time MLA and minister, her diligence and unwavering loyalty to Kejriwal ensured her rise to the top. Party insiders highlighted her work ethic and ability to manage crises as key reasons for her elevation.

In 2024, amidst rising public dissatisfaction over governance delays and Kejriwal's continued detention, Atishi was chosen as the CM. This decision underscored her unique position within the party: a blend of intellectual rigour, political adaptability and loyalty.

Atishi's rise in the AAP was as dramatic as it was polarizing. From an Oxford-educated policymaker to a politician deeply embedded in the AAP's ideological shifts, her journey is as much about her capabilities as it is about her loyalty. But her comments on the communal violence in Jahangirpuri in 2022 – blaming 'Rohingyas' and 'illegal Bangladeshis' – left me puzzled, given her progressive background.[4]

I then reached out to a senior AAP leader, hoping to understand how someone like Atishi could align with such rhetoric. His response was both pragmatic and telling: 'In politics, moving on is the best policy. Atishi's greatest strength is that she is not stuck to her past but aligns with the present – the party line of Arvind Kejriwal. Her loyalty is unmatched.'

This statement encapsulates Atishi's political journey: one defined by adaptation and allegiance. Her early years in the AAP, marked by her contributions to the party's education model as mentioned before, showcased her intellect and vision. Yet, as her public persona evolved, so did her political strategies, aligning closely with Kejriwal's calculated balancing of governance and nationalism.

Critics, however, are quick to point out that Atishi's ascent is less about merit and more about necessity. Ashutosh, a former AAP leader, was candid in his assessment: 'Atishi's prominence today is because Kejriwal needs her. He uses people based on the needs of the hour.'

This sentiment underscores the transactional nature of the AAP's internal politics. Kejriwal, known for his shrewd political instincts, has often built and rebuilt his team around loyalty rather than ideological consistency. Atishi's unwavering support for him, even at the cost of compromising her progressive ideals, seems to be a cornerstone of her rise within the party.

Her trajectory raises critical questions: Is Atishi a reflection of the AAP's ability to nurture talent or is she merely a product of Kejriwal's tactical manoeuvring? The truth likely lies somewhere in between. While her capabilities are undeniable, her journey also highlights the compromises that define contemporary Indian politics – where adaptability and loyalty often trump steadfast principles.

Kejriwal's Strategic Choice for Delhi's Top Post

Kejriwal's decision to appoint Atishi as Delhi's CM was not merely a reflection of her administrative capabilities but a strategic move driven by political pragmatism and loyalty.Selecting Atishi was a way to consolidate the AAP's growing support among women voters – a demographic that has become central to the party's electoral success. Until 2015, Kejriwal and the AAP struggled to resonate with women voters. However, a slew of pro-women policies, such as free bus travel for women and widespread installation of CCTV cameras for enhanced safety, began to shift this dynamic. By the 2020 Delhi Assembly elections, women had emerged as a strong support base for the AAP (as discussed earlier).

Building on this momentum, the AAP government introduced a direct benefit scheme in March 2024, offering ₹1,000 per month (later increased to ₹2,100) to women above 18 years as Mahila Samman Yojana. Bringing Atishi to the forefront as CM later in the year reinforced this outreach. Her leadership symbolized the party's commitment to women's empowerment, sending a strong signal ahead of the 2025 Delhi elections.

Kejriwal's trust in Atishi extends beyond her administrative prowess. Her loyalty to the party, and to him personally, played a crucial role in her appointment. Atishi has consistently stood by Kejriwal through the AAP's highs and lows, even during internal party rifts. Her allegiance was underscored by symbolic gestures, such as keeping an empty chair beside her during meetings as a tribute to Kejriwal. This act encapsulated her role as a caretaker rather than a competitor for the top post.

In contrast, as we know, other prominent leaders like Raghav Chadha, once a star face of the party, distanced themselves from the internal struggle following Kejriwal's arrest. Chadha, tainted by allegations in the excise policy case, lacked the clean slate that Atishi brought to the table.[5]

Atishi's leadership also highlighted her ability to navigate political alliances. She led protests across Delhi, coordinated with national opposition parties like the Congress, TMC and Samajwadi Party, and kept the AAP's political machinery functional. Her rise to prominence, while criticized by some as driven by loyalty rather than merit, also reflects her adaptability and political acumen.

For Kejriwal, Atishi represents a bridge between governance and political strategy—a leader who can hold the fort while ensuring the party's ideological and electoral goals remain intact.

24

The AAP vs Centre: Tale of Three Lieutenant Governors

As I have described the Delhi liquor policy scam and the aftermath in this part of the book, it is also important to look into the fundamental reason behind the entire turmoil. This fundamental reason is the constant conflict between the AAP and the central government. The Centre tries to keep a check on the Delhi government in two ways. One is through LGs, and the other one is through bureaucracy. In this chapter, we look into the conflict between the AAP and the LGs.

I remember vividly the morning of August 2016 in Delhi, a city that was still new to me. I was a fresh-faced journalism student at a media school nestled in the heart of Old Delhi. The city, with its chaotic charm and historical grandeur, was both overwhelming and exhilarating. That morning, however, was different. My phone buzzed incessantly and on the other end were my parents, their voices tinged with worry. They had just read about a shootout in Old Delhi, and their concern was palpable.

'What is Chief Minister Arvind Kejriwal doing?' my father demanded. 'He hasn't even issued a statement. It's his jurisdiction; he should speak up.' I was still groggy, the remnants of sleep clouding my thoughts, and I struggled to piece together a coherent response. The situation was confusing, and I was still trying to grasp the intricacies of Delhi's governance.

Many people, including my parents, believed that the police and the administration of Delhi were under the control of the Delhi government. However, the reality was far more complex. Despite being the capital of India, Delhi is not a full-fledged state but a Union territory. This distinction means that the central government holds significant authority over the city's police administration.

The AAP government, despite its electoral mandate at that time, had control over only a few fundamental issues. Delhi's administrative structure is trifurcated, with different bodies handling various aspects of governance.[1] The Delhi government oversees education, health, electricity, transport, water and other essential services. Meanwhile, civic issues fall under the purview of the municipal corporations. For a long time, Delhi had three separate municipal corporations, but they were recently merged into one entity by a central government law. Another key player in Delhi's governance is the Delhi Development Authority (DDA), which is under the central government's control. The DDA manages a significant portion of Delhi's land, adding another layer of complexity to the city's administration.[2]

Unlike other states, Delhi does not have a governor. Instead, it has a lieutenant governor (LG), a powerful figure appointed directly by the Ministry of Home Affairs. The LG oversees the police administration and reports to the central government.

This unique administrative setup often led to friction between the AAP government and the LG. The AAP government frequently accused the different LGs of overstepping his bounds and hindering their ability to govern effectively. On the other hand, the LGs claimed that the AAP government was not functioning properly. This constant tussle made governing Delhi a challenging task.

Kejriwal vs Jung

The power tussle between Kejriwal and then LG Najeeb Jung began almost as soon as the AAP took office in 2013. What initially seemed like a clash of constitutional interpretations quickly escalated into a relentless struggle for administrative control, with power dynamics and governance frequently coming under the spotlight. There have been numerous clashes between Kejriwal and Jung, but here, I have focused on the most significant ones that I witnessed firsthand as a rookie trainee journalist. The conflicts with the LG can be broadly categorized into two main areas: disputes over the transfer and posting of officials, and disagreements regarding the policies implemented by the Delhi government.

As mentioned earlier in the book, the first major flashpoint occurred when Kejriwal's government drafted the Jan Lokpal Bill. Before the bill could be tabled in the Delhi Assembly, LG Jung intervened, demanding that the draft be sent to him for review. Jung, citing constitutional protocol, forwarded the bill to the then solicitor general, Mohan Parasaran, who deemed it 'unconstitutional' without prior approval from the Centre. This marked the beginning of a contentious relationship between Kejriwal and Jung. The AAP government retaliated by calling Jung a 'Congress agent', setting a tone for future confrontations.[3]

Kejriwal's first term, as we know, was short-lived. In 2015, after a resounding electoral victory, Kejriwal returned as CM with renewed zeal. Yet, the friction with Jung only intensified. In April 2015, Kejriwal issued a directive mandating that all files, even those pertaining to police, public order and land – subjects under the Centre's jurisdiction – be routed through his office. This provoked a sharp reaction from the LG. Jung reminded the CM that under Article 239AA of the Constitution, the LG retained authority over these subjects, emphasizing there was no constitutional obligation to route such files through the CM. Kejriwal, in turn, approached the Delhi High Court to challenge Jung's interpretation.[4]

The month after, the AAP government soon found itself embroiled in a public spat over the appointment of senior bureaucrats. In May 2015, Jung appointed Shakuntala Gamlin as acting chief secretary while then chief secretary, K.K. Sharma, was on leave. This appointment outraged Kejriwal, who accused Gamlin of lobbying on behalf of power companies. Kejriwal publicly alleged that Gamlin had pressured the Power Minister to sign off on a ₹11,000 crore loan guarantee for private power companies – a move that, he claimed, would burden Delhi's residents with steep tariff hikes. The LG, however, defended his decision, asserting his constitutional prerogative to make such appointments.[5]

The conflict escalated further with the controversial appointment of Swati Maliwal as chairperson of the Delhi Commission for Women (DCW). Maliwal, a close associate of Kejriwal from the IAC movement became the centre of accusations of nepotism, as we have already discussed earlier. Jung declared the appointment 'ultra vires' (beyond legal authority), arguing that his approval was mandatory for such postings. The Opposition seized the opportunity to accuse the AAP of favouritism, while the party insisted that Maliwal was chosen for her credentials. Despite the controversy, Maliwal asserted her dedication to women's welfare, but the row once again underscored the deep-rooted administrative conflict.[6]

Thereafter, again tensions peaked with the water tanker scam, a case involving alleged corruption in awarding contracts during Sheila Dikshit's tenure as CM. Jung ordered the Anti-Corruption Branch (ACB) to investigate both Dikshit and Kejriwal. The AAP government accused the LG of orchestrating political vendettas at the behest of the Centre. Kejriwal's administration argued that the ACB should report to the Delhi government, not the LG – a point of contention that had long fuelled the power struggle.[7]

The turning point came in August 2016 when the Delhi High Court ruled that the LG was not bound by the advice of the Delhi cabinet. The ruling reinforced the LG as the administrative head of Delhi, delivering a significant setback to Kejriwal's attempts to consolidate power. The court dismissed the AAP's petitions challenging the LG's authority, prompting the Delhi government to appeal the decision in the Supreme Court.[8]

The LG–CM tussle flared up again in October 2016 when Jung appointed IAS officer Alka Diwan as DCW member secretary. Kejriwal rejected the appointment and replaced Diwan with another officer, Dilraj Kaur, without seeking the LG's approval. The move was seen as a direct challenge to Jung's authority and added to the ever-growing list of disputes between the two.[9]

For Kejriwal and the AAP, this power struggle is not merely administrative but symbolic of their larger fight against centralization. From the *Janlokpal Bill* to bureaucratic appointments, the AAP consistently accused Jung of obstructing governance at the behest of the Centre. Conversely, the LG's office has maintained that its interventions are constitutional and necessary to ensure lawful administration.

The Kejriwal government has often argued that these tussles have stymied its ability to govern effectively. The delays in decision-making, coupled with public disagreements, have created a perception of dysfunction. Critics of the AAP point to these conflicts as evidence of its inability to work within constitutional boundaries. Supporters, however, see Kejriwal's defiance as a necessary pushback against excessive central control.

Najeeb Jung resigned from his post on 22 December 2016.[10]

Kejriwal vs Baijal

The relationship between Kejriwal and former LG Anil Baijal has been marked by numerous conflicts, each highlighting the ongoing power struggle within Delhi's administrative framework.

In 2017, then Samajwadi Party MP Naresh Agarwal had accused the LG Baijal of treating Kejriwal like a peon.[11] Then Deputy Chairman P.J. Kurien, who was chairing the proceedings, requested then Housing and Urban Affairs Minister Hardeep Singh Puri to mediate the friction between the two. The issue dominated discussions on a bill related to Delhi, with Opposition members raising concerns about the CM not being invited to the inauguration of the Delhi Metro's Magenta Line. Kurien suggested that Puri take the initiative to resolve the friction between the LG and Kejriwal. Puri accepted the challenge, acknowledging it as a significant task, even more challenging than negotiating with terrorists during his four-decade public life. He humorously proposed inviting both parties for lunch to sort out the differences.[12]

Another significant tussle occurred in August 2017 over the issue of mohalla clinics. The Delhi government claimed that the LG was sitting on files related to the clinics' proposals, which the LG's office denied.[13] This led to protests by several AAP leaders and supporters outside the LG house, resulting in chaos. The LG's office issued a statement explaining the current status of the proposal and outlining the progress made so far. However, the behaviour of the protesting members was described as increasingly rude and discourteous.

The first major flashpoint occurred in February 2018, involving an alleged assault on then Chief Secretary Anshu Prakash.[14] According to sources and Prakash himself, he was summoned to Kejriwal's official residence at midnight for a meeting where several AAP MLAs were present. It was alleged that they attacked, abused and assaulted him.

In June 2018, Kejriwal staged a protest at the LG House against the strike by IAS officers following the alleged assault on Anshu Prakash. Although the issue was eventually resolved, another conflict soon arose over the implementation of CCTV cameras across Delhi. The Delhi government proposed installing CCTV cameras, but Baijal intervened and formed a high-level committee to draft a policy framework. The AAP criticized this decision, claiming it would only delay the project.

Another conflict with LG Anil Baijal in 2018 was when the AAP demanded approval for the proposal of doorstep delivery of ration. Baijal denied the nod and referred the proposal to the Centre, which Kejriwal argued was unnecessary according to the law. Kejriwal and the AAP accused Baijal of rejecting the proposal over 'petty politics'.[15]

The handling of the COVID-19 pandemic further strained relations between Kejriwal and Baijal. Disagreements arose over the implementation of lockdown measures, testing protocols and the management of healthcare resources. In June 2020, Baijal overturned Kejriwal's decision to reserve Delhi hospitals for the city's residents, arguing it was discriminatory.[16] The AAP viewed this move as an overreach of the LG's powers and an attempt to undermine their efforts to manage the crisis.

Despite the numerous conflicts between Baijal and Kejriwal, it must be acknowledged that the number of flashpoints was fewer compared to Kejriwal's relationship with Jung and later with Vinai Kumar Saxena. It is also important to mention that in July 2018, the Supreme Court ruled that the LG must work under the aid and advice of the CM. This verdict reduced the LG's intervention in the Delhi government's affairs, providing some relief to the ongoing power struggle.

In conclusion, the relationship between Kejriwal and Baijal has been marked by significant conflicts, each highlighting the complexities of governance in Delhi. From the alleged assault on Prakash to the handling of the COVID-19 pandemic, these tussles underscore the challenges of balancing power between the elected government and the LG. As Delhi continues to navigate these challenges, the need for clear and effective governance remains paramount.

The AAP vs Vinai Kumar Saxena

The appointment of Vinai Kumar Saxena as the LG of Delhi on May 2022 marked the beginning of a new chapter in the ongoing power struggle between the Delhi government and the LG's office. Saxena, known for his administrative acumen and no-nonsense approach, quickly found himself at odds with the AAP government led by Kejriwal.

The conflict between Saxena and the AAP government over the bus marshal scheme underscores the ongoing power struggle between the two authorities.[17] Introduced in 2015 by the Kejriwal-led government, the scheme aimed to enhance women's safety in Delhi's buses by deploying civil defence volunteers as marshals. The initiative, widely hailed for reducing harassment and ensuring safer public transport, became a political flashpoint in late 2022 when the LG raised concerns about its legality, finances and operational accountability. Saxena questioned the use of civil defence volunteers outside their mandated emergency duties, the transparency of their appointments and the fiscal burden of their salaries. The Delhi government, however, defended the programme, touting its success and accusing the LG of political interference to undermine their welfare agenda.

Saxena criticized the AAP government for not having a comprehensive, law-backed scheme for bus marshals, accusing them of making empty promises on the reappointment of the bus marshals. The LG's office emphasized the need for a well-defined scheme with proper budgetary support, while the AAP government argued that the proposal had been sent to the LG for approval. This disagreement highlighted the differing approaches to governance and the challenges of implementing policies in a politically charged environment.

One of the most contentious battles between Saxena and the Kejriwal government was over the education sector, particularly the 'Schools of Excellence' project. The AAP government, which had earned widespread praise for its education reforms, sought approval to send teachers to Finland for advanced training. Saxena rejected the proposal multiple times, citing concerns over financial prudence and suggesting online alternatives instead.[18] The move sparked outrage within the AAP, which accused Saxena of trying to derail one of its flagship initiatives.

Then Deputy Chief Minister Manish Sisodia, who was also in charge of education, accused the Lieutenant Governor of obstructing efforts to enhance Delhi's schools and halting teacher training programs purely out of political malice.

Saxena hit back, insisting that taxpayer money must be spent responsibly and transparently.[19]

In 2022, the polluted Yamuna became another flashpoint. The AAP government announced a massive clean-up operation as part of its pre-election promises, but Saxena criticized the project for its lack of accountability and concrete planning. He publicly chastized the Delhi government for failing to act on time and convened meetings with various agencies to expedite the clean-up.[20]

In 2022, LG V.K. Saxena and Chief Minister Arvind Kejriwal clashed over the Yamuna River's persistent pollution, highlighting jurisdictional tensions and political rivalry. The conflict intensified ahead of Chhath Puja in October, when toxic foam marred the river's surface. Saxena wrote to Kejriwal, urging immediate action to ensure clean ghats for devotees.[21] The AAP's Saurabh Bharadwaj dismissed the letter as vague, accusing Saxena of seeking publicity and undermining his office's dignity. Earlier, in June, Saxena initiated cleaning the Najafgarh Drain, a major pollutant source, claiming progress. The AAP, however, viewed this as an overreach, fuelling tensions. The LG claimed that the AAP government moved to court to stop his efforts.There was also a major conflict between Saxena and the AAP government on bus procurement. The bus procurement row centres around allegations of irregularities in the procurement of 1,000 low-floor buses by the Delhi Transport Corporation (DTC). The controversy began in September 2022 when the CBI initiated a probe into the alleged discrepancies in the tender process and the appointment of the Delhi Integrated Multi-Modal Transit System as the management consultant.[22]

The AAP government argued that the procurement process was transparent and that they had followed all necessary guidelines. However, Saxena approved the CBI investigation, which the AAP viewed as an attempt to malign their image and disrupt their governance. The AAP leaders claimed that the probe was based on unfounded allegations and aimed at creating hurdles in their development projects. The LG's office maintained that the investigation was necessary to ensure transparency and accountability in the procurement process.

In July 2023, Saxena directed the immediate termination of services of around 400 private persons appointed by the Delhi government as advisors, consultants and fellows. The LG's office alleged that these appointments were made by flouting constitutional provisions of reservation, depriving Scheduled Castes, Scheduled Tribes and OBCs of their rights. The AAP government, on the other hand, argued that these appointments were essential for the effective functioning of various departments. This move by Saxena was seen as an attempt to assert control over the administrative machinery and curb the influence of the AAP government.[23]

The tussle between Saxena and the AAP escalated with the removal of Shailendra Sharma and Jasmine Shah, and the subsequent closure of the DDCD office. The DDCD, as discussed earlier, was an advisory body established to provide policy recommendations to the Delhi government, which became a focal point of the power struggle.[24] The controversy began when LG Saxena ordered the removal of Jasmine Shah (vice-chairman of the DDCD) and Shailendra Sharma (then education advisor to the Delhi government), citing allegations of misuse of office for political purposes.[25] The LG claimed that Shah had acted as an AAP spokesperson while holding a government position, violating service conduct rules. Additionally, concerns were raised about procedural irregularities in the functioning of the DDCD. The Kejriwal government criticized Saxena's decision, accusing him of political vendetta and overreach. They argued that both Shah and Sharma were making critical contributions to the education and policy sectors, calling their removal a deliberate attempt to derail Delhi's governance reforms.

The 2018 Supreme Court Verdict

This chapter cannot end without mentioning the landmark verdict of the Supreme Court on the power of LG and Delhi government.

I remember it vividly – it was the midnight of 3 July 2018, when my phone rang. On the other end was an excited leader from the AAP. 'Tomorrow morning, please reach the Supreme Court as early as possible. The LG vs Delhi government verdict will come tomorrow,' he exclaimed. The anticipation in his voice was palpable.

As a journalist, I knew this was monumental news. The next day could either be a significant setback for Kejriwal and his team or a transformative moment for Delhi's governance. The stakes were high. By 10.30 the next morning, I found myself amidst a throng of journalists, AAP supporters and BJP loyalists outside the Supreme Court. The air was thick with anticipation. We all waited with bated breath for the verdict that could reshape the political landscape of Delhi.

When the order was finally announced, the atmosphere erupted. I vividly recall then AAP MLA Saurabh Bharadwaj shouting with joy and laughter. The Supreme Court had ruled that the LG must act on the aid and advice of the cabinet, effectively curbing the LG's power to stall the Delhi government's initiatives at will.

This was, at the time, a victory for the Delhi government. With the 2019 Lok Sabha elections on the horizon and the 2020 Delhi Assembly elections not far behind, the timing couldn't have been more critical. The AAP was invigorated, ready to push forward with renewed energy. Projects that had been languishing in bureaucratic limbo began to move forward. The stalled CCTV installation project was revived, and issues plaguing the mohalla clinics were swiftly addressed. There was a newfound motivation and energy among the AAP workers, a sense that they could finally implement their vision for Delhi without undue interference.

The 2018 Supreme Court verdict was more than just a legal ruling – it was a turning point that empowered the elected government. First, it unequivocally stated that the LG does not have independent decision-making powers and must act on the aid and advice of the Council of Ministers, except in matters of land, police and public order. This was a significant shift from the previous status quo, where the LG's concurrence was deemed necessary for most decisions, effectively paralysing the elected government's functioning.

Second, the verdict underscored the importance of a representative government. By affirming that the elected government of Delhi has legislative and executive powers over all subjects except the three reserved ones, the court reinforced the democratic mandate given by the people of Delhi. This empowered the then Delhi government to implement its policies and vision without undue interference, fostering a more accountable and responsive administration.

Moreover, the judgment highlighted the principle of collective responsibility. It emphasized that civil servants must report to the ministers and follow their directives – ensuring that the elected representatives could effectively govern. This was crucial for the implementation of policies and the day-to-day administration of the region.

I remember a senior journalist outside the Supreme Court that day telling me that the verdict restored the balance of power in Delhi's governance. It not only curtailed the LG's overarching authority but also bolstered the functioning of the elected government, paving the way for a more democratic and efficient administration. This judgment stands as a testament to the judiciary's role in upholding democratic principles and ensuring that the will of the people prevails in the governance of the National Capital Territory.

Part 6

Expansion and Prospects

25

A New Frontier: The Rise of the AAP in Punjab

As I pen this chapter, the AAP governs Punjab with an overwhelming majority. The rise of the AAP in Punjab is not merely a political victory – it is the result of a long, arduous journey marked by struggles, strategic moves and a deep connection with the evolving sociopolitical sentiments of the state. If the AAP's rise in Delhi was a narrative of meteoric success, its conquest of Punjab has been a much more complex story, filled with setbacks, resilience and gradual recognition by the people of Punjab.

The journey of the AAP in Punjab began in earnest in 2014, during the Lok Sabha elections.

The AAP's decision to contest in Punjab was born out of a combination of practical political strategy and the party's ideological alignment with the prevailing sentiments of the state.

Professor Ronki Ram, a noted political scientist at Panjab University, observed that Punjab was experiencing significant political and social challenges. The Shiromani Akali Dal (SAD) faced accusations of corruption involving several leaders allegedly tied to the state's drug issues and poor governance. The Congress also dealt with allegations that contributed to public dissatisfaction with existing political options. Amidst this backdrop, the AAP emerged as an alternative advocating for change. Although the party initially struggled, it gradually established its presence and eventually gained power, offering prospects for new governance.

Kejriwal, ever the strategist, saw Punjab as a potential foothold outside Delhi. The state was crucial for a number of reasons. First, Punjab, Delhi and Haryana form a contiguous belt, with significant demographic, cultural and economic overlaps. For Kejriwal, ruling this region could provide the AAP with a strong foundation for broader national expansion. Kejriwal himself hails from Hisar, Haryana, and had a personal connection to the region. This sense of familiarity was crucial as the AAP began to build its narrative in Punjab, presenting itself as a party for the common man, free from the entrenched corruption of the SAD–BJP coalition and the Congress.

The party also benefited from the support of key personalities like Bhagwant Mann, a popular comedian and social activist who joined the AAP during its early foray into Punjab politics. Mann's presence gave the AAP a relatable figure who could connect with the masses on an emotional level, something that the Congress and the SAD struggled with at the time. Just like in Delhi, the AAP began to focus on grassroots campaigning, emphasizing door-to-door engagement and using social media to spread its message of clean, transparent governance. Mann's rise within the party has mirrored the AAP's growing influence in Punjab. His ability to speak to the common man, especially the rural electorate, gave the AAP a strong foothold in the countryside, where traditional party loyalties had begun to erode.

As Punjab reeled from corruption, governance failure and the rise of the drug mafia, the AAP's focus on these pressing issues resonated with large sections of the electorate. The party promised a drug-free Punjab, with better healthcare and education – issues that found immense support among both the urban middle class and rural farmers. While its initial entry into Punjab politics during the 2014 elections was met with scepticism, the AAP surprised everyone by winning 4 out of 13 parliamentary seats (more on this later).[1] This performance was nothing short of remarkable for a party that had only recently ventured into the national political scene.

However, the AAP's journey in Punjab was far from smooth. The 2017 Assembly elections proved to be a mixed bag for the party. While it had hoped to secure a decisive victory, it fell short, winning only 20 out of 117 seats. The Congress, led by Captain Amarinder Singh, secured a comfortable majority, while the SAD–BJP alliance was relegated to a distant third. The result was a disappointment for the AAP, but it also underscored that the party had established itself as a formidable player in Punjab's political landscape. The 20 seats marked the beginning of a more sustained engagement with the state, and Kejriwal and his team knew that their moment in Punjab would eventually come.

Fast forward to 2022, and the AAP achieved what it had long set out to do – win Punjab decisively. With Bhagwant Mann as its chief ministerial candidate, the AAP secured a resounding victory, winning 92 out of 117 seats in the state assembly. The victory was not only a mandate for Mann's leadership but also an endorsement of Kejriwal's governance model, which had already seen success in Delhi. The AAP's governance in Delhi became the central plank of its Punjab campaign. The promise of replicating the 'Delhi Model' in Punjab, along with tackling the drug problem, played a significant role in winning the hearts of the electorate.[2]

The story of the AAP in Punjab is a testament to the party's resilience, its ability to tap into the pulse of the people and its strategic foresight. From winning four parliamentary seats in 2014 to a landslide victory in the 2022 Assembly elections, the AAP's rise in Punjab has been nothing short of remarkable. It demonstrates how a party, born out of an anti-corruption movement in Delhi, was able to connect with a diverse electorate in another state by focusing on the issues that matter most to the people.

Today (as of 2025), as the AAP governs Punjab, it faces new challenges – delivering on its promises, maintaining its connection with the electorate and navigating the complexities of state politics. However, its journey to power serves as a blueprint for its future ambitions, not only in Punjab but also across India. The success in Punjab has given the AAP a much-needed boost to further its national aspirations, solidifying its position as a party that can transcend regional boundaries and emerge as a key player in Indian politics.

2014 Lok Sabha Elections: A Promising Start

The 2014 Lok Sabha elections marked a significant moment for the AAP, as it made its first major foray outside Delhi, specifically in the politically turbulent state of Punjab. While much of the AAP's national focus was on Kejriwal's high-stakes contest against Narendra Modi in Varanasi, the campaign in Punjab followed a different trajectory. The AAP leaders adopted a localized, grassroots approach that mirrored their successful 2013 Delhi campaign, concentrating on door-to-door outreach, meeting voters at the ground level and forming direct, personal connections with the electorate. This strategy helped the party position itself as a fresh alternative to Punjab's entrenched political forces – the SAD and the Congress.

The 2014 elections in Punjab offered a unique opportunity for the AAP to capitalize on the dissatisfaction among voters. As mentioned previously, the political landscape in the state was fraught with growing anti-incumbency against the SAD–BJP alliance, which had been in power since 2007. Unemployment, deteriorating law and order, widespread drug abuse and the agrarian crisis had reached alarming levels, making it easier for the AAP to emerge as a viable alternative to the traditional parties. The party's focus on localized, issue-based campaigning allowed it to strike a chord with various sections of the electorate, particularly the urban middle class, youth and farmers.

One of the AAP's key strategies in Punjab was to present itself as a people's movement, working from the ground up. The AAP candidates were encouraged to develop personal relationships with voters, visiting their homes, listening to their concerns and positioning themselves as different from the established political elite. This grassroots method, which had worked wonders for the

AAP in Delhi back then, was adapted to Punjab. As a result, the AAP's emphasis on issues like corruption, unemployment and the drug crisis resonated deeply, particularly in the Malwa region.

In terms of messaging, the AAP focused on a platform of clean governance and social justice. The party targeted the SAD–BJP alliance on its failure to address the drug menace that had ravaged the state. Reports of widespread addiction, particularly among Punjab's youth, had become an epidemic by 2014. The SAD leaders were accused of either turning a blind eye to the issue or, worse, being complicit in drug smuggling and peddling. The AAP insiders highlighted how the party made drug abuse a core electoral issue, calling for urgent reforms and accusing the SAD–BJP government of neglect and corruption.

A senior journalist from Punjab, who wished to remain anonymous, shared insights into the political undercurrents at the time: 'It was an open secret that certain leaders within the SAD were involved in the drug trade. The Panthic (individuals or groups committed to Sikh religious and political interests, often advocating for Sikh identity) voters, who traditionally supported the SAD, were also frustrated by the alliance's partnership with the BJP, a party associated with Hindutva ideology. This discontent, particularly among the youth, helped swing a large chunk of voters towards AAP.'

The AAP's focus on the youth was another cornerstone of its campaign. Punjab's younger generation had borne the brunt of the state's socio-economic problems, from unemployment to drug addiction. Many young people viewed the AAP as the only party that addressed their concerns directly. The AAP's clean, anti-corruption image at that time and its promises to revitalize the state's economy and combat the drug crisis made it particularly appealing to younger voters, who were looking for change. The party's slogan of 'honest politics' resonated well with this demographic, helping it secure a significant portion of the youth vote.

Moreover, the Congress, which was the principal opposition to the SAD–BJP alliance, failed to provide a credible alternative. The Congress campaign lacked the grassroots engagement and issue-based focus that the AAP offered. As the Congress struggled to gain momentum, the AAP capitalized on the vacuum, presenting itself as the only party with a real chance of delivering change. Many voters who were disillusioned with both the SAD and Congress saw the AAP as a new hope for Punjab's future.

In its debut performance in the 2014 Lok Sabha elections in Punjab, the AAP won an impressive 4 out of 13 seats, all from the Malwa region – Faridkot, Fatehgarh Sahib, Sangrur and Patiala. This success was a remarkable feat, given that the party had ventured into an area where the SAD had traditionally held sway. The AAP's victory in these constituencies was not just a reflection of its grassroots campaigning but also a testament to the political disillusionment that had taken hold of the state.[3]

The Malwa region, in particular, had been a stronghold of the SAD, but by 2014, it had become a hotbed of anti-incumbency sentiment. The combination of rampant unemployment, the agrarian crisis and drug abuse had left the people of this region yearning for change. There were also widespread allegations of nepotism, particularly regarding the distribution of land and infrastructure projects. The AAP's message of clean governance, coupled with its focus on addressing these pressing issues, resonated strongly with voters in the region.

As Professor Ronki Ram aptly noted, 'There was widespread dissatisfaction among the youth and urban voters against the SAD and Congress. They were looking for an alternative. The situation was much similar to that of Delhi in 2013 when AAP came to power due to the discontent among people against CM Sheila Dikshit and Congress.'

However, the AAP's rise in Punjab also highlighted the deep-rooted problems facing the state. The party's success was as much about its own campaign as it was about the failures of the existing political establishment. The SAD–BJP alliance had alienated large sections of the electorate through its perceived complicity in drug trafficking, corruption and the mishandling of key resources. These scandals had severely tarnished the SAD's image, which had once prided itself on being a party for the common people. By 2014, many rural voters, who had previously supported the SAD, were ready to embrace the AAP as a legitimate alternative.

The Lost Opportunity: Why the AAP Failed in the 2017 Punjab Assembly Elections

In the run-up to the 2017 Punjab Assembly elections, the AAP seemed poised for a breakthrough. After its impressive debut in Punjab in the 2014 Lok Sabha elections, the AAP emerged as a formidable political force. Public enthusiasm, particularly among the urban middle class and youth, was palpable, and there was a widespread belief that the party could disrupt the status quo in Punjab's politics. Yet, despite the momentum, the AAP's dream of forming the government was shattered. The party managed to win only 20 out of 117 seats in the Punjab Assembly, falling far short of the majority needed to rule. Several factors contributed to this defeat, ranging from organizational shortcomings to damaging allegations that tarnished its image.[4]

One of the fundamental reasons the AAP faltered in the 2017 elections was its inability to penetrate rural Punjab. While the party's support base in urban centres like Ludhiana, Amritsar and Jalandhar was strong, it struggled to connect with voters in the countryside. Punjab's rural electorate, deeply entrenched in traditional party loyalties, was wary of the AAP's urban-centric approach. Despite its anti-corruption agenda and promises of change, the party could not resonate with the concerns of rural voters, many of whom felt alienated by the AAP's perceived lack of understanding of Punjab's agrarian challenges.

As discussed earlier, the rural electorate had long been under the influence of the SAD and the Congress, which had deep roots in Punjab's villages. In 2017, the AAP, being a relatively new player, could not match the organizational depth or grassroots networks that these traditional parties had built over decades. As a result, it failed to capitalize on the anti-incumbency sentiment against the SAD–BJP alliance, which had ruled Punjab for a decade.

Another key factor that worked against the AAP was the absence of a strong, homegrown leadership in Punjab. While Kejriwal was the face of the campaign, he was perceived as an outsider. This perception was cleverly exploited by the AAP's rivals who painted Kejriwal as someone who did not understand Punjab's unique sociopolitical dynamics.[5]

The lack of a credible local leader further compounded the AAP's problems. While Kejriwal had successfully led his party to victory in Delhi, his leadership style did not resonate with Punjab's voters, who wanted a local figure to lead the state. The AAP's national leadership often overshadowed its local leaders, leading to confusion about who would be the party's chief ministerial candidate if it won the election. This uncertainty left voters unsure of the AAP's leadership credentials. As Professor Ronki Ram observed, 'In AAP, till today, this is a major issue. The Delhi leadership is at the helm of affairs in Punjab, and this is not an idea which the people of Punjab like that much.'

The Congress, under the leadership of Captain Amarinder Singh, had a well-established political network, and the SAD–BJP alliance, backed by the powerful Badal family, had entrenched itself in Punjab's political landscape over decades. The AAP, on the other hand, was relatively new to the state's politics and could not match the organizational might of its traditional rivals. This organizational deficiency became particularly evident in rural areas, as mentioned earlier.

Internal factionalism further weakened the AAP's campaign in Punjab. As the election approached, cracks within the party began to emerge. Some of the AAP's key leaders in Punjab, including Sucha Singh Chhotepur (then the state convenor) were sidelined or expelled, leading to public disagreements and infighting. These internal rifts damaged the party's unity and distracted from its core message of governance reform and anti-corruption.[6]

Moreover, the AAP faced significant criticism for its candidate selection process. In many constituencies, the party fielded political novices or individuals with limited appeal among voters. In some cases, the AAP was accused of selecting candidates without proper scrutiny, which led to dissatisfaction within the party ranks and scepticism among voters. This lack of experienced, well-established candidates hurt the AAP's credibility, especially in rural areas where voters tended to favour familiar, seasoned politicians.

A senior Punjab-based journalist, speaking on condition of anonymity, pointed out that the AAP's campaign strategy also had some notable missteps. The party's focus on attacking both the Congress and the SAD–BJP alliance simultaneously created confusion among voters about its main opposition. Instead of focusing its energy on one rival, the AAP spread its attacks, which diluted its message and made it harder for voters to see the party as the definitive alternative to the ruling SAD–BJP alliance.

The AAP's aggressive campaign, which cantered on portraying Punjab as being ravaged by drugs, corruption and misgovernance, did not sit well with a significant section of voters. While the AAP's rhetoric on these issues was not entirely baseless, its portrayal of the state as a disaster zone alienated many voters, especially in rural areas. The party's focus on Punjab's drug problem, in particular, struck a nerve with voters who felt that the AAP was exaggerating the issue for political gain.

The Congress capitalized on this backlash by positioning itself as a more moderate, stable alternative. Singh's campaign, which promised loan waivers for farmers and economic development, resonated with voters who were looking for a more constructive vision for Punjab's future. Singh's personal popularity, coupled with the anti-incumbency sentiment against the SAD–BJP government, helped the Congress win the trust of voters who might have otherwise considered voting for the AAP.

Perhaps the most damaging blow to the AAP's campaign in Punjab came in the form of allegations that the party was sympathetic to separatist elements.[7] These accusations, which were spread by the AAP's political opponents and amplified by sections of the media, played a critical role in eroding the party's support among moderate and nationalist voters in Punjab.

The roots of these allegations lay in Punjab's troubled history with separatism, particularly the Khalistan movement of the 1980s and 1990s. Although the movement had largely subsided, the scars it left behind were still fresh, and any political association with it was seen as dangerous. In this context, the AAP's outreach to segments of the Sikh diaspora and its perceived pandering to radical elements during the campaign raised suspicions.

A key moment that fuelled these allegations was when Kejriwal stayed at the house of an ex-Khalistan sympathizer during one of his campaign visits to Punjab. This incident was quickly seized upon by the AAP's opponents, who accused Kejriwal of aligning with forces that wanted to destabilize Punjab's hard-won peace. Although Kejriwal defended himself by calling it an innocent oversight, the damage was already done.

Both the Congress and the SAD launched sustained campaigns to paint the AAP as sympathetic to separatist elements. They repeatedly questioned Kejriwal's intent and portrayed him as an outsider who did not understand the sensitivities of Punjab's history. The SAD–BJP alliance, in particular, used this narrative to dissuade moderate Sikh and Hindu voters from supporting the AAP, warning that a vote for the AAP could lead to a revival of the dark days of violence and insurgency.

Captain Amarinder Singh, too, played a pivotal role in fuelling this narrative. He accused the AAP of being in cahoots with radical elements and alleged that the party had received financial support from extremist groups abroad. This narrative resonated strongly with voters, particularly in rural areas, where memories of the insurgency were still vivid.

By the time the election was held, the separatist sympathizer narrative had significantly damaged the AAP's image in Punjab. The party, which had entered the election with high hopes and substantial momentum, found itself on the defensive. While the AAP still managed to win 20 seats, it fell far short of the expectations it had set for itself.

A senior AAP leader revealed that internal polls showed an AAP win in Punjab until allegations of separatist sympathies surfaced 72 hours before voting. The Congress capitalized on this issue, with Singh's strategy and credibility leading to their victory.

The AAP's 2017 campaign in Punjab serves as a cautionary tale about the importance of understanding local dynamics, building grassroots support and effectively countering political attacks.

Paradigm Shift in Punjab Politics (2020–22)

In the 2019 Lok Sabha elections, the AAP won only one seat in Punjab – Bhagwant Mann from the Sangrur constituency.[8] However, from 2020 to 2022, a paradigm shift in Punjab politics took place due to several reasons. The fundamental reason behind this shift was the farmers protest against three controversial farm bills brought by the BJP-led central government. The passage of these three farm bills led to massive protests from the farmers. The discontent against the SAD was at its peak. Similarly, during this time, the Congress party in Punjab was suffering from massive infighting. In this political environment the AAP got the advantage and grew in such a way in Punjab that in 2022 it came in power in Punjab with a humongous majority.

Senior journalist and political editor of *The Quint* Aditya Menon said, 'During this time the anger of people grew against the SAD because of farm bills and also the sacrilege cases. On the other hand, the Congress was facing infighting and there was anti-incumbency sentiment across the state. The people thought that AAP is the only alternative and people voted for the AAP.'

A Storm of Discontent: The Fall of the SAD and the Rise of the AAP Amidst Punjab's Farmer Protests

The introduction of three contentious farm laws in September 2020 by the central government sparked unprecedented unrest, especially in Punjab, where agriculture is the lifeblood of the economy. The SAD, once a trusted ally of the BJP, found itself mired in controversy, as its initial endorsement of the farm bills incited widespread fury among the very farmers it had long relied on for political support.[9] The three farm laws aimed at liberalizing the agricultural market, purportedly to empower farmers by allowing them to sell their produce beyond government-regulated *mandis*. These changes were framed as modernizing reforms, designed to create more flexible and competitive opportunities for farmers. However, farmers in Punjab and Haryana saw these laws not as opportunities but as threats to their livelihoods. The dismantling of the mandi system was perceived as the first step towards the erosion of the minimum support price (MSP) mechanism, a vital safety net for farmers, which ensured that they were not at the mercy of volatile market forces and large corporations.[10]

This fear acted as a catalyst for one of the largest farmer-led movements in modern India. The protests, which began in Punjab, quickly spread across the country. Thousands of farmers mobilized, marching towards Delhi and setting up camps at its borders in defiance of the new laws. Their movement was marked by resilience, unity and a steadfast refusal to compromise on their demands. Soon, the world took notice, as the protests became emblematic of the larger struggle against government policies, which many felt catered more to corporate interests than the welfare of ordinary citizens.

At the centre of this turmoil was the SAD. As mentioned previously, the SAD initially stood by the central government's farm reforms, a decision that ignited rage among the farming community. For the farmers, this was nothing short of a betrayal – the SAD, the party that had for decades championed their interests, had seemingly aligned itself with policies that had endangered their future.

As the protests swelled and pressure mounted, the SAD leadership found itself cornered. In a bid to salvage its reputation and distance itself from the growing unrest, Harsimrat Kaur Badal, a senior SAD leader and then Union Minister, resigned from the BJP-led government in September 2020. Shortly afterward, the SAD officially severed ties with the NDA. However, this political pivot did little to quell the fury. Many saw the SAD's decision to leave the alliance as a belated and politically motivated attempt to regain lost ground rather than a genuine act of solidarity with the farmers.[11]

While the SAD was reeling from the backlash over the farm laws, another issue resurfaced, further tarnishing its image – the sacrilege incidents of 2015. These incidents involved the desecration of the Guru Granth Sahib, the sacred scripture of the Sikh faith, a deeply emotional issue for Punjab's majority Sikh population. The handling of these incidents by the then SAD–BJP government was seen as inadequate, with many accusing the leadership of complicity in shielding the perpetrators.[12]

For the protesters, the farm agitation was not just an economic struggle – it became a broader fight for justice and dignity. The sacrilege incidents, a festering wound, now fuelled a second wave of resentment against the SAD. Farmers, many of whom were Sikhs, viewed the party not only as betrayers of their economic security but also as enablers of sacrilege. This dual anger, rooted in both economic and spiritual grievances, created an insurmountable wall between the SAD and the people it had once represented.

Meanwhile, new political actors were quick to seize the opportunity presented by the SAD's decline. Among them, the AAP emerged as a formidable contender.

The AAP's promises of transparent governance and its vocal support for the farmers' cause resonated strongly with the disillusioned electorate. The AAP opposed the farm bills in Parliament and supported the protests. Kejriwal arranged food, toilets and medicines for the protesters at the Delhi border. An AAP leader stated they aided the farmers without party flags to respect the apolitical nature of the protest, following Kejriwal's instructions.

In November 2021, after more than a year of continuous protests, the Indian government finally repealed the controversial farm laws. This was seen as a historic victory for the farmers and a testament to the power of sustained, collective action. Yet, the political fallout for the SAD lingered. While the repeal of the laws was celebrated, it did little to erase the memories of the SAD's initial support for them or its failure to address the sacrilege crisis.

The 2022 elections underscored how deeply the farmer protests and related events had reshaped Punjab's political narrative. The SAD's downfall was complete, while the AAP capitalized on the changing winds to establish itself as the new political heavyweight. The protests had become more than just a reaction to farm laws – they symbolized a broader call for political accountability and change.

Infighting in the Congress: A House Divided

The period between 2020 and 2022 was one of profound turmoil for the Congress in Punjab. As the state was engulfed by the historic farmer protests, the Congress, which had been in power since 2017, found itself entangled in a bitter internal struggle that not only fractured its leadership but also destabilized its future. The infighting, marked by factionalism and a clash of egos, came to a head in 2021– unleashing a series of dramatic events that reshaped both the party and the political landscape of Punjab.

The roots of discord within the Punjab Congress were planted long before the farmer protests erupted. As explained earlier, in 2017, under the seasoned leadership of Captain Amarinder Singh, the party had secured a convincing electoral victory, seemingly on solid ground. However, as the years wore on, fault lines began to emerge. Singh, a towering figure in Punjab politics, was respected for his experience but soon faced growing opposition from within his own ranks. Many within the party accused him of being aloof, dictatorial and failing to address the pressing issues plaguing the state, such as the rampant drug problem and economic stagnation. Critics also pointed to his perceived failure to honour several of the promises made during the 2017 election campaign, which further stoked dissatisfaction.

One of the most prominent critics of Singh's leadership was Navjot Singh Sidhu, a former cricketer who had joined the Congress in 2017 after parting ways with the BJP. Sidhu, with his energetic personality and fiery speeches, quickly ascended the ranks of the Congress, gaining considerable influence. He was not content to remain in the shadow of Singh and openly challenged his leadership. Sidhu accused Singh of being too complacent and not doing enough to defend Punjab's interests, especially in the context of the farmer protests. He castigated Singh for being too soft on the central government and failing to take a stronger stand in support of the protesting farmers.

As 2021 progressed, tensions between Singh and Sidhu grew increasingly public, with their power struggle playing out in the media. What had begun as internal dissent transformed into a full-blown rebellion, dividing the party into two warring factions. In a move that escalated the conflict further, Sidhu resigned from his position in the state cabinet in June 2019, citing his dissatisfaction with Singh's leadership. This public display of defiance further polarized the party, leading to a series of urgent interventions by the Congress high command.[13]

Despite multiple attempts by the party's national leadership to mediate between the warring camps, no resolution was forthcoming. The Congress President Sonia Gandhi and her son Rahul Gandhi held several high-level meetings with both Singh and Sidhu in an effort to restore order, but the rift only deepened. Both leaders dug in their heels, with neither side willing to concede ground. The resulting stalemate made the situation untenable for the Congress leadership and set the stage for an explosive outcome.

In September 2021, the infighting reached its zenith when Singh resigned as CM of Punjab. In his resignation speech, Singh did not mince words, making it clear that he felt abandoned by the Congress leadership and undermined by Sidhu and his faction. Singh's departure was a monumental moment in Punjab's political history, and marked the end of an era. The Congress had lost one of its most experienced leaders in the state, and the party was left to navigate the aftermath of this internal implosion.

In the wake of Singh's resignation, the Congress leadership moved swiftly to appoint a new CM. Charanjit Singh Channi, a Dalit leader, was chosen to fill the position, making history as Punjab's first Dalit CM. His appointment was seen as a politically astute move, aimed at consolidating the Dalit vote in the run-up to the 2022 state elections. Channi's rise was initially met with optimism, and for a brief moment, it appeared as though the Congress might be able to regroup and present a united front.[14]

However, the internal strife was far from over. Sidhu, who had been appointed as Punjab Congress president earlier that year, continued to assert his authority, often at the expense of Channi's leadership. The power struggle between Sidhu and Channi created further instability within the party, as both leaders jostled for control and influence. Sidhu, emboldened by his rising popularity, sought to dominate the party's agenda, while Channi struggled to assert his authority as the CM. The result was a disjointed and chaotic leadership, with conflicting messages emanating from the party's top brass, further eroding the Congress's credibility.

As the 2022 state elections approached, the internal discord within the Congress took its toll. The party – once seen as the natural choice for governance in Punjab – appeared fractured and disorganized. The public spats and power plays between its leaders created the image of a party in disarray, unable to offer stable leadership at a time when Punjab was grappling with serious challenges. This perception of dysfunction proved to be a significant liability in the upcoming elections, as voters lost confidence in the party's ability to deliver effective governance.

The fallout from the infighting was not confined to the Congress alone. The political instability within the party created an opening for the AAP, which had been steadily building its presence in Punjab. The party capitalized on the disillusionment with the Congress and positioned itself as a viable alternative. In the 2022 state elections, the AAP's strategy paid off, as it secured a decisive victory, emerging as the dominant political force in Punjab.

The infighting within the Punjab Congress was symptomatic of a broader malaise afflicting the party at the national level. Once the dominant force in Indian politics, the Congress has been steadily losing ground due to leadership crises, factionalism and an inability to present a coherent vision to the electorate. The events in Punjab highlighted the challenges faced by the party in maintaining internal cohesion and responding to the aspirations of its voters. As the Congress continued to grapple with these issues, the political landscape of Punjab – and indeed India – shifted, with new players like the AAP gaining prominence.

The AAP's 2022 Punjab Assembly Elections Victory and Beyond

The AAP's 2022 Assembly elections victory in Punjab was nothing short of a political phenomenon, marking a decisive shift in the state's political landscape. The AAP secured 92 out of 117 seats – a sweeping majority that not only stunned its rivals but also catapulted it from a fringe player to a dominant force in Punjab politics. The scale of the victory reflected a deep undercurrent of public disenchantment with traditional parties.

The AAP's rise in Punjab can be traced back to its persistent grassroots campaigning, a focus on delivering clean governance and addressing pressing local issues such as unemployment, education and the agrarian crisis. The party positioned itself as the voice of change, promising to uproot corruption and mismanagement that had long plagued the state. This resonated particularly well with Punjab's youth and rural voters, who were increasingly disillusioned by the failures of the incumbent Congress government led by Channi.

One of the critical factors behind the AAP's victory was its strong performance in rural areas, where it won 64 out of 77 seats. This was largely due to the AAP's ability to capitalize on the frustrations of the farming community, which had been at the forefront of protests against the central government's controversial farm laws. The party's promise of pro-farmer policies, along with Kejriwal's reputation as a leader who delivers on governance, struck a chord with voters.

The 2022 election also marked the collapse of the once-dominant SAD, which managed to win only three seats, its worst-ever performance. The AAP's victory, with over 42 per cent of the popular vote, set the stage for a potential long-term realignment in Punjab's politics, and its ripple effects may extend beyond the state.[15]

As the AAP began its governance in Punjab, it became evident that the party would face several challenges that went beyond mere electoral promises. While the electoral victory was a clear rejection of the traditional political forces in the state, it also placed enormous expectations on the AAP's shoulders to deliver on promises of good governance, economic revival and addressing deep-rooted social and political issues. However, the reality on the ground has been far from easy, with the AAP government facing significant obstacles ranging from law and order deterioration to the resurgence of separatist sentiments, all under the looming shadow of populism and dependence on the central leadership in Delhi.

One of the most pressing challenges for the AAP government in Punjab has been the deterioration of law and order in the state. The murder of Sidhu Moose Wala, a popular singer and youth icon, in May 2022 was a glaring example of how fragile the state's security apparatus had become. Moose Wala, who had joined the Congress shortly before the 2022 elections, was gunned down in broad daylight, sparking outrage across the state and country. His murder not only highlighted the rise in gang-related violence but also brought to the fore concerns over political vendettas, organized crime and a general breakdown of law and order.[16]

It is widely believed that shortly before the incident, the AAP government had announced a reduction and withdrawal of security for several individuals and published their names (including Moose Wala's), which may have contributed to the event.

The incident sent shockwaves through the state, with many questioning the AAP government's ability to maintain peace and security. Law and order is a sensitive issue in Punjab – a border state that has historically faced threats from militancy and cross-border infiltration. The Moose Wala murder, coupled with other high-profile crimes, raised questions about the AAP government's effectiveness in controlling rising crime and ensuring the safety of its citizens. The AAP's critics were quick to point out that despite its promises of clean governance, the party was struggling to rein in criminal elements and create a secure environment.

Professor Ronki Ram remarked, 'One of the biggest challenges facing the AAP is maintaining law and order in Punjab. Currently, there is a perception that under the Bhagwant Mann government, the law-and-order situation has worsened. Given Punjab's history of insurgency and separatism, such a perception among the people is detrimental. Therefore, the AAP should concentrate on addressing and improving this situation.'

Punjab's history bears the marks of separatist violence, especially during the 1980s and early 1990s insurgency. Despite decades of relative peace, recent years have seen a resurgence of pro-Khalistan sentiments, raising concerns about radical elements exploiting sociopolitical vulnerabilities. The rise of leaders like Amritpal Singh and his group, Waris Punjab De, highlights this issue. Additionally, in the 2024 Lok Sabha elections, Sarabjeet Singh Khalsa, known for his pro-separatist views and as the son of one of Indira Gandhi's assassins, won the Faridkot constituency as an independent candidate.

The AAP government, which campaigned on the promise of development and clean governance, now finds itself in a tricky position. Addressing separatism requires a delicate balance – asserting the authority of the state while avoiding alienation of any community. Furthermore, given that Punjab shares a sensitive border with Pakistan, the resurgence of separatist calls has significant national security implications. The AAP government's response to these developments has been cautious, but many believe that a more proactive and firmer stance is needed to prevent the situation from spiralling out of control.

The growing influence of social media and diaspora groups in fuelling separatist ideologies has further complicated matters. The state government faces the challenge of countering these narratives while ensuring that legitimate grievances of the people are addressed in a democratic manner. The rise of such sentiments, if left unchecked, could lead to further instability and undermine the progress that Punjab has made in the post-militancy era.

Professor Ronki Ram opined, 'Punjab has witnessed much bloodshed in the past and will never go back to such days. The victory of pro-separatist elements in isolated cases is unlikely to have much effect in Punjab's broader political dynamics.' However, some political analysts argue that the ascent of the AAP has led to a notable decline in the SAD's influence, resulting in a lack of moderate voices in Punjab's Panthic politics. The SAD has traditionally upheld a moderate stance in Sikh politics, but their voice is now less prominent. Shortly after Bhagwant Mann became the CM, a by-election in the Sangrur Lok constituency saw Simranjit Singh Mann of the SAD-Amritsar, known for his pro-separatist views, emerge victorious.

A senior journalist from Punjab, speaking on condition of anonymity, commented:

> Bhagwant Mann may have the potential to be an effective administrator in Punjab, but when it comes to Sikh politics, he lacks popularity. The AAP has indeed fallen short in addressing the gap in Panthic politics, and this failure has allowed pro-separatist elements to gain a platform. Moving forward, the AAP will need to strike a balance between effective governance and addressing the void in Sikh political representation.

While the rise of separatism is alarming, one of the defining features of the AAP's rise, both in Delhi earlier and in Punjab now, has been its reliance on populist measures to win electoral support. In Punjab, the party promised a host of welfare schemes aimed at providing free electricity, water, healthcare and education. While these promises played a crucial role in the AAP's landslide victory, the challenge now lies in delivering on these commitments without compromising the state's fiscal health.

Punjab is already one of the most indebted states in India, with a staggering debt burden that leaves little room for extravagant populist measures. The implementation of the AAP's promised welfare schemes will require significant financial resources, which are hard to come by in a state grappling with stagnant economic growth, declining agricultural productivity and an over-reliance on subsidies. The party's promise of providing free electricity up to 300 units per household is already placing strain on the state's finances, with concerns that it could lead to a fiscal crisis if not managed properly.

The AAP government's challenge is twofold – it must balance the populist promises that brought it to power with the need for prudent fiscal management. Failure to strike this balance could lead to economic instability and erode public confidence in the government's ability to deliver long-term development. Furthermore, the party's reliance on populism as a political strategy raises questions about its ability to implement sustainable reforms that address Punjab's deeper structural issues, such as its agrarian crisis and unemployment.

Another challenge facing the AAP government in Punjab is its perceived dependence on the central leadership of the party in Delhi, particularly Kejriwal. While Mann holds the position of CM in Punjab, many observers have noted that key decisions are being influenced, if not directly controlled, by the Delhi leadership. This has raised concerns about the autonomy of the Punjab government and its ability to make independent decisions that cater to the unique needs of the state.

The centralization of decision-making in Delhi is problematic for several reasons. First, it undermines the credibility of the Punjab leadership and creates a perception that the state is being run by remote control. Second, it limits the government's ability to respond swiftly and effectively to local challenges, as decisions often need to be vetted by the party leadership in Delhi. Finally, it stifles the emergence of strong regional leaders within AAP who can build a long-term political base in Punjab.

To elaborate on how Kejriwal and the Delhi leadership control Punjab's affairs, it is important to look at Raghav Chadha's appointment as the chairman of the advisory committee. His appointment ensures that Kejriwal's vision and policies are directly implemented in Punjab. Chadha's role as the chairman of the advisory committee allows him to oversee key initiatives and provide strategic guidance, effectively making him a conduit for Kejriwal's directives. By placing a trusted ally in a pivotal advisory position, Kejriwal can maintain a tight grip on Punjab's administration. This centralization is evident from Chadha's previous roles, including his significant involvement in the Delhi government and his instrumental role in the AAP's electoral strategy in Punjab. His presence in Punjab's governance structure ensures that the Delhi leadership's influence remains strong and unchallenged.

Senior journalist Aditya Menon stated, 'There is a perception that Bhagwant Mann does not make decisions independently. He is seen as reliant on Arvind Kejriwal through Raghav Chadha and also follows Home Minister Amit Shah's instructions regarding law and order.'

For the AAP to establish itself as a durable political force in Punjab, it will need to decentralize its decision-making process, and allow the state leadership more autonomy in addressing local issues. The AAP's previous success in Delhi was largely attributed to its focus on local governance and strong leadership under Kejriwal. Replicating this model in Punjab requires empowering local leaders who understand the state's unique challenges and can offer tailored solutions.

To overcome its challenges, the AAP will need to recalibrate its approach to governance. Strengthening law and order, addressing the underlying causes of separatist sentiments, managing fiscal responsibility and empowering the state leadership are crucial steps that the government must take to restore public confidence and ensure long-term stability in Punjab. As the party grapples with these issues, the future of both the AAP and Punjab's political landscape hangs in the balance.

Professor Ronki Ram opined, 'The Lok Sabha election result says that the AAP enjoys the support of people in Punjab. The implementation of the policies, Bhagwant Mann's autonomy in taking decisions and materialization of the promises are key for AAP's future in the state. If the AAP can do these things properly then they will remain the key force in Punjab's politics in the coming days as well.'

26

Expansion Dreams and Realities

It was the first week of November in 2016. I was a journalism student in Delhi, navigating the sprawling city in search of stories that would help me understand the complex world of politics and reporting. At the time, Jawaharlal Nehru University (JNU) was a hub of political unrest, with a massive student protest underway over the disappearance of a student, Najeeb Ahmed. The tension was palpable, and students from across the campus had united in a powerful demonstration – their voices reverberating through the walls of academia.

Amidst the protest, there was a flurry of activity as Delhi's CM made an unexpected visit to address the students. Kejriwal's presence at JNU, where political activism had often found fertile ground, brought with it a wave of curiosity and excitement. Senior political figures from various parties like Shashi Tharoor from the Congress also joined the students.

I found myself standing next to an AAP leader who had accompanied Kejriwal. I asked him a simple question, 'Why did Arvind Kejriwal suddenly visit JNU? What is the plan?'

The leader smiled, and before answering, asked me about myself. I introduced myself as a journalism student, trying to grasp the complexities of political reporting. His smile broadened, and he replied, 'We are a new political party, and we want to expand our reach. Not just in Delhi, but across many states, and among every section of society.' Tapping a CPI(M) student leader's shoulder, he added with a grin, 'Just like them, we also want to become a national party.' The young leader smiled back, offering a nod of goodwill – a subtle recognition that in the world of politics, ambitions often mirror one another.

By then, Kejriwal's speech had concluded, and the leader I was speaking with had to leave, swept away by the tide of political duties. During his speech I remember he attacked the ABVP, the RSS and the BJP at one go. He said, 'The Delhi police has not questioned the accused ABVP students. This is a message that now the ABVP–RSS–BJP goons' supremacy will continue…'

Even as it won in Delhi in 2015, the AAP had already set its sights on expanding beyond the capital. Their mission was not just to govern a city, but to create a national movement across the country.

As of today (2025), the AAP stands as a national political party, with a government in Punjab and a growing presence in states like Goa and Gujarat. The party is also making inroads in Himachal Pradesh, Uttar Pradesh, Assam, Maharashtra and Karnataka. The seeds of ambition sown in those early years have borne fruit, as the party continues to evolve – embodying the very national aspiration that was so casually expressed to me that day at JNU.

I recall another striking encounter from my early days of covering the AAP, this time with a man called Farhan (a pseudonym). The AAP's headquarters were, at the time, located at Deendayal Upadhyay Marg in Delhi. After attending a press conference addressed by Rajya Sabha MP Sanjay Singh, I was preparing to leave when Farhan stopped me outside the office, his face full of anticipation. He asked me about myself, and I briefly told him I was a journalist covering the day's event. Without much hesitation, he asked if I could connect him with Sanjay Singh. Curious, I asked why.

Farhan's answer left me momentarily speechless. 'I am from Kashmir,' he said, with a sense of urgency in his voice. 'I want to contest the local body elections there and need approval from AAP's central leadership.'

At that time, I hadn't heard much about the AAP's presence in Kashmir. The politics of the Valley felt a world apart from Delhi's, with deep-rooted issues of autonomy, militancy and traditional political parties dominating the conversation. I couldn't help but ask, 'How do you plan to fight an election in Kashmir? Does AAP even have an organization there?'

Farhan, sensing my scepticism, patiently explained. 'We have a small but committed group in Kashmir,' he said. 'The people are tired of the same old political dynasties and want an alternative. There is curiosity about AAP, and we want to channel that curiosity into something meaningful.'

His confidence was startling, and though I was running late, I could not ignore his conviction. Before leaving, I connected him with a party member to guide him in his quest. I do not know what became of Farhan. Whether he succeeded in securing an AAP ticket for the local elections in Kashmir remains a mystery. But his ambition was not lost on me. As I write this chapter (in 2024), the AAP has secured an Assembly seat in Kashmir. Mehraj Malik of the AAP emerged victorious in the Doda constituency.[1]

The AAP's appeal has never been confined to Delhi alone. Its potential to expand is not just because of Kejriwal's popularity but because people across India have been yearning for an alternative not only in politics but in governance. People want leaders who prioritize their everyday concerns over political theatrics.

As Sisodia said in a TV interview after his bail in the Delhi liquor policy scam, 'The meaning of alternative politics has evolved. Today, when mainstream politics is about dislodging elected governments by any means, AAP's vision of governance truly stands as an alternative.'[2]

The AAP's initial foray beyond Delhi was marked by ambition, hope and a whirlwind of hasty decisions. As mentioned earlier, in 2013, when it swept to power in Delhi, the party's leadership believed they were riding the crest of a national wave. The resounding success in the capital filled them with a sense of possibility. However, the expansion that followed was far from smooth and revealed deep fissures in the party's structure. The fact that the AAP emerged from the IAC movement ensured that it had supporters across the nation who had rallied behind the ideals of the movement. Yet, having a widespread base of supporters is not the same as the cadre of a well-organized political machinery. The party, in its early days, lacked the structural foundation necessary for long-term success outside of its Delhi stronghold.

'The AAP was born from a movement, and our first priority should have been to establish a solid organizational structure. But I feel that it did not happen,' says Ashutosh. Kejriwal's charismatic leadership and singular vision, while appealing, often sidelined crucial organizational needs, leaving the party vulnerable as it sought to expand into other states.

In the 2014 general elections, the AAP took a daring leap, fielding candidates in over 400 constituencies across India, with a focus on states like Haryana, Punjab, Uttar Pradesh and Maharasthra. The general elections proved to be a bitter lesson. The AAP's ambitions collided with the harsh realities of Indian politics.

Despite this electoral debacle, the AAP attempted to frame the elections as a stepping stone to greater things, rather than a failure. The intent, it said, had not been to secure victories across the 400 seats it contested from but to send a powerful signal: that the AAP was here to stay and had the courage to challenge entrenched power. The election campaign, though fruitless in terms of seats, was an effort to solidify their commitment to serious, nationwide electoral battles in the future and also begin to build a cadre outside of Delhi.

What this and other debacles showed were the limits of charisma without organizational depth and that thc AAP lacked a stable foundation from where it could launch its campaigns. The AAP's strategic errors during this time, according to Amitabh Tiwari, included opposing the Congress but later allying with them to form the Delhi government in 2013 and Kejriwal challenging

Modi in Varanasi in 2014 Lok Sabha election despite the BJP not being a major rival at the time. These actions confused voters.

Goa Gameplan

The AAP's foray into Goa began in earnest during the 2017 Legislative Assembly elections. The party fielded candidates in 40 out of the state's 40 constituencies.[3] Despite a high-profile campaign, it failed to win any seats. This initial setback highlighted the challenges of establishing a foothold in a state with a well-entrenched political landscape dominated by the BJP and the Congress. The party received around 6 per cent vote share.

Undeterred, the AAP continued to build its organizational structure in Goa, focusing on strengthening its grassroots network, engaging with local communities and addressing issues specific to the state. It retained its emphasis on transparency, anti-corruption measures and people-centric policies, gradually building a dedicated support base.

In the 2022 Assembly elections, the AAP's persistence seemed to pay off. It won two seats but the vote percentage did not increase much. Winning 2 out of 40 seats is not as grand a success as the AAP had hoped it would be but it did help them enter the politics of Goa. The AAP's candidates, Captain Venzy Viegas and Cruz Silva, won in the Benaulim and Velim constituencies, respectively.[4] An AAP functionary from Goa told me that the reason of their victory is the party's focus on local issues, such as unemployment, environmental conservation and corruption. Also, the AAP's grassroots mobilization efforts, including door-to-door campaigns and community meetings, helped the party connect with voters on a personal level.

However, according to a senior journalist who covered Goa for a long time, 'In Goa, more than political party the popularity of the candidate is important. Both these candidates were popular local faces that is why they won.'

During the 2022 elections, the AAP strategically focused on the Bhandari community in Goa, recognizing its significant influence in the state's political landscape. The Bhandari community, which is in the OBC category, constitutes a substantial portion of Goa's population. The AAP's efforts to engage with this community have been a key aspect of its expansion strategy in the state. According to reports OBCs constitute around 27 per cent of the total population of Goa, and the Bhandari community is 61 per cent of the total OBC population of Goa.[5]

The AAP's commitment to the Bhandari community was evident in its decision to project a member of this community as its chief ministerial candidate for the 2022 Assembly elections. Amit Palekar, a lawyer-turned-politician, was chosen as the AAP's CM face in Goa. This was a strategic move aimed at garnering support from the Bhandari community. His background as a social worker and his involvement in local issues made him a suitable candidate to represent the community's interests.

The party's focus on the Bhandari community was further emphasized by its promise to give representation to the community in the Assembly and cabinet. The AAP leadership, including Sisodia, highlighted the importance of the Bhandari community in Goa's political landscape and assured them of significant roles in the government. This approach was part of the AAP's broader strategy to build a coalition of support among various communities in Goa.

In addition to focusing on the Bhandari community, the AAP also aimed to address the concerns of other significant groups in Goa. The party announced that its deputy chief ministerial candidate would be from the Catholic community, which also forms around 25 per cent of Goa's total population, according to the last census.

The AAP sought to build alliances with other political parties to enhance its electoral prospects. In 2024, the AAP and the Congress announced a seat-sharing arrangement for the upcoming Lok Sabha elections. The alliance won one out of two seats in the state from the South Goa Lok Sabha constituency, where the Congress candidate won with the support of the AAP. This alliance was seen as a strategic move to consolidate the anti-BJP vote and increase the chances of electoral success.

Success in Gujarat

The AAP's foray in Gujarat is a fascinating journey marked by strategic efforts, grassroots mobilization and electoral tests. It began in earnest during the 2021 local body elections. The party contested the Surat Municipal Corporation elections and won 27 seats,[6] emerging as the main opposition to the BJP. This success was significant, as it demonstrated the party's ability to challenge the established political order in the state. Its performance in Surat was attributed to its focus on local issues, such as sanitation, water supply and public health.

Following this success, the AAP launched a series of campaigns and initiatives to connect with voters across the state. Its leadership frequently visited Gujarat to engage with local communities and understand their concerns. The party's emphasis on transparency, anti-corruption measures and people-centric policies resonated with many Gujaratis, and gradually helped build a dedicated support base.

In the run-up to the 2022 Gujarat Assembly elections, the AAP announced its intention to contest all 182 seats in the state. The party's campaign focused on replicating the Delhi Model of Governance, which included initiatives such as free electricity, free water and improved public services, as we know. The AAP tried to present the Delhi Model as opposed to PM Narendra Modi's Gujarat Model. The AAP's promise to provide high-quality education and healthcare, along with its commitment to clean politics, struck a chord with the disenchanted Congress voters.

The party organized door-to-door campaigns, community meetings and public rallies to connect with voters on a personal level. The AAP's volunteers, known as 'foot soldiers', played a crucial role in spreading the party's message and mobilizing support. The AAP's emphasis on participatory governance and citizen engagement helped build a strong grassroots network across the state.

The 2022 elections marked a significant milestone in the AAP's expansion in Gujarat. The party won five seats and secured about 13 per cent of the vote share.[7] While this performance fell short of its expectations, it was a notable achievement for a relatively new party in Gujarat's political landscape, where the BJP has been uninterruptedly in power since 1998. The AAP's success was attributed to its focus on local issues, effective grassroots mobilization and the appeal of its clean politics agenda.

Following the 2022 elections, the AAP initiated a series of meetings with key leaders and booth in-charges across constituencies to strengthen its grassroots network. These efforts were part of its long-term strategy to solidify its organizational presence and prepare for future elections. The AAP also sought to build alliances with other political parties like the Bharatiya Tribal Party to enhance its electoral prospects. Finally, the alliance talk failed over seat-sharing agreement.

As a result of it gaining 12.5 per cent vote share in the 2022 Gujarat Assembly elections, the Election Commission granted the AAP the status of a national party – the sixth party to receive this recognition in the country. It provided the AAP with certain privileges, such as access to electoral rolls and the ability to contest elections under a common symbol, which further strengthened its organizational capabilities.

Nistula Hebbar told me, 'In Gujarat, the rise of the AAP occurred due to significant sections of the Congress party being dissatisfied with their own party. The AAP successfully capitalized on this discontent and disillusionment among Congress supporters at the ground level. A portion of these disenchanted Congress leaders and supporters cast their votes for the AAP.'

According to political analyst Amitabh Tiwari, in the 2017 Gujarat Assembly elections, the Congress party secured approximately 42 per cent of the vote. This decreased to around 27 per cent in the 2022 Gujarat Assembly elections, reflecting a decline of 15 per cent even as the AAP garnered approximately 12.5 per cent of the vote share. The BJP, on the other hand, experienced a modest increase in vote share, rising by about 3 per cent from the 2017 to the 2022 elections. The rise in the AAP's vote share therefore appears to correlate directly with the decline in the Congress's vote share.'[The] AAP leveraged the dissatisfaction with the Congress in Gujarat and engaged in caste-focused politics,' said Tiwari. 'For instance, selecting Isudan Gadhvi, an OBC, as the chief minister candidate was a strategic decision by AAP.'

Gujarat has long been a stronghold of the BJP, particularly under the leadership of PM Narendra Modi and Home Minister Amit Shah, both of whom hail from the state. The BJP's dominance in Gujarat has been nearly unchallenged for decades, making any political breakthrough by another party noteworthy. In this scenario, the AAP's success in winning five seats and securing 13 per cent of the vote share in 2022 marks a substantial shift.

According to Mahashweta Jani, the state coordinator of CSDS-Lokniti, 'The AAP has stepped into the vacuum in Gujarat's Opposition space.'[8] She further elaborated that the Congress has largely stayed absent from street politics, contrasting sharply with the AAP, which drew attention in 2021 by highlighting the issue of examination papers being leaked. In Gujarat, the AAP's state president, Gopal Italia, has made a name for himself as a combative figure. His bold stance, including a high-profile incident in 2017 when he threw a shoe at the state's Home Minister over corruption, earned him the reputation of a rebel.

Jani also pointed out that Kejriwal has significantly increased the visibility of his party. She noted that while three-wheelers at traffic signals often display photos of Modi, it is now common to see some featuring Kejriwal as well – a level of visibility Rahul Gandhi has not achieved.

The BJP's 'B Team'?

In its expansion strategy, the AAP has targeted states where the political battlefield is dominated by a bipolar contest between the BJP and the Congress, with Punjab being an exception. By focusing on such states, the AAP has followed a calculated plan to rise by eroding the Congress's voter base, filling the vacuum created by the latter's internal struggles and voter disenchantment.

Since the beginning, the AAP has revealed a reliance on absorbing the vote share of opposition parties, especially the Congress. A notable example of this is Delhi itself, where the rise of the AAP effectively dismantled the Congress's support base, while the BSP saw a gradual decline in influence. Yet, what stands out in Delhi is how the BJP's vote share remained remarkably steady throughout the AAP's rise. Even as the AAP surged to prominence, the BJP's vote percentage consistently hovered around 35 per cent, showing little signs of decline. In fact, during each Lok Sabha election, the BJP's vote share rose, while the Congress found itself obliterated by the AAP's meteoric rise.

The AAP's growth, therefore, has been largely dependent on the weakening of the Congress across Delhi, Goa, Gujarat and Punjab, rather than any significant erosion of the BJP's vote bank. As Nistula Hebbar astutely told me, '[The]AAP's expansion is not dependent on the BJP but on the Congress party. In the states where the fight is between the BJP and Congress and the Congress party is either demoralized or broken due to infighting, there AAP rose. The core vote bank in the states where AAP expanded, like Goa, Gujarat and Punjab, is of the Congress party.'

The AAP has recognized the futility of attempting to build its organization from scratch in states where a deeply entrenched BJP or other regional powers hold sway. Instead, it has focused on states where the Congress once had a strong organizational structure but has since faltered due to internal discord and weakened leadership. In these states, the AAP has capitalized on the disillusionment of Congress workers and the electorate, positioning itself as a viable alternative. This approach has allowed the AAP to expand rapidly by leveraging pre-existing organizational frameworks, effectively turning the Congress's network into its own.

Nistula Hebbar recounts an anecdote from her coverage of the Gujarat Assembly elections:

> When I covered the 2017 Assembly elections in Gujarat, I noticed that in several crucial places, Congress had campaign offices. In 2022, when I returned to cover the Assembly elections, I saw that many of these same

> offices, which were once Congress strongholds, had been converted into AAP campaign centres. When I spoke to the leaders present, they openly admitted that they had previously been with the Congress but had left the party due to internal resentment and joined AAP. This is a fundamental phenomenon behind AAP's expansion.

A similar pattern can be seen in states like Gujarat and Goa, where the AAP's growth has been built on the foundations of a crumbling Congress apparatus. In Goa, for example, where the Congress once dominated, the AAP seized the opportunity as the Congress weakened due to factionalism, leadership disputes and defections.

The AAP's approach to growth, therefore, has been opportunistic. In states like Gujarat, Goa and Punjab, the party has stepped in not as a disruptor of the existing BJP–Congress dynamic, but as a beneficiary of the Congress's decline. In these states, the AAP has been able to present itself as a fresh, anti-establishment force, attracting both common voters and disillusioned Congress workers alike. Punjab stands as the best example of the AAP's ability to exploit the weakening of traditional parties. In 2017, after the Congress wrestled the state from the ruling SAD–BJP alliance, the AAP's rise to becoming the second-largest party in the state's legislature was powered largely by the support of disgruntled Congress voters and workers who sought change but didn't trust other, more established players.

However, the AAP's strategy is not without pitfalls. While it has proven adept at filling the vacuum left by a struggling Congress, it still faces the difficulty of solidifying its organizational base in states beyond Delhi. The party's rapid rise, though impressive, has often been driven by external factors like dissatisfaction with the Congress rather than a deeply ingrained support system or mass cadre strength. In states where the AAP lacks a clear organizational foundation, its ability to sustain its momentum remains uncertain. So, though it has increased its countrywide footprint, the question remains whether it can build the depth and resilience necessary to become a lasting national force.

Can the AAP Become a National Alternative?

The answer to whether the AAP can truly emerge as a national political alternative is an unequivocal no. While the AAP is the only political party apart from the BJP and the Congress to govern two states in India (until 2025), its trajectory reveals deep contradictions and fundamental shortcomings that undermine its ambitions. From its inception, the AAP presented itself as a pan-India force with a narrative that transcended regionalism. This distinguishing factor initially set it apart from other parties. However, over time, the AAP has morphed into a Delhi-centric entity, primarily by curbing the growth of its Punjab leadership and consolidating power within its Delhi-based core.

It is worth noting that the AAP has indeed succeeded in crafting and marketing its Delhi Model of Governance – a feat that the Congress, despite ruling multiple states, has failed to replicate. Yet, even this model comes with inherent limitations. Its cornerstone – welfare-centric and populist policies – has a finite appeal. Freebies like subsidized electricity or financial assistance to women may have won previous elections in Delhi, but such promises lose their sheen in states where similar schemes are already in place. As more regional parties adopt and adapt welfare measures tailored to their electorates, the AAP's ability to stand out diminishes. Its reliance on replicating the same strategies across diverse political landscapes reflects a lack of innovative vision and foresight.

Moreover, the lack of a robust ideology poses a significant handicap for the AAP in the current Indian political context. The party's attempt to emulate certain strategies of the BJP – albeit without overt calls for violence or inflammatory rhetoric – reveals a disconcerting opportunism. As discussed earlier, the AAP has repeatedly distanced itself from Muslim voters, shamed the community publicly and avoided standing against injustices targeted at them. The party seems to calculate that disillusioned Muslims, facing hostility from the BJP, will have no choice but to vote for the AAP. To secure votes in Muslim-majority constituencies, the party fields Muslim candidates but fails to demonstrate substantive support for the community's rights and concerns. This two-faced strategy – of exploiting Muslim discontent while refusing to take a principled stand – will inevitably backfire.

Whether you agree with the Congress's ideology or not, one thing that is undeniable in political parties like the Congress, Samajwadi Party, TMC, Rashtriya Janata Dal, DMK and JMM – they firmly oppose the RSS and the BJP's brand of politics. However, Kejriwal takes a bafflingly contradictory approach. While he occasionally targets the BJP, he conspicuously avoids criticizing the RSS, often signalling a subtle camaraderie with its ideology. This duplicitous stance raises serious questions about his political integrity.

Take, for instance, Kejriwal's claim about writing a letter[9] to RSS chief Mohan Bhagwat. Kejriwal said he wanted an answer to five things including whether Bhagwat approves of Modi inducting allegedly corrupt leaders into the BJP using the CBI and ED as tools of coercion. This is not an act of defiance but a calculated appeal to the RSS, as though pleading with Bhagwat to rein in Modi. Such a stance is not just politically fragile but reeks of opportunism designed to keep floating BJP voters reassured that Kejriwal harbours no ill will towards the RSS. It is a masterclass in playing both sides, and it is as unprincipled as it is transparent.

Kejriwal's contradictions don't end there. While posturing as a reformist, the AAP had openly welcomed over five defectors from the BJP and the Congress ahead of the 2025 Delhi Assembly elections. Yet, in his letter to Bhagwat, he questions the RSS's acceptance of BJP's strategy of sidelining its workers for 'carpet-laying duties' while prioritizing new entrants from rival parties. The hypocrisy is glaring: Kejriwal is doing precisely what he criticizes the BJP for, all while attempting to curry favour with the RSS.

This doublespeak lays bare the fragile and opportunistic nature of Kejriwal's politics – a calculated refusal to challenge the ideological roots of the BJP, all in the hope of appeasing a segment of the BJP's voter base. Such a strategy may be clever in the short term but is devoid of the conviction and clarity that true political leadership demands.

Before the 2025 Delhi Assembly election, the AAP's announcements had signalled a notable shift in its political strategy. The party vowed to bar illegal Bangladeshi immigrants[10] from accessing Delhi schools – a move subtly targeting Muslims under the pretext of immigration control. Simultaneously, Kejriwal had promised ₹18,000 monthly aid to Hindu and Sikh priests post-election, appealing directly to these communities.[11]

Let there be no ambiguity: a political party that lacks the courage to stand for India's minorities cannot credibly claim to be an alternative of any kind. The very essence of political opposition in today's India lies in challenging the politics of hatred and division. The AAP has repeatedly failed this test. Its refusal to confront systemic injustices, even as it builds schools and hospitals, reveals a party that prioritizes optics over ethics. Governance achievements, no matter how laudable, cannot substitute for a spine when it comes to standing against communal atrocities or divisive ideologies.

What is the AAP's Future in Coalition Politics?

The AAP's stance on opposition politics is blatantly opportunistic. The party recognized the necessity of Congress for the Lok Sabha elections in Delhi, and joins hands with them when it suits their parliamentary ambitions. Yet, during the Assembly elections, where the AAP held a strong footing, it swiftly sidelined and opposed the Congress. This dual strategy reveals a lack of consistency and conviction in the AAP's approach to coalition politics.

Historically, Kejriwal has demonstrated a troubled relationship with alliance politics. From its inception, the AAP positioned itself against many prominent opposition figures, including Lalu

Prasad Yadav, Mulayam Singh Yadav and Sharad Pawar. Yet, before the Lok Sabha elections, Kejriwal had no qualms about sharing the stage with these leaders and forging temporary alliances. Such tactical flip-flopping underscores the party's failure to establish a clear and credible position on coalition politics. Without a coherent strategy, the AAP's role in forming stable and enduring alliances will remain tenuous at best.

The 2024 Lok Sabha elections exposed a deeper issue: grassroots voters' mistrust of the Congress–AAP alliance. The AAP's very foundation was built on challenging the Congress, and this history of antagonism continues to erode trust when the two parties come together. Kejriwal's inability to form a cohesive and consistent alliance – one capable of contesting elections as a united front – raises serious concerns about the AAP's national ambitions.

Furthermore, the AAP's strained relationships with opposition leaders (barring Mamata Banerjee of the TMC) highlight the challenges it faces in coalition-building. As the AAP expands into other states, it does so largely at the expense of existing opposition parties. This strategy inherently limits its ability to foster collaborative opposition politics. The AAP's future in national politics will depend on its ability to reconcile its expansionist ambitions with a credible and principled stance on coalition politics.

What is the AAP's National Expansion Plan?

At this stage, the AAP does not have a concrete national expansion plan. The earlier strategy aimed to expand the party's presence in states like Uttarakhand, Goa, Gujarat, Haryana, Rajasthan, Uttar Pradesh and Madhya Pradesh. However, the fallout from the liquor policy scandal has significantly impacted these ambitions.

The Delhi liquor policy case, which led to the arrests of prominent AAP leaders like Kejriwal, Sisodia and Sanjay Singh, has cast a long shadow over the party's expansion efforts. The controversy not only tarnished the party's image but also diverted its focus from national ambitions to damage control and legal battles. The scandal provided ammunition to political rivals, particularly the BJP, to question the AAP's integrity and governance model.

In Gujarat, the AAP's expansion plans faced a significant setback when Bhupendra Bhayani,[12] one of its MLAs, defected to the BJP. This defection underscores the challenges the AAP faces in retaining its cadre and building a robust organizational structure in states beyond its strongholds of Delhi and Punjab. The party's inability to prevent such defections raises questions about its internal cohesion and strategic planning.

The AAP's national expansion is heavily dependent on its leadership. The reality is that, apart from Kejriwal, Sisodia and Sanjay Singh, there is a noticeable absence of prominent leaders who can spearhead the party's growth in other states. This leadership vacuum has hindered the AAP's ability to establish a strong local presence and connect with voters at the grassroots level. The party's centralized leadership approach, with a heavy reliance on Kejriwal's charisma and governance model, has not translated into effective local leadership in other states.

Moreover, the AAP's focus on Delhi and Punjab has meant that it has not given adequate prominence to local leadership in other states. This lack of focus on nurturing and promoting regional leaders has limited the party's ability to build a sustainable and widespread political base. The absence of strong local leaders who can resonate with the electorate and address state-specific issues has been a significant impediment to the AAP's national ambitions.

The party's earlier successes in Delhi and Punjab were driven by a combination of effective governance, innovative policies and a strong anti-corruption narrative. However, replicating this model in other states has proven to be challenging. The political dynamics, voter expectations and regional issues vary significantly across states, requiring a tailored approach that the AAP has struggled to develop.

27

National Prospect

The AAP is undeniably positioning itself for a larger role in Indian national politics. Kejriwal, with his distinct leadership style and populist appeal, has emerged as a significant face among opposition leaders. However, the party's national ambitions hinge on several critical factors that will shape its trajectory in the coming years.

Punjab, the only state where the AAP holds power, will be a litmus test. The 2027 Punjab Assembly elections will determine whether the party's governance model resonates with voters over the long term. Losing Punjab would leave the AAP with no state under its control, severely limiting its ability to claim a pan-Indian presence.

Additionally, the AAP's dismal performance in states like Gujarat and Goa highlights the challenges it faces in expanding its footprint. Despite considerable effort, the party has failed to make a significant impact in these regions. If this stagnation continues, it will call into question the viability of its national ambitions. The AAP must not only improve its performance in states where it already has a presence but also strategically target new regions to expand its base.

Haryana, for instance, offers an adjacent political terrain with potential for growth. Yet, the AAP has struggled to establish a robust organization or garner popular support there, raising doubts about its ability to replicate its Delhi–Punjab success in neighbouring states.

Another crucial aspect is the AAP's role within the broader opposition framework, particularly the INDIA alliance. The party's stance on coalition politics remains ambiguous. Aligning with the Congress for the Lok Sabha elections while contesting against it in state elections sends mixed signals to voters. This inconsistent strategy risks alienating the very electorate the AAP seeks to attract. Clarifying its coalition strategy – whether to work within the INDIA bloc or carve an independent path – will be vital for its long-term prospects. Recently, the AAP even raised a demand that the Congress should be ousted from the INDIA bloc.[1]

Moreover, the AAP must articulate a clear position on its ideological stance relative to both the BJP and the Congress. Can it offer a distinctive national alternative, or will it remain a regional player with sporadic influence? These questions will determine how the party is perceived by voters and political analysts alike.

While the AAP has made remarkable strides, the road to becoming a formidable national force is fraught with challenges. Success in upcoming elections, strategic expansion and clarity on coalition politics will be decisive factors. For Kejriwal and his party, the coming years will be critical in determining whether the AAP can truly transcend its regional roots and emerge as a significant player on the national stage. I will try to answer here the three most critical questions for the AAP in terms of its national prospect.

28

2025: The Delhi Challenge

The 2025 Delhi Assembly election was a defining moment for the AAP and Kejriwal. A victory would have cemented the AAP's position as a political force capable of defeating the BJP in direct contests for the third consecutive time – a feat no other party has achieved in recent history. While the JMM, under Hemant Soren, has twice defeated the BJP with Congress as an ally, and the TMC triumphed over the BJP in West Bengal in 2016 and 2021, these victories were in different political contexts. Notably, in West Bengal, the BJP only emerged as the primary opposition after 2016.

The AAP, on the other hand, has directly defeated the BJP in Delhi with overwhelming majorities – winning 67 of 70 seats in 2015 and 62 seats in 2020. This track record raises the stakes for the upcoming election. A reduced margin of victory, even if the AAP retains power, could embolden the BJP as a stronger opposition within the Delhi Assembly. Losing over 10 seats would make governance more challenging, especially under pressure from the central government through the LG.

If AAP were to lose the election entirely, it would be a major blow, putting Kejriwal's leadership and political credentials on the line. Notably, Kejriwal is not the incumbent CM, and he has stated he will only take the post if his party wins. This makes the 2025 election not just a test for the AAP but also a personal battle for Kejriwal, who must prove his continued relevance and leadership in Delhi politics. With its legacy and Kejriwal's future at stake, this election will shape the narrative for the AAP in the years to come.

Before the 2020 Delhi Assembly elections, the AAP had significant advantages that contributed to its landslide victory. Strategic guidance from Prashant Kishor and campaign management by I-PAC had bolstered its outreach, while popular schemes like free bus rides for women and free electricity up to 200 units appealed to voters. However, the political terrain has shifted dramatically since then, leaving the AAP on unstable ground.

Post 2020, the COVID-19 pandemic stalled governance and the introduction of new schemes. This period also brought controversies, including the alleged liquor policy scam, leading to the arrests of prominent AAP leaders. The most significant development, however, was the arrest of Kejriwal himself, marking a critical turning point. Kejriwal's arrest, presented by the party as political vendetta, was initially expected to evoke a wave of sympathy and solidarity among voters. Yet, the 2024 Lok Sabha elections proved otherwise, as the AAP failed to secure a single seat in Delhi despite its alliance with Congress.

This loss revealed a growing discontent among Delhiites, fuelled by perceptions of stalled governance and anti-incumbency after 12 years of AAP rule. The emotional appeal of Kejriwal's arrest did not translate into electoral support, leaving the party scrambling to reclaim its footing. The ongoing schemes have become a significant burden for many stakeholders. For instance, based on my personal interactions with several bus drivers, many expressed reluctance to operate their buses due to financial losses incurred from the free bus travel scheme for women. Similarly, electricity companies are reportedly grappling with massive financial challenges and operational losses, partly due to the free electricity provision for up to 300 units and the lack of a tariff increase for several years.

Despite these mounting issues, the authorities appear unwilling to address these pressing concerns and instead continue to introduce additional populist schemes, further compounding the strain on existing resources and infrastructure.

The AAP introduced two welfare schemes: the enhanced Mahila Samman Yojana, increasing monthly payouts to women above 18 from ₹1,000 to ₹2,100,[1] and free healthcare for residents above 60. While these initiatives aim to reinvigorate the party's voter base, their effectiveness remains uncertain in the face of growing political challenges.

As the AAP approached the 2025 elections, the stakes were higher than ever. With Kejriwal's leadership under scrutiny and public trust waning, the party faced a daunting task to reclaim its place as Delhi's ruling force.

Mahila Samman Yojana: A Gamechanger?

In a bid to solidify its position ahead of the high-stakes 2025 Delhi Assembly elections, the AAP unveiled the Mahila Samman Yojana, offering ₹2,100 monthly to women aged 18 and above. This marked the AAP's first venture into large-scale direct cash transfers, joining a broader trend popularized by parties like the TMC, the JMM and the BJP. Originally proposed at ₹1,000, the revised amount hinged on the party's re-election, underscoring its electoral significance.

The scheme's intent appears twofold: to mitigate the financial burden of inflation on women and to secure a critical voter demographic. Women voters have become pivotal in determining electoral outcomes, as evidenced by welfare-focused policies across India. The AAP's strategy to attract women's support mirrors its earlier promises in Punjab, where a similar pledge remains unfulfilled.

The initiative holds potential to provide real relief to women managing rising household expenses. However, critics question the fiscal sustainability of such populist measures, particularly in light of the AAP's ongoing flagship welfare programmes. Moreover, the delayed implementation raises scepticism. Despite cabinet approval, reports indicate the scheme will require at least three months to launch, leaving a glaring gap before elections.

Delhi's electoral math makes this demographic crucial. With 67 lakh women voters against 79 lakh men, the margin for swaying elections is narrow. Historically, women favoured the Congress, but the AAP disrupted this pattern in 2020 by introducing welfare schemes like free bus travel for women, which resonated widely. The BJP, however, has since gained traction among women voters, particularly since the 2024 Lok Sabha elections.

For Kejriwal, the stakes are high. The scheme is not just a ploy to consolidate women voters but a test of the AAP's credibility. In a political climate where trust is critical, Kejriwal's gamble hinges on whether voters perceive the scheme as a genuine commitment or a convenient electoral tactic. The 2025 elections will reveal whether the AAP's latest promise translates into sustained political support.

Sanjeevani Yojana

For years, the BJP in Delhi has criticized Arvind Kejriwal's government for allegedly depriving Delhiites – particularly senior citizens – of healthcare benefits by not implementing the Ayushman Bharat Yojana. In response, ahead of the 2025 Delhi Assembly elections, the AAP has introduced the Sanjeevani Yojana, a healthcare scheme promising free medical treatment for all senior citizens aged 60 and above in government and private hospitals.[2] Notably, there is no income cap for eligibility under this scheme, signalling an inclusive approach.

Prime Minister Narendra Modi had previously apologized to Delhi residents for the non-implementation of Ayushman Bharat,[3] which had heightened the pressure on Kejriwal's government to deliver an alternative narrative. With Sanjeevani Yojana, the AAP seeks to establish itself as a provider of superior healthcare facilities. While the policy's details are still being drafted, the *Indian Express* reported that the scheme might expand upon the Delhi government's existing surgery referral initiative. This initiative, operational since 2022, allows patients awaiting surgeries at government hospitals for over a month to be referred to private hospitals, with costs covered by the state.

Over 12,000 people have benefited from this scheme between 2022 and 2024, showcasing its potential scalability.

Unlike Ayushman Bharat, which imposes eligibility criteria based on economic status, the Sanjeevani Yojana offers universal access to senior citizens, irrespective of financial background. This inclusivity sets it apart and aligns with the AAP's voter-centric strategy, particularly targeting Delhi's senior citizen demographic. According to available data, Delhi has over 2.1 million senior citizens, constituting approximately 8.5 per cent of the city's population – a number that is likely to have grown.

The scheme's potential impact extends beyond senior citizens. In lower-income, lower-middle-class and middle-class families, healthcare expenses for elderly members often strain household finances. By promising free treatment in private and public hospitals, the scheme could alleviate financial burdens, indirectly benefiting entire families. This broader appeal enhances its political significance, as it positions the AAP as a party focused on addressing everyday challenges.

However, questions remain about its financial feasibility and implementation timeline. Critics argue that such schemes often remain election rhetoric, especially when announced close to polls without operational frameworks. Moreover, with the policy still in its drafting phase, voters may doubt its immediate benefits.

Nevertheless, the Sanjeevani Yojana is a calculated political move that highlights the AAP's effort to counter the BJP's narratives while reinforcing its governance credentials. The 2025 elections will ultimately reveal whether this promise resonates with voters or is dismissed as another populist ploy. For now, it underscores the AAP's bid to regain its narrative dominance in Delhi's political landscape.

No-Alliance with the Congress

In the 2025 elections, the AAP announced that they will not join hands with the Congress party.[4] The reason is that the Congress from 2013 onwards has not done well in the Assembly elections of Delhi, and from 2015 onwards the vote percentage of the

Congress has remained in single digits. That is why the AAP believed that an alliance with the Congress would not be helpful. However, it is not as simple as it sounds.

The AAP's decision to contest the 2025 Delhi Assembly elections without forming an alliance with the Congress poses significant risks, particularly regarding the fragmentation of key voter bases. Historically, Muslim voters have been instrumental in shaping electoral outcomes in Delhi, and their allegiance to the AAP has shown signs of wavering. In 2015, the AAP secured an overwhelming 77 per cent of the Muslim vote, winning 9 out of 10 Muslim-majority seats. However, this support declined to 69 per cent in 2020 and further eroded during the 2022 MCD elections, where the Congress gained ground in Muslim-dominated areas like Mustafabad and Shaheen Bagh. This shift was attributed to the AAP's perceived inaction during the 2020 riots and its ambivalence on contentious issues like the CAA.

Without an alliance, the Muslim vote risks splitting between the AAP and the Congress, weakening the secular bloc and potentially allowing the BJP to consolidate its position. The AAP faces the dual challenge of rebuilding trust with disillusioned Muslim voters while managing the broader implications of a divided opposition, which could erode its dominance in Delhi.

Dalit voters, another critical demographic, also present a challenge for the AAP. Traditionally aligned with the Congress, many Dalits shifted their support to the AAP due to its promises of social justice. However, recent controversies, such as the resignation of Dalit leaders Rajendra Pal Gautam and Raaj Kumar Anand[5], have strained this relationship. Gautam's resignation, following his participation in a Dalit conversion ceremony, highlighted the AAP's struggle to balance Dalit aspirations with broader political sensitivities. Anand's departure in 2024 further underscored growing dissatisfaction among Dalit leaders within the AAP, complicating the party's efforts to retain this crucial voter base. The Congress, meanwhile, has positioned itself as a champion of Dalit concerns, threatening to reclaim its lost support.

The absence of an alliance between the AAP and the Congress intensifies the risk of vote-splitting, particularly among anti-

BJP voters. This division could inadvertently benefit the BJP, undermining the Opposition's collective strength. The AAP's recent initiatives, such as the expanded Mahila Samman Yojana and free healthcare for senior citizens, reflect its attempt to appeal to a broad demographic and reinforce its governance credentials. However, these measures may not be sufficient to counter the effects of a fragmented vote.

Replacing Own People with Defectors

The AAP's strategy for the 2025 Delhi Assembly elections signals a marked departure from its earlier ideals, leaning heavily on replacing its old guard with leaders defected from rival parties like the Congress and the BJP. This approach reflects a shift in the AAP's political ethos, embracing a more conventional, realpolitik strategy. It also raises questions about the party's evolving identity, after once priding itself on grassroots leadership and anti-establishment values.

One of the most telling changes is the sidelining of senior AAP leader and two-time Delhi Assembly Speaker Ram Niwas Goel. A veteran in Delhi politics, Goel played a pivotal role in the AAP's rise and consolidation in Shahdara. However, in a twist of irony, his replacement is Jitender Singh Shunty, the BJP leader Goel defeated in the 2015 elections. According to insiders, Goel was unhappy with Shunty's induction into the AAP, especially given his personal history with him. While the AAP claims internal surveys indicated Goel's declining popularity due to his age, many expected his successor to come from within the party, not from the BJP. Shunty's selection underscores the AAP's apparent attempt to woo the BJP voters in key constituencies by co-opting their leaders.

Another notable shift was in Timarpur, where the AAP has replaced its loyal chief whip, Dilip Pandey, with former Congress MLA Surinder Pal Singh Bittoo.[6] This constituency, historically non-BJP, has consistently leaned towards the Congress or the AAP. While Bittoo's past victories as a Congress candidate add to his electoral appeal, his repeated losses to the AAP since 2013 highlight the risks of alienating the party's core supporters by sidelining steadfast leaders like Pandey.

Similarly, in Seelampur, the AAP replaced MLA Abdul Rehman, a prominent Muslim leader, with Chaudhary Zubair Ahmed, the son of long-time Congress leader Chaudhary Mateen Ahmed. This change comes against the backdrop of the AAP's perceived inaction during the 2020 North East Delhi riots and its ambiguous stance on issues like the CAA. Insiders suggest Rehman's disenchantment with the party's leadership led to his removal. Zubair Ahmed's candidacy, however, aligns with the AAP's broader strategy to consolidate votes in Muslim-majority areas where the Congress traditionally held sway.[7]

In Kirari, a North West Delhi constituency, the AAP replaced two-time MLA Rituraj Govind with former BJP MLA Anil Jha.[8] This move further underscored the party's bid to weaken the BJP's base while drawing on the electoral clout of defected leaders. Meanwhile, Deputy Speaker Rakhi Birla has been shifted from Mongolpuri to the relatively safer Madipur constituency, a calculated decision to mitigate challenges posed by the BJP heavyweight Raj Kumar Chauhan, a former Congress minister.[9]

Political editor and senior journalist Aditya Menon of *The Quint* has noted in an article that AAP's strategy hinges on appropriating the voter bases of its rivals. In areas like Seelampur and Seemapuri, the AAP's move to recruit prominent Congress leaders reflects its intent to consolidate anti-BJP votes, particularly in constituencies where the 2024 AAP–Congress alliance outperformed the BJP. Similarly, by inducting BJP leaders like Jitender Shunty and Anil Jha, the AAP aims to erode BJP's influence while depriving it of key faces in critical constituencies.[10]

While these tactics may bolster the AAP's electoral prospects, they risk alienating the party's core supporters who were drawn to its promise of clean, issue-driven politics. By prioritizing short-term gains over long-standing loyalties, the AAP must tread carefully to avoid undermining its identity as a party of the people. As the election approaches, it remains to be seen whether this gamble will pay off or further fragment Delhi's political landscape.

29

Death of a Dream: The AAP's 2025 Delhi Assembly Election Defeat

The 2025 Delhi Assembly elections, held on 5 February, marked a crucial moment in the capital's political landscape. As evening set in, exit poll results began pouring in, triggering a wave of speculation. Most pollsters indicated that the BJP had gained an edge, setting the stage for what could be a historic victory. The thought lingered in my mind – if these predictions were accurate, it would be the first time in 27 years that the BJP would form a government in Delhi.

Curious about how the AAP supporters were reacting, I reached out to my former neighbour, Pathikrit Mishra, a dedicated AAP worker from Mayur Vihar. Unlike the nervous chatter dominating news channels, Pathikrit remained confident. 'We have conducted our own surveys, and we are winning in all of them. Just look at the names of these exit poll agencies – they lack credibility,' he asserted. His confidence was unwavering, unfiltered by media scrutiny, suggesting a deep belief in the party's internal assessments.

Indeed, exit polls have often been unreliable, sometimes wildly missing the mark. Yet, Delhi is not a sprawling state with rural complexities – it is a metropolitan city where electoral trends are relatively easier to gauge. The AAP leaders quickly dismissed the exit polls, alleging a political agenda behind them.

They claimed that such projections were designed to create an atmosphere that would enable the BJP to poach the AAP MLAs.

The AAP's Rajya Sabha MP, Sanjay Singh, ridiculed the credibility of the exit polls. 'If companies that give massages and run spas, conduct exit polls then you know what will be the condition of exit polls,' he quipped,[1] urging supporters to wait for the final results on 8 February. However, the numbers coming in were not easy to ignore. A sense of urgency gripped the AAP's leadership, leading to a late-night strategy meeting at Kejriwal's residence. The top brass decided on a counter-narrative – that the BJP was attempting to engineer defections.

On 6 February, Kejriwal made an explosive allegation. He claimed that 16 AAP candidates had received calls from BJP operatives, offering ₹15 crore each and ministerial positions in exchange for switching sides. 'Some agencies are showing that the abusive party (BJP) is getting more than 55 seats. In the last two hours, 16 of our candidates have received calls that if they leave the AAP and join their party, they will be made ministers and given Rs 15 crore each,' he wrote in Hindi on X (formerly Twitter).[2] The AAP leaders began circulating phone numbers they alleged were being used for these calls, fuelling a social media storm.

The BJP swiftly dismissed these allegations as baseless, accusing the AAP of playing the victim card in anticipation of an electoral defeat. The controversy escalated when LG Vinai Kumar Saxena ordered an investigation. The ACB and Delhi Police were directed to probe the claims, adding another layer of political drama to an already charged election.

As Delhi awaited the final verdict, the battle was no longer just about votes – it had become a high-stakes war of narratives, with both parties fiercely defending their turf in a politically volatile environment.

The morning of 8 February began with an air of anticipation at 1 Canning Lane, the AAP's new headquarters in Lutyens'

Delhi. As counting commenced, party supporters gathered in large numbers, filling the grounds with banners, tents and hopeful chatter. A massive screen displayed live election trends, while the AAP spokespersons engaged with media channels from makeshift camps. The scene was bustling with energy – OB vans lined the streets, cameras rolled and microphones captured every moment of the unfolding drama.

As the first results trickled in, senior AAP leader Jasmine Shah emerged from the party office, waving confidently at the crowd. Despite early setbacks in postal ballots, he remained optimistic. 'We believe that AAP is going to form the government with a huge majority. It was not a normal election. On one side it was AAP, whereas on the other side, it was the entire system … It was an election between two models of AAP and of the BJP,' he declared, flashing a determined smile.[3] But the numbers told a different story.

Each time the AAP took the lead in a constituency, cheers erupted. But there was an underlying anxiety – an unease masked by forced celebration. The party was struggling in key battlegrounds, including New Delhi, where Kejriwal was trailing. Sisodia, contesting from Jangpura, was unable to close the gap, while Satyendar Jain faced a tough fight in Shakur Basti. Even incumbent CM Atishi was behind in her constituency. Cabinet minister Saurabh Bharadwaj, along with senior leaders like Somnath Bharti, Rakhi Bidlan and Durgesh Pathak, all found themselves on the back foot. By 10.00 a.m., the trajectory was clear – the AAP was in trouble.

By noon, the writing was on the wall. The optimism that had filled the AAP headquarters just hours earlier had evaporated, replaced by a quiet, uneasy acceptance of defeat. Supporters who had gathered in large numbers slowly began trickling out, the once-celebratory atmosphere giving way to silence. The unthinkable was happening – the Lotus was blooming in Delhi after 27 years.

The AAP, which once promised to redefine politics and rid the system of corruption, was now struggling to touch 30 seats. The sense of loss was profound. Anup Singh, a party loyalist from Shalimar Bagh, expressed his disappointment: 'We gave it everything. We campaigned relentlessly. But the results are devastating – it feels like people no longer trust us.'

As the day wore on, the reality set in – the AAP's meteoric rise had hit a hard stop. What had once been a political revolution now seemed like a fading dream. The capital, which had overwhelmingly backed Kejriwal's party for nearly a decade, had turned away, signalling a dramatic shift in Delhi's political landscape.

By the evening, results were declared which saw the AAP secure only 22 of the 70 seats, a steep decline from its landslide victories of 67 seats in 2015 and 62 in 2020. This loss stripped the AAP of power, ceding control to the BJP, which clinched 48 seats. The AAP's vote share dropped to 43.57 per cent, down from 53.57 per cent in 2020, reflecting voter fatigue after 10 years of governance.[4] The party retained strongholds among Dalit and Muslim communities, winning 11 of 12 Scheduled Caste seats and 6 of 7 Muslim-dominated constituencies, though its victory margins shrank significantly – most notably in Ambedkar Nagar, where it fell from 43.58 per cent in 2015 to 4.37 per cent.[5] Senior AAP leader Priyanka Kakkar told me, 'I do not say that there were no shortcomings from our side. Of course we went wrong in certain areas and we are still examining the result. But you must acknowledge that we did not fight against the BJP as a political party. We fought against ED, CBI, other central agencies and also the Election Commission of India. It is this nexus we fought against.'

Why Did the AAP Lose?

Famous Urdu poet Mirza Ghalib once wrote, '*Ik roz apni rooh se poocha, ki Dilli kya hai, to yun jawab main keh gaye, yeh duniya mano jism hai aur Dilli uski jaan* (I asked my soul: What is Delhi? She replied: The world is the body, and Delhi its life).'

Delhi is a wonder in its own right – a microcosm of India encapsulated within a city. From the narrow, bustling lanes of Daryaganj and Matia Mahal to the opulent expanses of Greater

Kailash, Delhi accommodates everyone, yet remains divided – not by caste, but by class. This class divide plays a pivotal role in Delhi's politics, shaping electoral outcomes and governance priorities.

Former CM Sheila Dikshit strived to uphold the pluralism and modernism of Delhi. She worked relentlessly to improve the city's infrastructure and garnered support across different classes. However, with time, the middle class (particularly the lower middle class) grew disillusioned with her governance. Enter Kejriwal, a middle-class professional who understood the socio-economic hierarchy of Delhi like no other. The AAP came to power and retained its hold by strategically appealing to the poor, lower middle class and segments of the upper middle class.

Governance in Delhi is unique in its immediacy – the city-state's relatively small size means that government policies have a direct and tangible impact on its residents. The AAP's early success was rooted in its focus on key public sectors and its well-crafted welfare policies. However, by the 2025 Delhi Assembly elections, the party's governance record was under scrutiny. The anti-incumbency sentiment against the AAP after 10 years in power was at its peak. With the arrests of Kejriwal, Sisodia and other key leaders, the party struggled with a leadership vacuum. In their absence, Atishi, Saurabh Bharadwaj, Kailash Gahlot (who later joined the BJP), Gopal Rai and Imran Hussain attempted to manage governance while simultaneously campaigning against the arrests of their top brass. The result was a glaring administrative failure.

Sanjeer Alam, associate professor at the CSDS, noted in the Lokniti-CSDS Delhi election survey: 'The results of the 2025 Assembly elections show that the AAP lost more than two-thirds of the seats it had bagged in 2020.'[6]

An Anti-Kejriwal Election

After resigning as CM and securing bail from the Supreme Court, Kejriwal emerged from jail, declaring the Delhi Assembly election his 'agnipariksha'. The entire campaign revolved around him, underscoring a clear message – the waning popularity of the AAP supremo.

Kejriwal's declining popularity was not an overnight phenomenon. While the AAP's own missteps played a crucial role, the BJP's sustained narrative-building against him also contributed significantly.

Until 2020, Kejriwal was functioning smoothly, delivering on his promises and enjoying considerable public support. If we compare him with other populist leaders like Mamata Banerjee, Hemant Soren, M.K. Stalin, Yogi Adityanath or Himanta Biswa Sarma, a common factor emerges – their ability to deliver on schemes, even amidst challenges. Many of them faced opposition from the central government, yet they managed to implement their policies effectively.

Kejriwal, however, faltered in this aspect over time. While his contributions to education and healthcare remain undeniable, the past five years have seen a decline in these sectors. Many mohalla clinics shut down or ran out of medicines, and after Sisodia's imprisonment, the AAP's hallmark education reforms also lost momentum.

As mentioned before, at the heart of Kejriwal's appeal was a threefold promise – good governance, honesty and his image as a 'common man'. The BJP systematically dismantled all three. While the AAP blamed the central government and the LG for obstructing its work, the average citizen was less concerned with the reasons and more affected by the fact that progress had stalled.

Kejriwal's arrest further eroded public confidence. Initially, many still believed he was not corrupt. However, as he faced repeated rejections of bail and a prolonged legal battle, public perception shifted. Unlike Hemant Soren, whose singular arrest allowed room for a conspiracy theory, the AAP saw multiple top leaders taken into custody in the liquor policy scam. Gradually, the belief solidified that the party that had once stood against corruption had itself succumbed to it.

The final blow came with the 'Sheesh Mahal' controversy (more on this later). Even those who were hesitant to accept the corruption allegations found their doubts shattered when the BJP strategically circulated videos showcasing Kejriwal's opulent lifestyle. The footage was widely shared on WhatsApp, ensuring that no Delhi voter remained unaware of it. This narrative destroyed the very foundation of his 'aam aadmi' image. By the time elections arrived, public sympathy had evaporated and Kejriwal himself had become the focal point of voter resentment.

Ultimately, Delhi's mandate was not a resounding endorsement of the BJP – it was an unmistakable rejection of Kejriwal.

Middle-Class Factor

The middle class of Delhi has historically played a crucial role in electoral victories. In previous elections, a pattern had emerged: while Delhi's middle class voted for the BJP in the Lok Sabha elections, they leaned towards the AAP in the Assembly elections. In 2025, this trend shifted. Alam observed, 'Compared to 2020, AAP's support among the poor fell by 11 percentage points. Its vote share among the lower classes declined even more sharply – by 18 percentage points. Although the AAP saw a section of the middle-class voters also move away from it, it was among the rich that the party lost hugely.'[7]

The CSDS data highlights a gradual shift in Delhi's middle-class voting patterns. In 2015, the AAP secured approximately 55 per cent of the middle-class vote. By 2020, this figure had dropped slightly to 53 per cent, with the BJP's support rising from 35 per cent to 39 per cent. This indicated a growing inclination towards the BJP among the middle class, forcing the AAP to recalibrate its strategy.

Recognizing this, Kejriwal made an unprecedented move before the 2025 Delhi elections – he released a 'Middle-Class Manifesto'.[8] This manifesto, accompanied by a seven-point charter of demands for the Union Budget, aimed to address the middle class's economic concerns.

The key demands included a significant increase in education spending, urging the government to allocate 10 per cent of the budget to education (up from the current 2 per cent), capping private school fees and expanding scholarships. In healthcare, the AAP advocated for a 10 per cent budget allocation and the removal of taxes on health insurance. The manifesto also proposed raising the income tax exemption limit from ₹7 lakh to ₹10 lakh and removing GST on essential commodities. For senior citizens, it promised free medical services, robust pension schemes and a 50 per cent concession on rail travel.

By highlighting these tangible issues, the AAP sought to position itself as the party that understood and prioritized middle-class aspirations. However, the BJP, well aware of the significance of this demographic, played its trump card just days before the election. On 1 February (four days before polling), Finance Minister Nirmala Sitharaman announced a massive tax relief: individuals earning up to ₹12 lakh annually would pay no income tax. This single move resonated deeply with the middle class and tilted the electoral balance in the BJP's favour.

Ashish Bhattacharya, a 56-year-old banker from Chittaranjan Park, summed up the middle-class sentiment: 'What was Kejriwal giving us? We don't send our children to government schools, we don't go to mohalla clinics, we always get electricity bills above 300 units, so we don't get any relief. Our wives and daughters don't travel by bus. Yet, our tax money was funding freebies for others. We were being used.'

This sentiment was prevalent across Delhi's middle class. The AAP spokesperson Priyanka Kakkar, however, offered a different perspective: 'It would be incorrect to attribute our defeat solely to the middle class. We lost by only a few percentage points to the BJP, which means we still enjoyed support across various sections for our work and honest governance.'

Echoing his concerns, 38-year-old IT professional Ritesh Verma from Malviya Nagar told me:

> I voted for AAP in three consecutive assembly elections because I believed they were challenging the status quo. Even when the party shifted its focus to freebies, I continued to support them, as they were helping the lower middle class and the poor while ensuring basic services

remained intact. But look at Delhi today – the roads are crumbling, drains are clogged, water shortages are rampant and pollution worsens every year. Despite AAP being in power in Punjab, they have failed to address stubble burning. Instead of governance, all we see is constant confrontation with the Centre. At this point, it seems more practical to have the same party ruling both Delhi and the Centre to ensure better coordination and essential services.

Governance Issues

From what Ritesh Verma shared with me, his concerns echoed a larger sentiment reflected in the CSDS study, which identified critical governance failures as key factors behind the AAP's electoral setback in Delhi. Among these, the issue of Yamuna's pollution emerged as a decisive voter concern. The CSDS-Lokniti survey, conducted between 29 January and 6 February, highlighted how the river's deteriorating condition influenced electoral choices, transforming an environmental crisis into a political liability for the AAP government.[9]

The study, which surveyed 3,137 respondents across 28 constituencies, revealed that local governance concerns dominated voter priorities. Over 80 per cent of respondents cited the Yamuna's filth as a major issue, a direct indictment of the AAP's failure to fulfil its 2020 promise of cleaning the river. Kejriwal had staked his credibility on this commitment, even stating that voters should reject him if he failed. Well, they did. The river, choked with sewage and industrial waste, came to symbolize the AAP's broader governance lapses. More than 90 per cent of respondents expressed disappointment over the city's cleanliness, further fuelling anti-incumbency sentiments. Kejriwal's last-minute campaign claim that Haryana had 'poisoned' the Yamuna failed to resonate – voters dismissed it as yet another excuse.

This growing disenchantment handed the BJP a powerful narrative. Narendra Modi, in a rally in Rohini, labelled the AAP as an '*AAPda*' (disaster), citing Yamuna's neglect, the water crisis and pollution as emblematic of the party's administrative failures. Following the BJP's victory, Parvesh Verma pledged to 'revamp the Yamuna riverfront', tapping into voter expectations for concrete action. The survey also found that over half of the electorate had decided their votes before the campaign began, with the BJP successfully consolidating anti-AAP sentiments among upper castes and OBCs.

Political analysts of CSDS, Sandeep Shastri and Sanjay Kumar, noted, '[...]More than nine of every 10 respondents were disappointed with "the lack of cleanliness" in the city and more than eight of every 10 upset over pollution and the non-availability of clean drinking water...'[10]

Systematic Undermining of Delhi's Elected Government

While the AAP bears responsibility for its governance failures, it is essential to recognize that the party was not solely to blame. Since the AAP's resounding victory in the 2020 Delhi Assembly elections, the BJP-led central government has systematically weakened its authority – both by stalling its initiatives and through legislative manoeuvres designed to curb its powers.

One of the most significant moves in this direction came in 2021 when the Centre passed the Government of NCT of Delhi (Amendment) Act or the GNCTD (Amendment) Act. This legislation fundamentally altered Delhi's governance structure by shifting power from the elected government to the LG. The amendment redefined 'government' to mean the LG, effectively reducing the CM and council of ministers to secondary players. It mandated that the LG be consulted on all executive decisions, significantly delaying policy implementation. Additionally, the Act stripped the Delhi Assembly of its rule-making powers, requiring that certain bills be routed through the LG to the President, further entangling governance in bureaucratic red tape.

The AAP and its allies condemned the move as an outright assault on democracy, arguing that it disenfranchised Delhi's voters. The BJP, however, defended the amendment, citing Article 239AA of the Constitution, which grants Delhi a unique status as a Union Territory requiring central oversight. Instead of resolving disputes, the amendment escalated tensions, setting the stage for future confrontations – most notably the 2023 ordinance.

In a landmark judgment on 11 May 2023, the Supreme Court ruled in favour of the AAP government, affirming its control over services, including bureaucratic appointments, except in areas reserved for the Centre, such as police and land (this is separate from the 2018 judgment). The five-judge bench, led by then Chief Justice D.Y. Chandrachud, reaffirmed the democratic principle that an elected government must have authority over its administration.[11] This ruling should have strengthened the AAP's governance, but its victory was short-lived.

Barely a week later, on 19 May 2023, the Centre retaliated with the GNCTD (Amendment) Ordinance, overturning the Supreme Court's decision.[12] This ordinance created the National Capital Civil Service Authority, once again placing the LG above the CM in matters of bureaucratic appointments. Justified under Delhi's status as the national capital, this move stripped the elected government of a crucial aspect of governance, sparking fresh legal and political battles. The ordinance was later enacted into law, ensuring the continued dominance of the Centre over Delhi's administration.

Alongside these legislative curbs, the BJP also wielded the office of the LG as a tool for political pressure. Lieutenant Governor Vinai Kumar Saxena intensified crackdowns on the AAP leaders, further crippling the party's functioning. As the AAP struggled to implement policies amidst these constraints, the visible decline in Delhi's infrastructure – overflowing sewers, deteriorating roads and an escalating water crisis – became ammunition for its critics.

The AAP leader Akshay Marathe captured this reality succinctly:

> The BJP's systematic disempowerment of AAP [...] had severe consequences for Delhi's people. The city fell into a state of disrepair: sewers choked and overflowed, roads

> crumbled, water pipelines leaked, and garbage piled up in colonies. Delhi's citizens were subjected to deliberate suffering as punishment for their political choice. By the time the Delhi elections of 2025 arrived, one section of the city – those who did not rely on Kejriwal's free education, healthcare, power, water, and transport – yearned for more visible signs of a functioning government. The ransom was finally paid to the BJP in the form of votes.[13]

This erosion of the AAP's governing capacity played a pivotal role in shifting public sentiment. What began as a clash over governance soon turned into a broader political struggle, ultimately reshaping Delhi's electoral landscape.

Corruption and Credibility

Another significant blow to the AAP's credibility came from corruption allegations, particularly the 'Sheesh Mahal' controversy. According to CSDS-Lokniti study nearly two-thirds of respondents perceived the AAP as corrupt, with 28 per cent labelling it 'very corrupt' – a dramatic shift for a party that had emerged from the 2011 anti-corruption movement.[14]

The controversy centred on the lavish renovation of Kejriwal's official residence at 6 Flagstaff Road. Initially budgeted at ₹7.91 crore in 2020, costs ballooned to ₹33.66 crore by 2022 – a staggering increase, according to a leaked CAG report.[15] The BJP seized this opportunity to attack the AAP, branding Kejriwal's residence a 'Sheesh Mahal' of extravagance, replete with imported curtains, marble fittings and luxury appliances. This image of opulence starkly contrasted with Kejriwal's earlier portrayal as a humble leader who once drove a WagonR. The survey found that 4 in 10 respondents viewed the expenditure as wasteful, undermining the AAP's claims of fiscal prudence.

The BJP capitalized on this scandal alongside the liquor policy controversy, in which Kejriwal, Sisodia and Satyendra Jain faced legal action. Union Home Minister Amit Shah declared that Delhi's electorate had demolished Kejriwal's 'Sheesh Mahal of lies'. The BJP's sustained campaign effectively linked these scandals to broader governance failures – unfulfilled promises on Yamuna's cleanup and declining civic management – further eroding the AAP's moral high ground.

As Shastri and Kumar observed, '[T]he AAP and its leadership faced a severe "credibility deficit". Not just the defeat of the party but the defeat of its key leaders in their constituencies was an indicator of the same. [...] Lokniti-CSDS Survey showed that half the respondents were disappointed with the work done by their representatives. [N]early one in every three (35%) of those disappointed with their MLA's performance were "strongly disappointed".'[16]

However, the AAP leaders rejected the notion that corruption allegations swayed voters. In an interview for this book, AAP spokesperson Priyanka Kakkar told me, 'I do not believe people think we are corrupt. Around 43 per cent still voted for us because of our ideology. We did not lose credibility – the BJP orchestrated the liquor policy case and Sheesh Mahal narrative. There is no truth in these allegations. However, I agree that the arrests of our top leaders affected us politically.'

Shift in Women's Vote

In the 2020 Delhi Assembly elections, women voters had played a crucial role in the AAP's sweeping victory. However, in the latest election, this support dwindled significantly. Despite a higher female turnout – 60.92 per cent compared to 60.21 per cent for men – political analysts suggest that women did not back the AAP as they did before.[17]

The AAP attempted to woo women voters with ambitious financial promises. Before the 2024 Lok Sabha elections, it pledged ₹1,000 monthly under the Mahila Samman Yojana, later increasing it to ₹2,100 ahead of the Assembly polls. However, this strategy failed. The party's credibility had already taken a hit due to corruption allegations. Women who had once embraced the AAP's free bus rides in 2020 now saw these new pledges as empty rhetoric. Adding to the AAP's woes was its track record in Punjab, where a similar ₹1,000-aid promise remains unfulfilled despite the party being in power. Delhi's women voters noticed this failure, further deepening distrust.

Based on the Lokniti-CSDS survey data, the AAP's vote share among female voters dropped by 11 percentage points compared to the 2020 elections. While the AAP still outperformed the BJP among women, securing 49 per cent of their votes compared to the BJP's 43 per cent, this decline marked a significant shift that weakened the party's overall electoral performance.[18]

Several factors explain why women's support for the AAP declined. One key reason is the limited reach and impact of the AAP's women-centric welfare schemes, particularly among non-beneficiaries. The free bus travel scheme, a flagship initiative of the AAP government, did sway beneficiaries in its favour, with 55 per cent of these women voting for the AAP, giving it a 17-point lead over the BJP among this group. However, among women who did not benefit from the scheme, the AAP's support plummeted to just 29 per cent, while the BJP captured a commanding 61 per cent of their votes.[19] This stark contrast suggests that the AAP failed to convince non-beneficiary women of its broader governance or welfare credentials, limiting the scheme's electoral dividend to a narrower segment of the female electorate.

Over the past five years, the AAP has failed to introduce any significant new schemes specifically for women. The only initiative it proposed was never implemented – a point I have detailed in my analysis. Another major commitment the AAP made was the installation of CCTV cameras across Delhi to enhance women's safety. However, this project, too, remained incomplete.

The issue of 'non-beneficiary' women, as highlighted in the CSDS survey, further underscores the growing dissatisfaction with the AAP. This segment, largely comprising upper-middle-class and affluent women, exhibited the highest levels of disenchantment. Unlike previous elections, which were often shaped by community-based voting patterns, this election was largely driven by class dynamics. Women's disillusionment with the AAP was no exception, reflecting a broader shift in electoral behaviour.

Meanwhile, the BJP successfully capitalized on this discontent. Its Mahila Samridhi Yojana, offering ₹2,500 per month, gained significant traction. Launched post-election under CM Rekha Gupta, the scheme mirrored BJP's successful welfare strategies in Madhya Pradesh and Maharashtra. Coupled with the party's focus on safety and well-executed outreach efforts – like closed-door meetings under the Pink Parcha campaign – the BJP's narrative of governance reliability under Narendra Modi resonated more effectively than the AAP's last-minute populism.

The AAP's inability to counter the BJP's strategic groundwork and its failure to adapt to the evolving political landscape cost it dearly. The loss of women's trust played a decisive role in its defeat, highlighting a critical miscalculation in its electoral strategy.

The Congress Effect

Beyond governance failures, the AAP's shifting political alliances also played a role in its decline. Poll strategist Prashant Kishor remarked, 'His [Kejriwal] fluctuating stance – first aligning with the INDIA bloc and then exiting it – hurt his credibility.'[20] This proved true on the ground. Despite Kejriwal's arrest and the party's efforts to frame it as political persecution, there was no sympathy wave in Delhi. By contrast, JMM leader Hemant Soren, arrested under similar circumstances, received massive voter backing upon his release, securing a significant victory in Jharkhand's elections.

A major setback for the AAP was its failure to form an alliance with the Congress, despite both parties being part of the INDIA bloc. This division fragmented the anti-BJP vote, directly costing the AAP at least 11 key constituencies where Congress's vote tally exceeded the margin of AAP's defeat, ultimately helping the BJP break its 27-year losing streak in Delhi.

Take New Delhi, where Kejriwal lost to BJP's Parvesh Verma by 4,089 votes. Congress's Sandeep Dikshit polled 4,568 votes. Had these shifted via an alliance, Kejriwal might have eked out a win. In Jangpura, Sisodia fell to BJP's Tarvinder Singh Marwah by just 675 votes, while Congress's Farhad Suri drew 7,350 votes – enough for a comfortable AAP victory if united. Greater Kailash saw Saurabh Bharadwaj lose to BJP's Shikha Roy by 3,188 votes, with Congress's Garvit Singhvi siphoning off 6,711 votes. Malviya Nagar mirrored this: Somnath Bharti trailed BJP's Satish Upadhyay by 2,131 votes, as Congress's Jitender Kumar Kochar took 6,770 votes.

The pattern held elsewhere. In Rajinder Nagar, Durgesh Pathak lost to BJP's Umang Bajaj by 1,231 votes, with Congress's Vineet Yadav grabbing 4,105 votes. Chhatarpur's Brahm Singh Tanwar fell to BJP's Kartar Singh Tanwar by 6,239 votes, while Congress's Rajender Singh Tanwar polled 6,601 votes. Sangam Vihar's razor-thin race saw AAP's Dinesh Mohaniya lose to BJP's Chandan Kumar Choudhary by 344 votes, dwarfed by Congress's 15,863 votes. Trilokpuri (392-vote margin, Congress: 6,147), Timarpur (1,168-vote margin, Congress: 8,361), Badli (15,163-vote margin, Congress: 41,071) and Nangloi Jat (26,251-vote margin, Congress: 32,028) followed suit. Without Congress's spoiler role, the AAP could have clinched a tighter race, perhaps nearing the 35 seats needed to challenge BJP's dominance. Division proved fatal.

Priyanka Kakkar of the AAP reflected on this dynamic, stating, 'It was very clear that the Congress wanted to play this role of a spoiler. They are exposed now. Congress leaders openly admitted that this defeat was different from their past defeats in Delhi – their goal was to weaken AAP.'

Community Disenchantment

It is important to acknowledge that disenchantment of different communities also played a crucial role in the AAP's debacle. For example, particularly in constituencies with a high Muslim population the AAP did not perform well. Once a dominant force in these areas, the AAP's performance reflects a shifting political landscape that raises questions about its enduring appeal among key voter groups.

In the 2020 elections, the AAP secured a commanding 62 out of 70 seats, bolstered by robust support from Muslim-majority constituencies like Okhla, Mustafabad and Seelampur. However, in 2025, the party's vote share in seats where Muslims exceed 25 per cent of the electorate dropped by over 10 percentage points, settling at around 51 per cent. This erosion did not benefit the BJP, which saw a marginal decline of 1.1 per cent in these areas, but rather signalled a fragmentation of votes. The All India Majlis-e-Ittehadul Muslimeen (AIMIM) and the Congress emerged as key players, siphoning off significant portions of the AAP's traditional Muslim support base. In Okhla, AIMIM's candidate garnered 27.1 per cent, finishing second, while in Mustafabad, the party secured 16.6 per cent, contributing to the AAP's loss to the BJP.[21]

Analysts point to multiple factors behind this shift. The AAP's perceived inability to address Muslim community concerns – such as post-2020 riot rehabilitation and opposition to the CAA – may have fuelled disillusionment. Meanwhile, the AIMIM's targeted outreach and the Congress's resurgence, with a 4 per cent vote share increase in these seats, split the anti-BJP vote. Despite retaining six of seven Muslim-majority seats, the AAP's reduced margins underscore a vulnerability.

The AAP's defeat in Delhi can be attributed to several factors, many of which have been discussed in the chapter. However, one of the most decisive elements was also the BJP's highly strategic and localized campaign. The saffron party focused singularly on allegations of corruption against the AAP and its record of misgovernance, ensuring that these issues dominated public discourse.

The RSS also played a crucial role in BJP's victory. Its grassroots network mobilized support through small neighbourhood meetings and door-to-door outreach, consolidating voter sentiment in favour of the BJP. The result is now clear – Rekha Gupta has been sworn in as the CM of Delhi, marking the end of the AAP's rule in the national capital.

For the AAP, the challenges ahead are manifold. The first and most immediate task is to keep the party intact in Delhi. Defections have become a political norm, and the BJP will likely use every tactic at its disposal to weaken the AAP's ranks. Holding the flock together will require not just damage control but also a clear vision for the party's future. Additionally, without a thorough organizational overhaul, the AAP's survival in the capital will become increasingly difficult.

Another pressing issue is the need for a new political narrative. Kejriwal's once-powerful slogan of 'Kaam ki Rajneeti' has lost its resonance. The party must craft a fresh appeal that can reconnect with voters and counter the BJP's aggressive messaging. Most importantly, the AAP must work to rebuild its credibility. The loss in Delhi has left the party in a precarious position, and Kejriwal's response has only compounded the crisis. His failure to directly address the people of Delhi or engage with the press has created a vacuum – one that the BJP has been quick to exploit. Instead of focusing on damage control in Delhi, Kejriwal appears preoccupied with Punjab, further alienating his core voter base.

For Kejriwal and the AAP, the way forward is clear: they must re-establish their connect with the people of Delhi. Political survival hinges on engagement, and unless Kejriwal steps out of his defensive posture and actively reaches out to the electorate, the party risks further decline.

Acknowledgements

Writing a book on politics that traces the evolution and journey of the AAP was no small task. This book represents countless hours of reflection, research and writing, but it would not have been possible without the unwavering support of so many people who stood beside me through every step of this journey.

First and foremost, I must thank my daughter, Aishiki (Ginnu), who, at just six years old, displayed patience and understanding beyond her years. She endured my long hours of writing and deadlines with love and affection that made this journey unforgettable. My wife, Anindita, deserves heartfelt gratitude for managing everything at home and ensuring that I had the peace and space to write. Her sacrifices during this time were immense, and I owe her the time and attention I could not give during this process.

This book is also a tribute to my parents, Ratna Ghosh and Professor Amit Kumar Ghosh. My father instilled in me a deep appreciation for politics, the discipline of reading and the importance of analysing society with a critical eye. Without their support and guidance, my intellectual journey – and this book – would not have been possible.

I am indebted to my friends, Aupala and Modhura, who tolerated my absence and supported me unconditionally during this project. My editors, both in journalism and as a columnist, played an instrumental role. Durbar Ganguly (*Millennium Post*), Arya Rudra (*The Statesman*), Anup Verma (*Morning Standard*), Utpal Kumar (*CNN News18* and *Firstpost.*), Sanghamitra Mazumdar

(*ABP Live*), Saptarshi Basak (*Indian Express*), Aditya Menon (*The Quint*), Nardeep Singh Dahiya (formerly *Firstpost.*), Viju Cherian (*Deccan Herald*), C.H. Unnikrishnan (*CNBC TV18*), Vidya Heble (*Mid-day*), Sanjiv Shankaran (*Moneycontrol*) and others stood by me like a rock, offering guidance and encouragement that made this work possible.

I extend my gratitude to Aurangzeb Naqshbandi, Ashutosh, Nistula Hebbar, Ambar Kumar Ghosh, Amitabh Tiwari, Shailendra Sharma, Aditya Menon and Professor Ronki Ram for their time, insights and invaluable support. I would also like to thank my mentors – Ramu Patil, Josy Joseph, Bhavdeep Kang and the late Kingshuk Mukherjee – for their invaluable guidance and support.

During my time at the DARC, I was fortunate to receive mentorship and guidance from many individuals, including Jasmine Shah, then vice-chairperson of the DDCD, former Deputy CM Manish Sisodia, former AAP social media and IT head Ankit Lal, Shalin Mitra of the Health Department and others. My colleagues Mansha and Ramya, and mentors like Abhinandita Mathur, Atishi, Shailendra Sharma, Dilip Pandey and MP Sanjay Singh provided incredible support and encouragement throughout.

I also owe much to my alma mater, St Xavier's College (Autonomous), Kolkata, and its principal, Rev. Father Dominic Savio, for the constant support. I also wish to acknowledge the support of vice principal (Arts and Science) Prof. Bertram Da Silva; dean of Arts, Dr Farhat Bano; and dean of Science, Dr Indranath Chaudhuri for their constant encouragement and guidance. My academic mentors, Dr Ipsita Borat, Prof. Utsav Chakraborty and my PhD guide, Dr Romica Bhat, guided me through the world of academia, enriching my perspectives and work.

Lastly, I am deeply grateful to my editor, Swati Chopra, whose patience, constructive criticism and acknowledgment of my efforts kept me motivated. I also want to thank Wesley D'Souza and Sagareeka Pradhan for their meticulous editing, thoughtful suggestions and dedicated efforts. My thanks also goes to Chiki Sarkar of Juggernaut Books for believing in this project and giving me the platform to tell this story.

This book has been a journey of learning and unlearning, of gaining and losing, especially during the challenging times of the COVID-19 pandemic. While I may have inadvertently missed some names, every single individual mentioned – and those unmentioned – has played a vital role in making this book a reality. Thank you all.

A Note on the Author

Sayantan Ghosh is an accomplished journalist and academic based in Kolkata. He currently teaches journalism in the Department of Mass Communication, Videography and Journalism at St Xavier's College (Autonomous), Kolkata. With over eight years of experience in journalism, Sayantan began his career as a political correspondent with *Millennium Post* in Delhi. His journey later led him to the Delhi Assembly Research Centre, where he served as an associate fellow, working closely with the office of the then deputy chief minister of Delhi, Manish Sisodia.

Alongside his teaching responsibilities, Sayantan is pursuing a PhD in Journalism at the Amity School of Communication, Amity University, Kolkata. His research and academic interests are complemented by his role as a regular political commentator for numerous esteemed publications, including *The Quint*, *Moneycontrol*, *CNBC-TV18*, *CNN News18*, *Firstpost.*, *Deccan Herald*, *ABP Live* and *ETV Bharat Digital*, among others. Additionally, he contributes a monthly column titled 'Here, There and Everywhere' for the *Free Press Journal*.

Sayantan's work reflects his deep engagement with contemporary political discourse and media practices. He lives with his wife and young daughter, balancing his roles as a teacher, researcher, commentator and family man.

Endnotes

PART 1: ORGIN STORY

1: Anna vs Arvind

1. Abhinav Rajput, ‘“Quit AAP” as It Moved Away from Core Values, Says Minister Kailash Gahlot’, *The Times of India*, 21 November 2024, https://tinyurl.com/5y5bhy2c.
2. Kailash Gahlot (@kgahlot), X (formerly Twitter), 17 November 2024, 12.17 p.m., https://tinyurl.com/mruws4by.
3. TNN, ‘Anna Hazare Confirms Rift with Arvind Kejriwal, Says His Apolitical Mass Movement Will Continue’, *The Times of India*, 19 September 2012, https://tinyurl.com/mu3an23b.
4. Mayank Gandhi and Shrey Shah, *AAP and Down: The Rise and Fall of the Aam Aadmi Party*, Simon and Schuster India, 2018, p. 7.
5. Ibid. 34.
6. Ibid. 103.
7. Jiby Kattakayam, ‘Kejriwal Urges “Total Revolution”’, *The Hindu*, 16 November 2021, https://tinyurl.com/ysc68wnc. .
8. Mayank Gandhi and Shrey Shah, *AAP and Down: The Rise and Fall of the Aam Aadmi Party*, Simon and Schuster India, 2018, p. 104.
9. PTI, ‘Anna Hazare Tells Arvind Kejriwal Not to Use His Name, Photo for Votes as They Part Ways’, *India Today*, 20 September 2012, https://tinyurl.com/4b6r2nkh.

2: RSS Support

1. Praveen Donthi, ‘How Ties with the Think Tanks Vivekananda International Foundation and India Foundation Enhance Ajit Doval’s Influence’, *The Caravan*, 5 November 2017, https://tinyurl.com/34kwsamu.

2. Ibid.
3. ITGD Bureau, 'Anna Hazare to End His Fast as Govt Agrees to Redraft Lokpal Bill', *India* Today, 9 April 2011, https://tinyurl.com/bddr4776.
4. Gargi Parsai, 'Hazare Begins Fast on Ramlila Grounds', *The Hindu*, 17 November 2021, https://tinyurl.com/3aecu4vt.
5. TNN, 'Problems Mount for Govt as Anna Joins Ramdev's Fight', *The Times of India*, 3 June 2011, https://tinyurl.com/2tsmwupa.
6. Nistula Hebbar, 'Kejriwal May Not Be Able to Come Out of Chakravyuh Laid by His Opponents: KN Govindacharya', *The Economic Times*, 7 February 2014, https://tinyurl.com/bd3znzwd.
7. Ibid.
8. VOI, 'Political AAP Hid Behind Apolitical IAC: S Gurumurthy', Bharata Bharati, 5 February 2014, https://tinyurl.com/hcefheax.
9. Ibid.
10. Mayank Gandhi and Shrey Shah, *AAP and Down: The Rise and Fall of the Aam Aadmi Party*, Simon and Schuster India, 2018, p. 91.
11. PTI, 'RSS Slams Anna Hazare', *Deccan Herald*, 5 February 2012, https://tinyurl.com/y3ej9buk.
12. 'Anna Hazare's Mumbai Fast', *NDTV*, 26 December 2011, https://tinyurl.com/u9mvf2kd.
13. 'Once Its Core Member, Prashant Bhushan Says IAC Propped up by RSS, BJP', *The Indian Express*, 15 September 2020, https://tinyurl.com/54r8kuus.
14. 'Shanti Bhushan & Prashant Bhushan in Conversation with Rajdeep Sardesai | India Today India Tomorrow', YouTube, 12 September 2020, https://tinyurl.com/47cc8pu9.

3: IAC to AAP

1. Mayank Gandhi and Shrey Shah, *AAP and Down: The Rise and Fall of the Aam Aadmi Party*, Simon and Schuster India, 2018, p. 117–18.
2. Ibid. 117.
3. IANS, 'Arvind Kejriwal Formally Launches Aam Aadmi Party', *NDTV*, 26 November 2012, https://tinyurl.com/4682wxwb.

4: Uncertain Beginnings

1. PTI, 'Don't Pay "Illegal" Power, Water Bills: Kejriwal', *Business Standard*, 22 March 2013, https://tinyurl.com/366kz4up.
2. Avijit Ghosh, '13 Days On, Arvind Kejriwal Still on Fast Track', *The Times of India*, 5 April 2013, https://tinyurl.com/6m4hhrmy.

3. 'Arvind Kejriwal Ends Hunger Strike' *The Times of India*, 6 April 2013, https://tinyurl.com/bdfsh4ec.
4. Dipankar Ghose, 'Delhi Assembly Polls: Nine Crorepatis in AAP List of 18, Shazia Ilmi the Richest', *The Indian Express*, 15 November 2013, https://tinyurl.com/ycywayen.
5. PTI, 'AAP Influence Over, Bubble Has Burst: Sheila', *Firstpost*, 22 November 2013, https://tinyurl.com/s22s23et.
6. 'War Over Aam Aadmi Party's Poster Campaign Against Sheila', *The Times of India*, 27 June 2013, https://tinyurl.com/3brfnbr6.
7. Mayank Gandhi and Shrey Shah, *AAP and Down: The Rise and Fall of the Aam Aadmi Party*, Simon and Schuster India, 2018, pp. 143–44.
8. Hemant Abhishek, 'Arvind Kejriwal Takes Oath as Delhi Chief Minister', Zee News, 29 December 2013, https://tinyurl.com/4w4kpk2d.

5: Calculated Exit

1. Vishal Kant, 'Kejriwal's New Year Gift to Delhi: 50% Power Subsidy', *The Hindu*, 4 December 2021, https://tinyurl.com/3epyc7ca.
2. 'Kejriwal Keeps His Promise, 20,000 Litres of Free Water to Delhi Households from January 1', *India Today*, 31 December 2013, https://tinyurl.com/mskur3ft.
3. 'Arvind Kejriwal's Government Launches an Anti-corruption Helpline in Delhi', *The Times of India*, 11 January 2014, https://tinyurl.com/7kz5tc8a.
4. Naziya Alvi Rahman, 'Delhi CM Arvind Kejriwal to Sit on Dharna If Cops Not Suspended', *The Times of India*, 18 January 2014, https://tinyurl.com/mrwsatuk.
5. 'AAP's National Executive Meeting in Delhi to Decide on Lok Sabha Strategy', *India Today*, 4 January 2014, https://tinyurl.com/nnhdy3n2.
6. PTI, 'Congress, BJP Oppose AAP's "Hasty" Move to Push Jan Lokpal Bill', *The Times of India*, 14 February 2014, https://tinyurl.com/4626um3s.

6: 'Get Rid of Gaddars'

1. PTI, 'Shanti Bhushan Attacks Arvind Kejriwal Again, Accuses Him of Accepting "Tainted Money"', NDTV, 12 February 2015, https://tinyurl.com/5bbjtz22.
2. 'Prashant Bhushan Submits List of 12 AAP Candidates with Dubious Reputation', ZEE News, 24 January 2015, https://tinyurl.com/y8dy7ptn.

3. PTI, 'AAP's National Executive Meet on Feb 26', *India Today*, 20 February 2015, https://tinyurl.com/4wefcz8a.
4. Mayank Gandhi and Shrey Shah, *AAP and Down: The Rise and Fall of the Aam Aadmi Party*, Simon and Schuster India, 2018, p. 193.
5. Ibid. 194–96.
6. Ibid. 208.

PART 2: POLICY, POLITICS AND POPULISM

7: Delhi Model of Governance

1. 'Delhi Elections 2015: Arvind Kejriwal Prepares Youngest Cabinet in India with Average Age of 37 Years', *The Economic Times*, 13 February 2015, https://tinyurl.com/2x28ukrz.
2. 'CBI Justifies Raid on Kejriwal's Office', *The Hindu*, 17 November 2021, https://tinyurl.com/46y465pp.
3. 'Highlights of AAP's Manifesto', *The Hindu*, 4 December 2021, https://tinyurl.com/3spxtcu4.
4. 'Delhi Elections 2015: Arvind Kejriwal-Led AAP Breaks Rules of Identity Politics, Dents Core Vote Bases of BJP & Congress', *The Economic Times*, 23 January 2015, https://tinyurl.com/mr2e9p5j.
5. Raj Singh, 'Delhi Assembly Elections 2015: Important Facts and Major Stakeholders', India TV, 21 January 2015, https://tinyurl.com/nkkamrjv.
6. 'Delhi Budget Updates | AAP Govt Allocates ₹16,396 Crore for Education; To Give ₹1,000 per Month to Every Woman', *The Hindu*, 4 March 2024, https://tinyurl.com/yc2chnry.
7. 'Delhi Government's Education Reform Scheme "Chunauti" Based on Abhijit Banerjee's Model: Kejriwal', *The New Indian Express*, 15 October 2019, https://tinyurl.com/5cv9wwcz.
8. 'Delhi Govt. Launches Course to Encourage Entrepreneurship', *The Hindu*, 8 September 2021, https://tinyurl.com/592x3u9h.
9. PTI, 'Delhi Govt's Mega PTM Has Helped Parents Get Involved in Children's Development Process: Research', India TV, 23 September 2021, https://tinyurl.com/mrpetm3f.
10. Atul Mathur, 'Delhi: Vigilance Submits Report Alleging "Grave Irregularities and Corruption" in Construction of 2,405 Classrooms', *The Times of India*, 25 November 2022, https://tinyurl.com/ynepmtz8.
11. 'Over 1 Lakh Ninth-Graders Fail in Academic Year 2023–24 in Delhi Govt Schools', *Business Today*, 11 July 2024, https://tinyurl.com/33fkt8a5.

12. 'State of Public (School) Education in Delhi', Praja.org, December 2017, https://tinyurl.com/3kd9xedk.
13. Ibid.
14. Ibid.
15. Chandrakant Lahariya, 'Mohalla Clinics of Delhi, India: Could These Become Platform to Strengthen Primary Healthcare?', *Journal of Family Medicine and Family Care*, Vol. 6, No. 1, 2017, https://tinyurl.com/mrjkbwnz.
16. Ashish Srivastava, 'Big Bang Launch of Arogya Mandirs', *The New Indian Express*, 26 May 2025, tinyurl.com/yntudprj.
17. Arvind Kejriwal (@ArvindKejriwal), X (formerly Twitter), 20 November 2023, 6.15 p.m., https://tinyurl.com/33dw8d6n.
18. Sumana Nandy, 'Explained: The Fraud Allegations Against AAP's Mohalla Clinics in Delhi', NDTV, 5 January 2024, https://tinyurl.com/4t6782pm.
19. 'Home Ministry Directs CBI to Probe Corruption Allegations Against Mohalla Clinics in Delhi', *The Indian Express*, 5 January 2024, https://tinyurl.com/y2axujyd.
20. Pallavi Ghosh, 'Delhi Mohalla Clinic "Scam" Gets Murkier with New Findings on "Fake Lab Tests"; Health Minister Reacts', News18, 4 January 2024, https://tinyurl.com/5hf7rxjn.
21. Gourav Mahendra Mishra, 'Explained | What Is the Mohalla Clinic Scam', *Deccan Herald*, 6 January 2024, https://tinyurl.com/3fdv3js3.
22. 'Home Ministry Directs CBI to Probe Corruption Allegations Against Mohalla Clinics in Delhi', *The Indian Express*, 5 January 2024, https://tinyurl.com/y2axujyd.
23. Durgesh Nandan Jha, 'Delhi: Not All Vitals of Public Health Infra Stable', *The Times of India*, 29 December 2020, https://tinyurl.com/bdzzt9sj.
24. Prachi Singh, Shamika Ravi and Sikim Chakravarty, 'COVID-19 | Is India's Health Infrastructure Equipped to Handle an Epidemic?', Brookings, 24 March 2020, https://tinyurl.com/bddmrns7.
25. Durgesh Nandan Jha, 'Delhi: Not All Vitals of Public Health Infra Stable', *The Times of India*, 29 December 2020, https://tinyurl.com/bdzzt9sj.
26. 'Free Electricity in Delhi up to 200 Units, Announces Arvind Kejriwal', *India Today*, 1 August 2019, https://tinyurl.com/5ebm6kbw.
27. Sumedha Awathy and Binit Das, 'Rooftop Solar Generation: Why Delhi Government Schools Fare Better than Others', *Down To Earth*, 17 August 2021, https://tinyurl.com/bdfk5v25.

28. Saurav Anand, 'High Losses and Debt Continue to Burden State Discoms Despite Tariff Hikes: Icra', ET EnergyWorld.com, 13 August 2024, https://tinyurl.com/2uas6jj2.
29. 'Delhi: Discoms Seek "Rational" Step on Domestic Tariff This Year', *The Times of India*, 5 April 2022, https://tinyurl.com/ycy9ufn2.
30. 'BJP Alleges "Financial Irregularities" in Delhi Discoms, Seeks Probe', *Hindustan Times*, 12 November 2024, https://tinyurl.com/25778m7m.
31. 'Delhi LG Orders FIR against Delhi Jal Board over ₹20 Crore "Embezzlement".' *Mint*, 24 September 2022. tinyurl.com/396mhtjh. Accessed 18 June 2025.

8: Experiments: Attack or Defend?

1. 'PM Narendra Modi a 'Coward, Psychopath,' Says Arvind Kejriwal After CBI Raid', *The Indian Express*, 16 December 2015, https://tinyurl.com/2a3dw2bk.
2. Arvind Kejriwal (@Arvind Kejriwal), X (formerly Twitter), 15 December 2015, 10.29 a.m., https://tinyurl.com/52xju8pk.
3. 'Centre Was Worried ACB Would Move Against Union Minister: Kejriwal', *The Times of India*, 18 July 2015, https://tinyurl.com/bdzxcrr4.
4. 'Centre Took Away My Most Potent Weapon Against Graft: Kejriwal', *Hindustan Times*, 12 February 2016, https://tinyurl.com/ynrwmvwp.
5. Jatin Anand and Soumya Pillai, 'Kapil Mishra Suspended from AAP a Day After Being Fired as Minister', *The Hindu*, 3 December 2021, https://tinyurl.com/243fjtd8.
6. Anindita Sanyal, 'Arvind Kejriwal Tweets "Truth Will Prevail". Barbs Come from Kapil Mishra', NDTV, 8 May 2017, https://tinyurl.com/2ke3djht.
7. PTI, 'Kejriwal Apologises to Majithia over Drugs Charge', *The Hindu*, 15 March 2018, https://tinyurl.com/2z5n8528.
8. 'Arvind Kejriwal Says Sorry to Arun Jaitley: Full Text of Apology Letter', *India Today*, 2 April 2018, https://tinyurl.com/7w73usma.
9. 'In More Trouble for AAP, Prominent Face Ashish Khetan Quits Party', *The Economic Times*, 22 August 2018, https://tinyurl.com/mw48ff7c
10. Alok K.N. Mishra, 'Ashutosh Quits AAP, Arvind Kejriwal Says: "Not in This Life"', *The Times of India*, 16 August 2018, https://tinyurl.com/4z364m79.
11. Alok K.N. Mishra, 'Arvind Kejriwal and His Cabinet Sit on Dharna at LG's Office', *The Times of India*, 12 June 2018, https://tinyurl.com/37v2uxy2.

12. PTI, '4 Non-BJP CMs Visit Kejriwal's Residence, Hold Talks Ahead of NITI Meet', *Business Standard*, 16 June 2018, https://tinyurl.com/5eysw4vu.
13. Sourav Roy Barman, 'As AAP Switches to Lok Sabha Poll Mode, Full Statehood Issue Takes Centre Stage', *The Indian Express*, 7 June 2018, https://tinyurl.com/ae423ybz.
14. Sourav Roy Barman, 'After Months, Kejriwal Attacks PM, Says Modi and LG Coordinating Bureaucrat Crisis in Delhi', *The Indian Express*, 11 June 2018, tinyurl.com/4a2ds8jc.

9: An Alliance that Never Was and the 2019 Jolt

1. ANI, 'Cong-AAP Alliance Finalised, Only "Fine-Tuning" Now, Says PC Chacko; AAP Leader Sanjay Singh Denies', *Business Standard*, 17 April 2019, https://tinyurl.com/2fumeaz4.
2. Gulam Jeelani, 'Congress Was Never Interested in Any Alliance with AAP: Sheila Dikshit', *India Today*, 22 January 2019, https://tinyurl.com/5n77ypw3.
3. 'Inside Story of Why AAP-Congress Talks Failed | Hear It from Arvind Kejriwal', *India Today*, 27 April 2019, https://tinyurl.com/538r7shb.
4. Archis Mohan, 'Arvind Kejriwal Did U-Turn on Delhi Seat-Sharing, Says Rahul Gandhi', *Business Standard*, 16 April 2019, https://tinyurl.com/4veuwru5.
5. ANI, 'NCP Chief Sharad Pawar Mediating Between Congress-AAP in Delhi: Sources', *India Today,* 19 March 2019, https://tinyurl.com/5shwcbj9.
6. 'Delhi CM Arvind Kejriwal Speech at Mamata Banerjee's United India Rally | Kolkata | V6 News', YouTube, 19 January 2019, https://tinyurl.com/ynx5mz68.

10: Populism and Prashant Kishor

1. 'Delhi Elections 2015: Arvind Kejriwal-Led AAP Breaks Rules of Identity Politics, Dents Core Vote Bases of BJP & Congress', *The Economic Times*, 23 January 2015, https://tinyurl.com/mr2e9p5j.
2. Avishek G. Dastidar, 'AAP, BJP and Delhi's Dalit Vote Swing', *India Today*, 18 April 2024, tinyurl.com/ynn6355s.
3. Anjishnu Das, 'Who Will Win Delhi, BJP or AAP? 5 Things to Watch out for Today', *The Indian Express*, 8 February 2025, tinyurl.com/4evbdj5a.

4. Shreyas Sardesai, 'Stunning Gender Gap: Women Voters Powered AAP's Landslide in Delhi', *The Indian Express*, 15 February 2020, https://tinyurl.com/3wdbw89e.
5. IANS, 'Delhi Polls: Arvind Kejriwal's 10 "Guarantees"', *The Economic Times*, 19 January 2020, https://tinyurl.com/mr44cxu5.
6. 'Gruha Jyothi Scheme: How to Get 200 Units of Free Power in Karnataka', *The Hindu*, 19 June 2023, https://tinyurl.com/w7j77k6d.

11: Shaheen Bagh to Welfare: 2020 Delhi Assembly Election

1. Ishita Mishra, 'RSS Welcomes SC Decision of Upholding Abrogation of Article 370', *The Hindu*, 12 December 2023, https://tinyurl.com/35c47rvt.
2. 'Arvind Kejriwal Tweets Support for Centre on Article 370', *Hindustan Times*, 10 June 2020, https://tinyurl.com/zytprr7n.
3. 'CAB Will Be Applicable in the Entire Country and Not Just Confined to West Bengal: Shri Amit Shah', YouTube, 23 April 2019, https://tinyurl.com/y7jfybhv.
4. PTI, 'Delhi Elections: Voting for BJP Will Prevent Thousands of Incidents Like Shaheen Bagh, Says Amit Shah', *The Times of India*, 26 January 2020, https://tinyurl.com/bdep2m9e.
5. Akhilesh Sharma, '"Press Button with Such Anger That Shaheen Bagh Feels Current": Amit Shah', NDTV, 27 January 2020, https://tinyurl.com/yh4x6wzz.
6. Saurabh Shukla, 'Delhi Elections: "Goli Not Biryani for Terrorists": Yogi Adityanath at First Delhi Rally', NDTV, 2 February 2020, https://tinyurl.com/5n9y29wv.
7. Shanker Arnimesh, 'Amit Shah, Adityanath, Anurag Thakur — 5 Most Provocative Speeches of Delhi Elections', *The Print*, 7 February 2020, https://tinyurl.com/2x27mnnc.
8. '"Pakistan Has Entered Shaheen Bagh": BJP's Kapil Mishra Raises Political Temperature in Delhi', *Hindustan Times*, 23 January 2020, https://tinyurl.com/y5dusfxz.
9. 'BJP's Parvesh Verma Courts Controversy Yet Again, Now Calls Arvind Kejriwal a Terrorist', YouTube, 29 January 2020, https://tinyurl.com/ydws7tjt.
10. 'I Stand with People of Shaheen Bagh: Manish Sisodia', India TV, 23 January 2020, https://tinyurl.com/y54fjaan.
11. 'If You Think I Am a "Terrorist" Then Vote for BJP: Kejriwal', ABP Live, 5 February 2020, https://tinyurl.com/y5782s7h.

12. 'Delhi Election 2020: AAP 1st Choice for Women and First-Time Voters, Shows India Today Exit Poll', *India Today*, 8 February 2020, tinyurl.com/4ht8pduu.

PART 3: SHIFTING IDEOLOGY

12: Janta-ism or Opportunism: The Ideology Question

1. 'If You Think I Am a "Terrorist" Then Vote for BJP: Kejriwal', ABP Live, 5 February 2020, https://tinyurl.com/y5782s7h.
2. R. Prasannan, 'AAP: Left, Right or Centre?', *The Week*, 15 February 2020, https://tinyurl.com/3spjrny6.
3. 'Extreme Patriotism, Honesty and Humanism Three Pillars of AAP, Claims Kejriwal', *The Economic Times*, 29 March 2022, https://tinyurl.com/ms55p5yh.
4. PTI, 'Goa Assembly Polls: AAP's CM Candidate to Be from Bhandari Community, Says Manish Sisodia', *The Hindu*, 11 November 2021, https://tinyurl.com/bdzbe7j5.
5. ANI, 'AAP CM Candidate for Punjab Will Be from Sikh Community, Announces Kejriwal', *Business Standard*, 21 June 2021, https://tinyurl.com/5n7xtj4s.

13: *Kam Ki Rajneeti* vs Hanuman Chalisa

1. 'AAP Minister in Delhi Rajendra Pal Gautam Resigns over Attending Conversion Ceremony', *The Hindu*, 13 October 2022, https://tinyurl.com/23hmpnps.
2. Badri Narayan, *Republic of Hindutva: How the Sangh is Reshaping Indian Democracy,* Penguin Viking, 2021, p. 55.
3. Utkarsh Mishra, 'Whoever Speaks against RSS, BJP Will Go Missing like Najeeb: Kejriwal in JNU', *Rediff*, 3 November 2016, tinyurl.com/4bwsveb7.
4. Amitabh Tiwari, 'Opinion | Delhi Elections: It's the Season of Swing Voters', NDTV, 6 December 2024, https://tinyurl.com/2hu529uj.
5. ANI, 'Lord Hanuman Has Blessed People of Delhi, Says Arvind Kejriwal over Poll Victory', mint, 11 February 2020, https://tinyurl.com/vnyzj2bf.
6. Devdutt Pattanaik, 'Was Hanuman a Dravidian, a Brahmin, or a Dalit?', *Deccan Herald*, 27 November 2024, https://tinyurl.com/4fmzphvz.
7. Shivam Vij, '10 Ambedkar Quotes That Show Why the BJP Can't Co-opt Him', *The Print*, 12 April 2018, https://tinyurl.com/ykrdz44v.

8. Ashutosh Sharma, 'AAP Doublespeak Belies Claim to Legacy of Ambedkar and Bhagat Singh', Frontline, 3 November 2022, https://tinyurl.com/56d56k59.
9. Ashutosh, 'AAP Has Appropriated Bhagat Singh Without Understanding Him', *The Indian Express*, 25 April 2022, https://tinyurl.com/mrjamsr3.
10. Shivam Vij, '10 Ambedkar Quotes That Show Why the BJP Can't Co-opt Him', *The Print*, 12 April 2018, https://tinyurl.com/ykrdz44v.
11. 'Son of Bhagat Singh, Not Savarkar: Kejriwal's Retort After Manish Sisodia Accused of Corruption', *India Today*, 22 July 2022, https://tinyurl.com/3nxk2bym.
12. Ashutosh, 'AAP Has Appropriated Bhagat Singh Without Understanding Him', *The Indian Express*, 25 April 2022, https://tinyurl.com/mrjamsr3.
13. Anurag Roushan, 'Aam Aadmi Party Launches "AAP Ka Ramrajya" Website Ahead of Lok Sabha Elections 2024: Here's All About It', India TV, 17 April 2024, https://tinyurl.com/nhkswyb8.
14. Gayathri Mani, 'AAP Launches "Ram Rajya" Website: What Is It About?', *The Indian Express*, 18 April 2024, https://tinyurl.com/4fmc7u6a.
15. PTI, 'Inspired by Ram Rajya, Delhi Govt Provides Good Health, Education, Free Water Supply: Arvind Kejriwal', *The Economic Times*, 25 January 2024, https://tinyurl.com/487wnvze.
16. Gayathri Mani, 'Sita, Hanuman, Bharat and a Vacant Chair as Atishi Takes Charge: For AAP, Ram the Refrain', *The Indian Express*, 24 September 2024, https://tinyurl.com/48mpp46t.
17. PTI, 'Kejriwal Launches Free Pilgrimage Scheme for Senior Citizens', *The Indian Express*, 5 December 2018, https://tinyurl.com/m9kfa5ze.
18. Sweta Goswami, 'Delhi Govt's Free Pilgrimage Scheme Now Includes Ayodhya, Says Arvind Kejriwal', *Hindustan Times*, 27 October 2021, https://tinyurl.com/5btsj84c.
19. 'Kejriwal Launches Ambitious Deshbhakti Curriculum', *The Hindu*, 29 September 2021, https://tinyurl.com/ek3c68h2.

14: Muslim Vote Matters But...

1. Shreyas Sardesai, '77% Muslims, 57% Sikhs Voted AAP', *The Indian Express*, 12 February 2015, https://tinyurl.com/mujb9bj6.
2. Ibid.
3. 'Delhi Election 2020: Muslim Voters Prefer AAP over Congress, Shows India Today Exit Poll', *India Today*, 9 February 2020, https://tinyurl.com/3wdwt6vb.

4. Verma, Lalmani, 'In Delhi Battle for Key Muslim Vote, AAP on Tenterhooks as Congress Turnws up Heat', *The Indian Express*, 3 February 2025. tinyurl.com/rkkxcpmj.
5. 'Delhi 2025 Assembly Elections: AAP's Vote Share Declines Considerably in Seats with High Muslim Presence', *The Hindu*, 2025, https://tinyurl.com/m3jbkyb7.
6. Ojha, Srishti, 'Tahir Hussain, 2020 Delhi Riots Accused, Gets Custody Parole to Campaign in Polls', *India Today*, 2025, https://tinyurl.com/44wdjebu.
7. Dushant Kumar, 'पत्रकार ने बिलकिस बानो पर सवाल किया, मनीष सिसोदिया का जवाब वायरल हो गया (Journalist Asked Question on Bilkis Bano, Manish Sisodia's Answer Went Viral)!', Lallantop, 19 October 2022, https://tinyurl.com/55zdvrb9.
8. Aditi Raja, and Parimal A. Dabhi, 'AAP Breaks Silence, Welcomes Bilkis Order; "Can't Comment," Says BJP Leader Who Justified Remission', *The Indian Express*, 2024, https://tinyurl.com/323esd5r.
9. Abhishek Dey, 'Gujarat Polls, Fear of "Muslim Appeasers" Tag: Why Aap Is Silent on Bilkis Bano Convicts' Release', *The Print*, 2022, https://tinyurl.com/294dkjbv.
10. Hanan Zaffar and Hasan Akram, 'Anti-Muslim Slogans Raised in Indian Capital, Suspects in Custody', Aljazeera, 10 August 2021, https://tinyurl.com/mrxs6ky7; Divya Trivedi, 'Hate Speech at Jantar Mantar Rally Latest Attempt by Hindutva Forces to Stoke Communal Passions', *Frontline*, 26 August 2021, https://tinyurl.com/582tsfvv.
11. Arnabjit Sur, 'Uttam Nagar Tense as Street Vendors Live in Fear', *Millenium Post*, 11 August 2021, https://tinyurl.com/mrx82zbc.
12. Mishra, Alok K.N., 'Reject CAA, Focus on Jobs: Arvind Kejriwal', *The Times of India*. 2020, https://tinyurl.com/5cc5dbdn.
13. Arnabjit Sur, 'Jahangirpuri Violence Chargesheet: Easy Access to Arms, Riot Pre-planned in Group Meetings', *The Hindu*, 19 July 2022, https://tinyurl.com/5xz6z9jz; 'Delhi Riots: From 2022's Jahangirpuri to Sadar Bazar in 1974, a History of Communal Clashes in the Capital', *Firstpost.*, 18 April 2022, https://tinyurl.com/mw4hrvcu.
14. Vibha Sharma and Abhay Singh, 'Bulldozers Crash into Livelihoods at Delhi's Jahangirpuri', *The Times of India*, 22 April 2022, https://tinyurl.com/4bhdd689.
15. Ifrah Mufti, 'BJP Using Bangladeshis & Rohingyas to Cause Violence, Claim AAP Leaders', *The New Indian Express*, 21 April 2022, https://tinyurl.com/45rvtadx.

16. 'Arvind Kejriwal Is Modi of 2013, Defamed Tablighi Jamaat, Alleges Asaduddin Owaisi', Scroll.in, 28 November 2022, https://tinyurl.com/3c8spb8h; Sweta Goswami, 'Kejriwal Warns of Rise in Cases After Tablighi Jamaat Episode', *Hindustan Times*, 1 April 2020, https://tinyurl.com/5n7xkfvp.
17. Akash Bisht and Sadiq Naqvi, 'How Tablighi Jamaat Event Became India's Worst Coronavirus Vector', Aljazeera, 7 April 2020, https://tinyurl.com/63m3e54f.
18. Aakash Joshi, 'AAP's Opposition to Rohingya Settlement Shows a Parochial Party, Unfit to Be a National Alternative', *The Indian Express*, 18 August 2022, https://tinyurl.com/3vavubxy.

PART 4: ONE MAN SHOW

15: Arvind Kejriwal-Centric AAP

1. 'Kejriwal Brings Out Another Report Card: Delhi Polls a Contest Between Two Models', *The Indian Express*, 10 January 2020, https://tinyurl.com/5f8nr2an.
2. IANS, 'Delhi Polls a Contest Between Two Models of Shaping India's Future: Sisodia', *Business Standard*, 11 January 2020, https://tinyurl.com/mrxy4nbm.
3. Deeksha Bhardwaj, 'Arvind Kejriwal Has Anger Issues, Calls Legislators "Tuccha" & "Gadha", Says Alka Lamba', *The Print*, 20 March 2019, https://tinyurl.com/4mazddar.
4. PTI, 'Atishi Appointed In-Charge of AAP's Goa Unit, Jarnail Singh of Punjab Unit', *The Economic Times*, 28 February 2020, https://tinyurl.com/529anbmz; Raj Kantak, 'Raghav Chadha Appointed Co-incharge of AAP's Punjab Unit', *Business World*, 20 December 2020, https://tinyurl.com/3x9h8uwh; Satish Jha, 'AAP Appoints Former IIT-D Professor Sandeep Pathak as Its Gujarat In-Charge', *Deccan Herald*, 21 March 2022, https://tinyurl.com/3cykhtxv.
5. Aarushi Maheshwari, 'Congress Refused Tie-Up, Is Planting Stories in Media: Kejriwal', inshorts, 20 March 2019, https://tinyurl.com/yv57jx9w.
6. PTI, 'Arvind Kejriwal to Take Strict Action After Bibhav Kumar "Misbehaved" with Swati Maliwal: Sanjay Singh', mint, 14 May 2024, https://tinyurl.com/mt9k6j4v.

16: Manish Sisodia: The Constant Deputy

1. Kushan Niyogi, 'Delhi Polls: Voters in Patparganj Demand Cleaner Water and Better Roads', *The Patriot*, 2025, https://tinyurl.com/2de2uv34.
2. 'Punjab MLA Sukhpal Singh Khaira Quits AAP, Faces Disqualification as MLA', *Hindustan Times*, 2019, https://tinyurl.com/4m2dpd49.
3. Mohan, Vibhor, 'Vote for Arvind Kejriwal as Punjab's CM Face, Says Manish Sisodia', *The Times of India*, 2017, https://tinyurl.com/mmvtypha.
4. 'Punjab's CM Will Be from Punjab: Kejriwal', *The New Indian Express*, 2017, https://tinyurl.com/jz9c7e2t.

18: Vijay Nair: 'The Blue-Eyed Boy of Arvind ji'

1. Nileena MS, 'Despite Allegations of Sexual Harassment, Former OML CEO Vijay Nair Finds Work with AAP', *The Caravan*, 31 October 2019, https://tinyurl.com/y3d6ysvy.
2. Surabhi Kanga, Bhanuj Kappal and Arnav Das Sharma, 'Facing the Music: How Only Much Louder Failed the Women in Its Ranks', *The Caravan*, 1 November 2018, https://tinyurl.com/y99s5b3h.
3. Nileena MS, 'Despite Allegations of Sexual Harassment, Former OML CEO Vijay Nair Finds Work with AAP', *The Caravan*, 31 October 2019, https://tinyurl.com/y3d6ysvy.

19: The Curious Case of Raghav Chadha: From Prominence to Absence

1. Arushi Jaiswal, 'Aap Ki Adalat: Parineeti, Raghav Share Their Love Journey from London Meeting to Udaipur Wedding', India TV, 7 December 2024, https://tinyurl.com/4zpzvje8.
2. Ibid.
3. Ibid.

20: Kejriwal's Coterie

1. PTI, 'Kejriwal Forms 9-Member Panel on Deliver on 70 Promises', *Business Standard*, 27 February 2015, https://tinyurl.com/2jtsweze.
2. PTI, 'Delhi Govt Raises Questions over Secretary-Level Salaries Paid to Non-official Members of DDCD', *The Times of India*, 3 September 2023, https://tinyurl.com/4kf3kzsk.
3. 'DDC Vice-Chairperson to Enjoy Cabinet Rank', *The Tribune*, 2015, https://tinyurl.com/mryj3wh9.

4. Sumit Kumar Singh, 'AAP Flayed for Splurging on Self-Publicity', *The New Indian Express*, 3 July 2015, https://tinyurl.com/mrsr4mbb.
5. ANI, 'Arvind Kejriwal's Personal Secretary Bibhav Kumar Sacked over Pending Criminal Case', *The Hindu*, 2024, https://tinyurl.com/3t5ndu8p.
6. Sourav Roy Barman, 'Fixing Kejriwal's Meetings & His Rivals — Bibhav Kumar of Swati Maliwal Row Is Ultimate AAP Insider', *The Print*, 16 May 2024, https://tinyurl.com/229tn3bw.
7. PTI, 'Maliwal Facing Corruption Case, Blackmailed by BJP to Be Part of Conspiracy against Kejriwal: AAP', *The Hindu*, 2024, https://tinyurl.com/7864e72t.
8. Bureau, The Hindu, 'Arvind Kejriwal's Aide Bibhav Kumar Granted Bail in Swati Maliwal Assault Case', *The Hindu*, 2024, https://tinyurl.com/5n7xhpww.
9. Bureau, Policy Watch, '9 MPs Including Arvind Sawant Get UNICEF Award for Advancing Child Rights', *PSU Watch*, 2020, https://tinyurl.com/396eut2b.

PART 5: AAP UNDER FIRE

21: Liquor-gate: The Delhi Liquor Policy Scam

1. Astha Oriel, 'Delhi Excise Policy Row: All You Need to Know', *Fortune India*, 2022, https://tinyurl.com/bd39au8k.
2. Gulam Jeelani, 'Explained | All You Need to Know about Delhi's New Excise Policy', *Moneycontrol*, 2021, https://tinyurl.com/my988ven.
3. Ibid.
4. Ibid.
5. Astha Oriel, 'Delhi Excise Policy Row: All You Need to Know', *Fortune India*, 2022, https://tinyurl.com/bd39au8k; AamAadmiParty, *X (Formerly Twitter)*, 2025, https://tinyurl.com/y735wptv.
6. Jalali, Ujwal, 'High on Liquor: What We Know so Far about Delhi Excise Policy Case', *The New Indian Express*, 2024, https://tinyurl.com/ye4rtz34. Accessed 20 June 2025.
7. 'Spirited Battle: On AAP and the Delhi Excise Policy', *The Hindu*, 22 August 2022, https://tinyurl.com/4nb5yn8y.
8. PTI, 'Enforcement Directorate Raids in Multiple States in Delhi Excise Policy Scam Case', NDTV, 6 September 2022, https://tinyurl.com/yvhdj3cv.

9. 'Arvind Kejriwal Denies Corruption in Delhi Liquor Policy', YouTube, 15 November 2022, https://tinyurl.com/3skn3axw.
10. Ashutosh Sharma, 'AAP Faces Existential Crisis as Liquor Scam Clouds Its Anti-corruption Image', 3 February 2024, https://tinyurl.com/556x7bzs.
11. 'Who Are the "South Group" Allegedly Involved in the Delhi Excise Policy Scam', CNBC TV18, 22 March 2024, https://tinyurl.com/3e534ppc.
12. Akriti Anand, 'Arvind Kejriwal Arrested: How "South Group" Is Linked to Delhi CM, K Kavitha's Arrest in Liquor Policy Scam | Explained', mint, 22 March 2024, https://tinyurl.com/47ca5cct.
13. Ibid.
14. PTI, 'Digital Evidence from Delhi Hotel's Business Centre Exposed Influence of "South Lobby" on Excise Policy: CBI', *Moneycontrol*, 2023, https://tinyurl.com/yjmsk5cs.
15. 'AAP's Big Revelation: "BJP's Direct Connection with South Lobby in Excise Policy"', AAP, 30 March 2024, https://tinyurl.com/2s39yzcr.
16. PTI, 'Hotel Evidence Exposed "South Lobby" Influence on Liquor Policy: Officials', NDTV, 28 February 2023, https://tinyurl.com/4fvyvcd6.
17. Ibid.
18. 'SC Notice to ED over Nair's Bail Plea, Hearing in 2 Weeks', *Hindustan Times*, 2024, https://tinyurl.com/msc6ktb8.
19. 'ED Must Probe "Direct Nexus" Between BJP and South Lobby, Says AAP', *The Hindu*, 30 March 2024, https://tinyurl.com/y8thj9ck.
20. Ibid.
21. Ibid.

22: Liquor Scam Aftermath: Kejriwal's Second Resignation

1. Pushkar Tiwari, 'Arvind Kejriwal Gets Interim Bail, but to Remain in Jail. Here's Why', NDTV, 12 July 2024, https://tinyurl.com/vzr99vz9.
2. Advay Vora, 'Arvind Kejriwal's Bail in CBI Case | Judgement Summary', SCO, 25 September 2024, https://tinyurl.com/4ukxppyw.
3. PTI, 'Will Resign as CM After 2 Days, Want to Give "Agnipariksha": Arvind Kejriwal; BJP Terms It "PR Exercise"', *The Telegraph Online*, 15 September 2024, https://tinyurl.com/yu7upun7.

23: Atishi: The New Delhi CM

1. Nikhil M. Babu, 'Atishi: From the Backroom to the Top', *The Hindu*, 16 May 2025, https://tinyurl.com/9y5r2sfn.

2. 'Why Did AAP's Atishi, Named as Delhi's New Chief Minister, Drop Her Second Name "Marlena"?', *Hindustan Times*, 17 September 2024, https://tinyurl.com/ys3bpvwf.
3. PTI, 'Atishi New Education Minister, Saurabh Bharadwaj New Health Minister of Delhi', *The Hindu*, 16 March 2023, https://tinyurl.com/mrx3faj6.
4. Ifrah Mufti, 'BJP Using Bangladeshis & Rohingyas to Cause Violence, Claim AAP Leaders', *The New Indian Express*, 21 April 2022, https://tinyurl.com/45rvtadx.
5. 'Delhi Excise Policy Case: ED Mentions Raghav Chadha in Chargesheet; "Reports That I Have Been Named as Accused Malicious," Says AAP Leader', *The Times of India*, 2 May 2023, https://tinyurl.com/4wcv2j9r.

24: The AAP vs Centre: Tale of Three Lieutenant Governors

1. 'An Overview of Governance in Delhi', *CivilsDaily*, 14 August 2024, https://tinyurl.com/575zxnww.
2. 'Land Policy (Chapter – 19 of MPD-2021) and Regulations for Operationalization of Land Policy', Delhi Development Authority, 2021, https://tinyurl.com/y2unjxet.
3. 'Jan Lokpal Bill: AAP Accuses Lieutenant Governor Najeeb Jung of Acting like a "Congress Agent"', *The Economic Times*, 8 February 2014, https://tinyurl.com/yrybuxxk.
4. Pragya Kaushika, 'Jung-Kejriwal Faceoff: Don't Bother LG with All Files, Orders CM', *The Indian Express*, 2 May 2015, https://tinyurl.com/32n6w22x.
5. PTI, 'Kejriwal Accuses Shakuntala Gamlin of Favouring Power Firms', *The Hindu*, 16 November 2021, https://tinyurl.com/4cw49r2p.
6. 'Maliwal Appointment: Jung Says Approval Not Taken', *The Hindu*, 16 November 2021, https://tinyurl.com/b3hfe58j.
7. Sumit Kumar Singh, 'Water Tanker Scam: Anti-Corruption Branch Files Fir Against Arvind Kejriwal and Sheila Dikshit', *The New Indian Express*, 21 June 2016, https://tinyurl.com/56m249h4.
8. 'Blow to Kejriwal: Lieutenant Governor Need Not Listen to Delhi Cabinet, Says Delhi High Court', *The Times of India*, 4 August 2016, https://tinyurl.com/4tcrzmbn.
9. PTI, '2 Officers Take Charge on One DCW Post, LG-Appointee Rejected', *The Economic Times*, 14 December 2016, https://tinyurl.com/47mb3uf6.

10. 'Najeeb Jung Resigns as Delhi Lt Governor; Thanks PM Modi for Help, Arvind Kejriwal for "Association"', *India Today*, 22 December 2016, https://tinyurl.com/3hcazct3.
11. 'Delhi's Lieutenant Governor Is Treating Arvind Kejriwal "Like a Peon", Say Opposition MPs', Scroll.in, 29 December 2017, https://tinyurl.com/yvj4np6y.
12. Ibid.
13. 'Delhi LG, AAP in War of Words over Meeting on Mohalla Clinics', *The Times of India*, 31 August 2017, https://tinyurl.com/5enyzxv7.
14. PTI, '"Attack Premeditated, a Conspiracy": Delhi Chief Secy Anshu Prakash Says in Complaint Against AAP', *Hindustan Times*, 20 February 2018, https://tinyurl.com/59rhuekw.
15. 'Delhi Lieutenant-Governor "Rejects" Doorstep Ration Delivery', *The Hindu*, 22 March 2018, https://tinyurl.com/2ab3urt4.
16. 'COVID-19: LG Overrules Arvind Kejriwal's Order on Hospital for Delhi Residents', *The Times of India*, 8 June 2020, https://tinyurl.com/384xs94v.
17. '"Unacceptable Proposition": L-G Vinai Kumar Saxena Slams Delhi Government over Bus Marshal Proposal', *The Indian Express*, 11 December 2024, https://tinyurl.com/c4nznb6n.
18. PTI, 'Delhi LG Bars Government School Teachers from Travelling to Finland for Training: Manish Sisodia', *The Times of India*, 12 January 2023, https://tinyurl.com/5y2pz874.
19. Paras Singh, 'Sisodia Accuses LG of Destroying Delhi Education Model', *Hindustan Times*, 14 January 2023, https://tinyurl.com/bdzduta8.
20. Saikat Kumar Bose, '"Who Talked About Yamuna Dip?" Delhi Lt Governor's Barb at Arvind Kejriwal', NDTV, 21 October 2024, https://tinyurl.com/4exxrbsv.
21. TNN, 'Before Chhath, Delhi LG V.K. Saxena Urges CM Arvind Kejriwal to Clean up Yamuna', *The Times of India*, 2022, https://tinyurl.com/abwxzfkj.
22. PTI, 'CBI to Probe AAP Govt for "Irregularities" in Purchase of 1,000 Buses', *Business Standard*, 11 September 2022, https://tinyurl.com/ms6szpfc.
23. 'Delhi Services Dept. Makes L-G's Call Official: 437 Appointments by Aap Govt. Declared "Void"', *The Hindu*, 6 July 2023, https://tinyurl.com/55zamt76.

24. Kumar Kunal, 'Delhi L-G Orders Removal of Jasmine Shah as Dialogue and Development Commission V-C', *India Today*, 18 November 2022, https://tinyurl.com/mr3xntd8.
25. Atul Mathur, 'Vigilance Orders Removal of Edu Adviser, Says Appointment Illegal', *The Times of India*, 10 April 2024, https://tinyurl.com/y3zzah2r.

PART 6: EXPANSION AND PROSPECT

25: A New Frontier: The Rise of the AAP in Punjab

1. '2014 Lok Sabha Election Results for Punjab', IndiaVotes, https://tinyurl.com/yfhzau3m.
2. 'Punjab Election Result 2022: AAP Wins 92 Seats; Bhagwant Mann to Take Oath as CM in Khatkarkalan', mint, 10 March 2022, https://tinyurl.com/yc4zp6cs.
3. PTI, 'Elections 2014: AAP Opens Lok Sabha Account in Punjab with Four Seats', *The Economic Times*, 16 May 2014, https://tinyurl.com/yc5d9795.
4. IANS, 'Big Win for Congress in Punjab, AAP Largest Opposition with 20 Seats', *The News Minute*, 11 March 2017, https://tinyurl.com/mpj5umus.
5. Chitleen K. Sethi, 'Punjab Poll Results: No CM Face, "Radical Link" Did AAP In', *Hindustan Times*, 12 March 2017, https://tinyurl.com/3e36meja.
6. I.P. Singh, 'Signs of Chhotepur Being Sidelined?', *The Times of India*, 5 August 2016, https://tinyurl.com/yczwxa4u.
7. 'Kejriwal Spends Night at Ex-Militant's House, Kicks off Political Row in Punjab', *Hindustan Times*, 2017, https://tinyurl.com/2y3jh4mx.
8. 'Lok Sabha Election Results 2019: Aam Aadmi Party Decimated in Punjab, Bhagwant Mann Its Lone MP', *Hindustan Times*, 24 May 2019, https://tinyurl.com/3cutdn8p.
9. Ikhhlaq Singh Aujla, 'SAD Walks Out of NDA', *The Times of India*, 27 September 2020, https://tinyurl.com/9ns2t869.
10. 'Legislations Will Enable Barrier-Free Trade In Agricultural Produce and Empower Farmers to Engage with Investors of Their Choice - Union Minister of Agriculture & Farmers' Welfare Shri Narendra Singh Tomar', PIB Delhi, 14 September 2020, https://tinyurl.com/e5x5dnaw.

11. Harpreet Bajwa, 'Farm Bills Fallout: Union Minister Harsimrat Kaur Badal Quits Modi Government', *The New Indian Express*, 18 September 2020, https://tinyurl.com/msn6kp5k.
12. Surjit Singh, 'Eight Years On, Sukhbir Tenders Apology for 2015 Sacrilege Case in Punjab', *Hindustan Times*, 15 December 2023, https://tinyurl.com/edt6wysc.
13. Vikas Vasudeva, 'Navjot Singh Sidhu Resigns from Punjab Cabinet', *The Hindu*, 14 July 2019, https://tinyurl.com/36b3j4sh.
14. 'Charanjit Singh Channi Takes Oath as Punjab Chief Minister', *The Hindu*, 20 September 2021, https://tinyurl.com/55m9tsbx.
15. 'Punjab Election Result 2022: AAP Wins 92 Seats; Bhagwant Mann to Take Oath as CM in Khatkarkalan', mint, 10 March 2022, https://tinyurl.com/yc4zp6cs.
16. Zoya Mateen, 'Sidhu Moose Wala: Murder of Popular Indian Singer Sparks Anger', BBC, 30 May 2022, https://tinyurl.com/5d9824rz.

26: Expansion Dreams and Realities

1. Suchitra Karthikeyan, 'AAP Wins Doda Poll Battle in Jammu and Kashmir; Makes Inroads in Fifth Territory', *The Hindu*, 8 October 2024, https://tinyurl.com/3afyppc2.
2. 'TV9 भारतवर्ष पर Manish Sisodia का अब तक का सबसे तगड़ा इंटरव्यू | Aam Aadmi Party', YouTube, 16 August 2024, https://tinyurl.com/5bzj4zc9.
3. 'Goa Election 2017: AAP Looks to Replicate Delhi Success Story, Projects Party as Alternative', *Firstpost.*, 3 February 2017, https://tinyurl.com/yc4ct4fe.
4. '2 Wins for AAP in Goa, Arvind Kejriwal Says "Honest Politics" Begins', NDTV, 10 March 2022, https://tinyurl.com/2v494jpj.
5. Pavneet Singh Chadha, 'Key Goa Groups Driving Its Power Play: Bhandaris to Kshatriya Marathas, Saraswat Brahmins to Christians', *The Indian Express*, 7 May 2024, https://tinyurl.com/2bwjeeu9.
6. D.P. Bhattacharya, 'AAP Wins 27 Seats in the Municipal Corporation Polls, Kejriwal Holds Roadshow', *The Economic Times*, 26 February 2021, https://tinyurl.com/2y5x2cys.
7. Kumar Anand and Prakash Kumar, 'AAP's Gujarat Gains: 5 Seats, 13% Vote Share and National Party Status', rediff, 8 December 2022, https://tinyurl.com/ucxkw6az.
8. Ashraf, Ajaz, 'Explaining AAP's Rise in Gujarat', *Mid-Day*, 2022, https://tinyurl.com/ywtxsbsv.

9. PTI, 'Arvind Kejriwal Writes to RSS Chief Mohan Bhagwat on BJP's Politics, PM Modi's Actions', *The Hindu*, 25 September 2024, https://tinyurl.com/56tyed4z.
10. 'Delhi Schools Told Not to Admit Wards of Illegal Immigrants', *The Hindu*, 24 December 2024, https://tinyurl.com/mwn4pjy8.
11. 'Kejriwal Promises ₹18,000 Honorarium for Temple, Gurdwara Priests If AAP Is Re-Elected in Delhi', *The Hindu*, 30 December 2024, https://tinyurl.com/5yubzvsx.
12. 'Ex-AAP MLA Bhupendra Bhayani Joins BJP in Gujarat', *The Hindu*, 4 February 2024, https://tinyurl.com/3tx69b22.

27: National Prospect

1. Saikat Kumar Bose, 'AAP Says Will Ask India Bloc to Remove Congress from Alliance If...', NDTV, 26 December 2024, https://tinyurl.com/3v23mpu7.

28: 2025: The Delhi Challenge

1. Abhinav Rajput, 'Arvind Kejriwal Launches Mukhyamantri Mahila Samman Yojana for Financial Aid to Women in Delhi', *The Times of India*, 23 December 2024, https://tinyurl.com/htwxhhmh.
2. Ira Alok Puranik, 'Free Healthcare for Senior Citizens Aged 60 and Above in Delhi: Arvind Kejriwal's Poll Promise; What Is Sanjeevani Yojana?', *The Economic Times*, 20 December 2024, https://tinyurl.com/6br34yws.
3. Tanushka Dutta, '"I Apologise to All Above 70": PM Slams Delhi, Bengal over Ayushman Bharat', NDTV, 29 October 2024, https://tinyurl.com/5ypk5bcx.
4. Alok K.N. Mishra, 'No Possibility of Alliance with Congress for Delhi Polls: Arvind Kejriwal', *Hindustan Times*, 11 December 2024, https://tinyurl.com/3rh985v4.
5. 'Delhi Minister Raaj Kumar Anand Resigns, Quits AAP', *The Hindu*, 11 April 2024, https://tinyurl.com/rvfw7pd2.
6. Abhinav Rajput, 'Bittu Joins AAP Hours After Timarpur MLA Pandey's Telling Post', *The Times of India*, 6 December 2024, https://tinyurl.com/59udfbnt.
7. Saikat Kumar Bose, 'In AAP's First List for Delhi Polls, 6 of 11 Candidates Are Defectors', NDTV, 21 November 2024, https://tinyurl.com/4tmy2btk.
8. Ibid.
9. Ibid.

10. Aditya Menon, 'Can AAP's New Strategy Help It Become the Only Party to Defeat BJP Thrice?', *The Quint*, 18 December 2024, https://tinyurl.com/3bc6fhmp.

Epilogue

1. '"If Massage, Spa Companies…": How AAP's Sanjay Singh Looked at Delhi Exit Poll Results', mint, 6 February 2025, https://tinyurl.com/2kp4bea8.
2. 'AAP vs BJP: Kejriwal's Poaching Allegations Rakes up a Storm on Eve of Delhi Election Result', *Moneycontrol*, 7 February 2025, https://tinyurl.com/5n6fftun.
3. ANI, 'AAP Going to Form Government with Huge Majority: Jasmine Shah on Delhi Polls', *The Economic Times*, 8 February 2025, https://tinyurl.com/mrxwk2cf.
4. Prabhash K. Dutta, 'Delhi Election Results: AAP Wins All 12 Seats Reserved for SC Candidates', *India Today*, 2020, https://tinyurl.com/32d2vp4p.
5. Lalmani Verma, 'In Delhi Battle for Key Muslim Vote, AAP on Tenterhooks as Congress Turns up Heat', *The Indian Express*, 2025, https://tinyurl.com/rkkxcpmj.
6. Sanjeer Alam, 'Rich as Well as Lower Classes Moved Away, but AAP Retains Support of Poorest Strata', *The Indian Express*, 10 February 2025, https://tinyurl.com/yeymu79e.
7. Ibid.
8. Mallica Joshi, 'AAP's Middle Path: A Manifesto for Middle Class, a Reframing of Welfare Schemes', *The Indian Express*, 23 January 2025, https://tinyurl.com/mehts2az.
9. Sandeep Shastri, Sanjay Kumar and Suhas Palshikar, 'Why Kejriwal Lost: Pollution, Lack of Clean Drinking Water Behind Voter Anger; Two-Thirds Saw AAP as Corrupt', *The Indian Express*, 10 February 2025, https://tinyurl.com/5c4p6s3v.
10. Ibid.
11. 'SC Verdict on Delhi Govt vs Centre: "Defeat for Dictatorial Actions of BJP," Say AAP Leaders', *The Indian Express*, 11 May 2023, https://tinyurl.com/yxez2ucb.
12. 'Negating Supreme Court Order, Centre Brings Ordinance on Delhi Officer Postings', *The Times of India*, 20 May 2023, https://tinyurl.com/yc4py9jn.

13. Akshay Marathe, 'Don't Misdiagnose AAP Defeat in Delhi Election Results. It Will Be Fatal to Democracy', *The Print*, 9 February 2025, https://tinyurl.com/3je83utt.
14. Sandeep Shastri, Sanjay Kumar and Suhas Palshikar, 'Why Kejriwal Lost: Pollution, Lack of Clean Drinking Water Behind Voter Anger; Two-Thirds Saw AAP as Corrupt', *The Indian Express*, 10 February 2025, https://tinyurl.com/5c4p6s3v.
15. Ritu Sarin and Jatin Anand, 'Audit Trail of Kejriwal's CM Residence: Cost up Thrice to Rs 33 Crore, Splurge on Curtains to Carpets', *The Indian Express*, 6 January 2025, https://tinyurl.com/4ubnxrcc.
16. Sandeep Shastri, Sanjay Kumar and Suhas Palshikar, 'Why Kejriwal Lost: Pollution, Lack of Clean Drinking Water Behind Voter Anger; Two-Thirds Saw AAP as Corrupt', *The Indian Express*, 10 February 2025, https://tinyurl.com/5c4p6s3v.
17. Subham Singh and Dipu Rai, 'Women Voters Turned Out in Greater Numbers, AAP Lost Big in 2025 Delhi Polls', 8 February 2025, https://tinyurl.com/mr2hr9z7.
18. Priyanka Mittal and Kirti Sharma, 'Gender Divide in Delhi Polls: Men Fuel BJP Surge, AAP Retains Edge Among Women', *The Indian Express*, 10 February 2025, https://tinyurl.com/kpa6wkdb.
19. Ibid.
20. Sahil Sinha, 'Arvind Kejriwal Should've Resigned After Arrest, Not Bail: Prashant Kishor on AAP Loss', *India Today*, 9 February 2025, https://tinyurl.com/2aczpszb.
21. 'Delhi Election Results 2025: AAP's Vote Share Declines Considerably in Seats with High Muslim Presence', *The Hindu*, 8 February 2025, https://tinyurl.com/7heh7rrh.